AN INTRODUCTION TO
Environmental Law and Policy in Canada

Paul Muldoon

Alastair Lucas

Robert Gibson

Peter Pickfield

2009
Emond Montgomery Publications
Toronto, Canada

Emond Montgomery Publications Limited
60 Shaftesbury Avenue
Toronto ON M4T 1A3
http://www.emp.ca/highered

Printed in Canada on 100 percent recycled paper.
Reprinted July 2014.

We acknowledge the financial support of the Government of Canada through the Canada
Book Fund for our publishing activities.

The views expressed in this book are those of the individual authors and contributors
and do not necessarily reflect those of the publisher or of the universities and organizations with which the authors and contributors are affiliated.

Acquisitions and developmental editor: Peggy Buchan
Marketing manager: Christine Davidson
Supervising editor: Jim Lyons
Copy editor: Kate Hawkins
Proofreader: David Handelsman
Typesetters: Debbie Gervais and Nancy Ennis
Text designer: Tara Wells
Indexer: Paula Pike
Cover designer: Janice Van Eck

Library and Archives Canada Cataloguing in Publication

An introduction to environmental law and policy in Canada / Paul Muldoon …
[et al.].

Includes index.
ISBN 978-1-55239-127-3

1. Environmental law—Canada—Textbooks.   I. Muldoon, Paul R. (Paul Robert),
1956-
KE3619.E68 2008   344.7104'6   C2008-901645-9
KF3775.ZA2E683 2008

CONTENTS

Chapter 4   Courts, Tribunals, and Dispute Settlement

Chapter 5   The Relationship Between Canadian and International Law

Chapter 6   The Development of Canadian Environmental Law

Chapter 7   The Basic Structure of Environmental Regimes

Chapter 8   Environmental ProtectionRegimes: Command and Control

Chapter 9   Sectoral Regulatory Regimes

Chapter 10   Environmental Assessment

Chapter 11   Planning and Management Regimes

Chapter 14   Using Administrative Decision-Making Processes to Protect the Environment

Chapter 15   Environmental Bill of Rights and Access to Information

Chapter 16   The Evolution of Environmental Law and the Challenges Ahead

Preface

"Do you care what happens to the air, the water, the land around you?" These were the opening words of *Environment on Trial: A Guide to Ontario Environmental Law and Policy* originally published 35 years ago—in 1973. *Environment on Trial,* an accomplishment of the Canadian Environmental Law Research Foundation (now the Canadian Institute for Environmental Law and Policy) was intended to empower the ordinary citizen in the legal and political exercise of environmental rights. The goal of an environmental bill of rights for Ontario has since been realized, but how well does it ensure maximum citizen participation in the achievement of a healthy and sustainable environment?

Much has changed since 1973. Challenges such as water pollution and landfills, while still significant in their potential for harm, seem trifling in comparison to the looming catastrophe of climate change. To many it appears that environmental issues have outpaced social, political, and legislative developments, and exponentially so.

An Introduction to Environmental Law and Policy in Canada has emerged out of that context. Much has been achieved—we now have an environmental bill of rights and an environmental commissioner in Ontario, and an environmental commissioner at the federal level. The public, both in Canada and globally, is taking notice of the environment like never before. However, we do not yet have the citizen participation needed to ensure a healthy and sustainable environment for future generations.

Indeed, we have seen an eroding of environmental protection for Canadians. Slowly, we are learning what happens when environmental safeguards are not in place—water pollution contaminates our drinking water; industrial emissions cause air pollution; and new biotechnologies create threats to biodiversity and food security. In many cases, the long-term consequences are unknown. We are now faced with rebuilding appropriate laws, policies, and governance processes to ensure a sustainable future.

We hope that *An Introduction to Environmental Law and Policy in Canada* will encourage students to learn more about our environmental laws and policies and to participate in the processes of improving them and implementing them. This was the objective in 1973 and it has become even more relevant and urgent today— 35 years later.

We are deeply indebted to David Estrin and John Swaigen, whose vision it was to create a citizens handbook in the 1970s. We are also deeply indebted to Paul Emond, Peggy Buchan, and the staff of Emond Montgomery and WordsWorth Communications, who took on this challenging project and saw it to its fruition, and the authors: Paul Muldoon, Alastair Lucas, Robert Gibson, and Peter Pickfield.

Anne Mitchell
Canadian Institute for Environmental Law and Policy

PART I

How the Legal System Works

CHAPTER 1

The Basics of Law

Law in Our Society

The law is a body of rules that governs the behaviour of whatever, or whomever, is subject to it. The laws of physics apply to all things—bungee jumpers as well as billiard balls. The laws of society apply mostly to people, and a particular set of laws applies only in the jurisdiction (the nation or other governing organization) that puts the laws in place. But all laws are authoritative, and this authority is their central quality. While the laws of society are generally more flexible than the laws of physics, all laws worthy of the name are binding.

The authority behind a human law may come from a long record of accepted customary practice that is enforced informally by the members of a community. More commonly today, the law's authority comes from formally established law-making bodies that are empowered constitutionally to ensure that the laws are accepted or enforced.

In Canada, the primary law-making bodies are the legislatures and the courts. Canadian legislatures (the federal Parliament and the provincial and territorial legislative assemblies) make law by enacting **statutes** and making **regulations** under these statutes. Courts make law in two ways: through decisions that interpret statutes and determine their constitutionality and through decisions that establish or adjust the principles of **common law** (judge-made decisions about similar cases stretching back in time).

We accept these law-making bodies as legitimate, and we accept their authority to make, within the limits of the constitution, laws that are binding on us. We must comply with their laws or risk enforcement action against us.

Legitimacy is important because the law works best if it is widely accepted. A military dictatorship may be able to impose oppressive laws through the use of brute force, but any regime whose legitimacy is not broadly recognized is difficult to maintain. And any law that is not generally accepted by those expected to obey it is difficult to apply. Enforcement action works best if it is not needed very often.

Law gains legitimacy by being made by legitimate authorities—duly elected legislative bodies and courts that operate with evident consistency and impartiality. But legitimacy is also closely tied to reasonableness. Indeed, a useful way to think about law is to imagine it as the work of a reasonable person.

In any community, the **reasonable person** is unlikely to be the most attractive or adventurous individual. More likely this person would be called "solid" and "responsible" and would be recognized as having characteristics and ideas common to most people in the community. This hypothetical reasonable person is the basis (though in different ways) for judgments about both civil and criminal liability under specific laws. She also provides the standard for legal decisions about environmental protection and management, including what should be anticipated or foreseen, how susceptibility to harm should be measured, and how care or precaution should be gauged.

Legitimacy and reasonableness are also tied to fairness, particularly in two fundamental principles of good law:

- the law must apply equally to all citizens, including public officials, and
- disputes between citizens and the government must be decided by properly authorized and impartial judicial bodies according to the law.

The first principle recognizes fundamental human equality before the law. The second emphasizes consistency and impartiality in the process of applying the law.

Finally, good law balances consistency and adaptability. Consistency is crucial because the law is a guide for behaviour. If the law and its enforcement are erratic, constantly shifting, or arbitrary, the law cannot be an effective guide. To be useful, the law must apply predictably to everyone, and it must be stable enough that people know what to expect. At the same time, the law must deal reasonably with a variety of different circumstances, and it must maintain its relevance in a world that is changing. In some areas, including environmental law, where improved behaviour is clearly needed, the law has the added challenge of encouraging change.

Formal law is not the only tool that society has for guiding and governing behaviour. Customary practice still applies. Education and economic incentives are also powerful. Nevertheless, the law figures prominently among our means of acting together to protect what we value, to correct what is dangerous, to foster greater understanding, and to ensure more effective and just steps to make our world happier and more sustainable.

The Historical Foundations

Law is as ancient as humanity. We have always depended on our fellow human beings and on nature. And we have always needed to maintain more or less amicable relations with them. In some instances, we have had no trouble discerning the right thing to do. But life has always been complicated. There have always been difficult situations, puzzles, tensions, potential conflicts to avoid, and actual ones to resolve. For these we have needed standardized systems for deciding what to do. This required a code of some sort, an accepted body of rules—in effect, law.

For well over 90 percent of human history, we were nomadic foragers on the land. During this time, law took the form of established customs and traditions. Although respected leaders, usually elders with decades of learning and experience, might make authoritative decisions, even they relied on the customs and traditions of their people. The old ways were favoured because they had worked in the past. Any deviation was risky.

With the gradual adoption of more sedentary agricultural life and especially with the rise of the great river valley civilizations, some of the customary rules were converted into written law. There were now more people to deal with, as well as large irrigation systems and other ambitious activities to manage. Most importantly, accumulation of property was now possible, and it proved to be a reliable source of tension and conflict.

For nomadic foragers, who hunted and gathered in different places according to the seasonal availability of various foods, property conflicts among community members were rare. No one had any incentive to accumulate material wealth because it had to be carried from one place to another. Wealth was a burden. This changed with settled agricultural life in which wealth could be accumulated and squabbled over. Moreover, control over good land (or at least reliable access to good land) was crucial. That too meant new tensions.

And so agriculture brought additional challenges for public decision making—for keeping the peace, providing security, managing the big projects, and organizing production and distribution. Tradition and custom still played a large role, but now there was also a class of authorities who assumed special responsibilities and powers. They made the decisions on matters when old traditions and customs failed to provide sufficient guidance.

The new authorities understandably found it impossible to make new rulings about every individual issue. They also wanted to ensure that everyone in society knew what the rules were. And so, gradually, they set out written laws for dealing with more or less predictable problems.

The first known written code of law is that of Hammurabi, king of Babylon, which was set down nearly 4,000 years ago. It refers to a system of contracts and judges that had been in place well before the code was carved in stone. The practice of codification spread. Sooner or later virtually all societies with written language also adopted some form of written law, though they all continued to rely on tradition and custom as well.

In some places—including England, which provides an important foundation for Canadian law—the formal authoritative statute laws made by kings and queens were accompanied by a gradually established common law. This law was based on court decisions and commentaries on important cases. The common law occupies a middle ground between ancient community custom and written statute law.

For most of history, the purpose of both written and customary law was essentially conservative. It was designed to maintain order among people and between people and their environment. This generally involved maintaining existing practices and keeping the peace. There was no expectation of progress and not much desire for change.

Much of this conservatism remains in the law today. But the law is no longer merely a reflection of codified tradition. It is also expected to be reasonable. This idea was advocated in the 4th century BCE by the Greek philosopher Aristotle, who argued that the law is properly an application of reason for the common good. If so, even the oldest of traditions could be challenged to pass the test of reason.

A more significant departure from a conservative agenda began about 500 years ago. At this time, some countries in Europe began to accept a set of what we now call "modern" ideas, all of them revolutionary at the time. Three are particularly important: the economic idea that it is acceptable, even desirable, for people to be self-interested profit seekers; the scientific idea that nature can be broken down into parts, understood, and manipulated for human benefit; and the combination of these two ideas that societies and individuals should pursue economic and scientific progress built on increasingly efficient and innovative exploitation of nature's resources.

Adopting the idea of progress brought many new opportunities and many new challenges. For the law, it introduced a basic tension. On the one hand, societies still needed to maintain order, support honest and peaceable behaviour, and preserve valued public goods. On the other hand, increasing numbers of individuals and powerful interests expected the law to promote economic and scientific advances that inevitably would be disruptive. While the overall results might be largely beneficial, they would undermine the old ways. Embracing progress meant facing new situations, new possibilities, and new problems.

Environmental law is a good example of the uncomfortable result. It is devoted both to preservation and to change. It is expected to protect resources and maintain biophysical and ecological systems that provide crucial services—for example, clean air and water, viable soil, productive forests, and reliable climate conditions. At the same time, it must facilitate advances that will minimize waste and enhance efficiency in resource use. And it must fit into the larger scheme of law and other tools and activities that aim to enhance social and economic as well as ecological well-being over time.

Like many other areas of law today, environmental law must be dynamic as well as conservative, ambitious as well as careful, and a broad contributor to society as well as an effective tool in its own realm.

CHAPTER 2

Environmental Law: Its Evolution in Canada

What Is Environmental Law?

Environmental law is the body of legislated statutes and judge-made common law that can be
used to protect and improve environmental conditions. Some of it deals with pollution control,
waste management, endangered species preservation, and other issues that clearly involve the nat-

ural environment. But "environment" is also often defined broadly to cover land,
water, air, and living organisms, including humans and their built environment,
and the interaction of these elements. This is sensible because many aspects of the
biophysical environment and the human social and economic environment are
deeply intertwined.

Some environmental law is aimed directly at the environment, narrowly or
broadly defined. In addition, there are many laws of more general application that
can be used to advance environmental objectives. Examples include the body of
common law that focuses on property and **tort** law (centred on private legal actions
concerning damages), both of which may be used to prevent environmental harm
or to compensate those harmed.

Some environmental laws focus on prevention of damage. Others are meant to
require, or at least to facilitate and encourage, rehabilitation of degraded environments or correction of environmentally damaging or dangerous behaviour. But all
of these have a positive environmental agenda. They aim to make things better or,
at least, less bad. In this, environmental law is unlike the neutral rules of, for

example, contract law, which is used to resolve disputes involving individuals or corporations. Environmental law is highly and openly value-laden.

Most of this positive agenda centres on human purposes, including immediate economic interests as well as long-term health and well-being and the political benefits of participation in decisions that affect our lives. At least to some degree, environmental law also seeks to benefit the environment itself and the ecosystems that sustain it. But this too serves human interests sooner or later, since we are permanently dependent on our environment for the basic prerequisites of survival and for the foundations of most of what enriches our lives.

Another way to understand environmental law is this: environmental law is the process whereby the common resources of society—the air we breathe, the water we drink, the minerals in the ground, the trees on the land, and the lakes—are allocated to those public and private interests that use those resources to provide goods and services for the public at large. Hence, licences are granted to extract aggregate from the ground for highway construction; permits to take water are granted to industry for manufacturing or to bottle water; and discharge approvals are granted to steel-making facilities to emit pollutants into the air. Environmental law asks whether such allocations should be made, how much is appropriate, and who should participate in such decisions.

Environmental law aims to protect and restore or improve the environment. It does not do this simply because some legislator or court had an idea. Rather, it reflects the values of many Canadians. Opinion polls have confirmed again and again that Canadians value their environment and support action to protect it. Environmental law supports these fundamental values.

The Scope of Environmental Law

Plenty of laws affect efforts to protect or improve the environment. Some of them do so directly, for example, by requiring pollution abatement. Others address environmental matters indirectly or as part of a related agenda, such as protecting health or property. As a result, the boundaries of environmental law are inexact.

The core of environmental law clearly includes **environmental regulatory laws**, which govern discharges of harmful substances into the air and water and onto land. **Environmental assessment law**, which requires careful attention to environmental considerations in the planning and approval of new undertakings, is also at the core of environmental law. So too is legislation that confers environmental rights on citizens—especially rights to receive environmental information, to participate in environmental regulatory decisions, and to demand that legally required standards be applied. Laws that protect endangered species and natural areas, and the environmental provisions in laws concerning agriculture, forestry, energy, and other major sectors of the economy are also important components of environmental law. Finally, we must include international laws, conventions, and treaties that are focused on environmental concerns such as persistent organic pollutants, substances that deplete the ozone layer, transboundary movement of hazardous wastes, and greenhouse gases. All of these subjects are discussed in later chapters.

Beyond this core, there are questions about how far environmental law should properly extend. Does it include national and provincial park legislation, a major part of which provides for public recreation? What about wildlife legislation concerned with "managing" wildlife mainly for hunting? Does environmental law include community and regional planning law, a subject that affects virtually all urban and regional economic activity through regulation of the built environment and its infrastructure? Human health is included in most statutory definitions of environment. But are the myriad of statutes, regulations, and bylaws that establish and regulate health and related social programs part of environmental law? Don't some tax and economic benefit laws concern or include environmental protection activities? What about the common law elements of property and tort law that have sometimes been used to halt property or natural resource development? And then there is international law, some of which deals with environmental issues. Which of all these areas of law deserve to be called "environmental"? Is there a logical end or a reasonable set of boundaries anywhere? Should we just accept that all law is in some sense environmental law? There is no neat answer to any of these questions.

One reason for the difficulties in defining the scope of environmental law is that much of it is quite recent and draws from a wide range of traditional legal concepts and subjects. For example, environmental regulatory law uses instruments (such as authorizations, prohibitions, and regulatory offences) and institutions (such as decision-making tribunals) that have counterparts in other regulatory areas such as health and safety and telecommunications.

Another reason for the impression of boundaries is that the environment underlies and supports everything. That is why environmental law overlaps other legal fields and why such areas as health law, planning law, and even tax law are, in a sense, part of environmental law. Laws in all of these areas can be used or adapted for the protection and enhancement of the environment. Recognizing these overlaps, we have included in this book sections on environmental laws in a variety of important sectors, as well as sections on common law tort, property rights, environmental offences, constitutional law, and the arcane administrative law concerning judicial review of environmental regulatory decisions.

All are important. We may look first to the core environmental rights and regulations or to specific environmental provisions in other laws. But we should remember that sometimes the environment can be protected most effectively by a court ruling that a threatening proposal is unconstitutional, or that granting an undesirable approval is outside the legal powers of a government board or official, or that the relevant decisions were made in a procedurally unfair way.

Ideas Underlying Modern Environmental Law

Formal environmental law can be traced back centuries, if not millennia, and customary rules about human–environment relations likely go back to our earliest ancestors. Most of what we now call environmental law, however, was introduced within the last few decades. Certainly it reflects the rising environmental concerns and the increasing environmental understanding of these years. But it has also been influenced by some other big ideas that have occupied recent debate on important public issues.

We will look at the nature, roots, and significance of these developments more closely when we examine the history of environmental law in Canada in part II of this book. For now, it is enough to note the main elements.

The first key point is that modern environmental laws have been as much about how we govern ourselves as about how we treat the environment. Many of the environmental laws in place today in Canada and other developed countries originated in a burst of environmental law-making in the late 1960s and early 1970s. These new laws focused on preventing as well as reducing pollution and signified a new understanding that environmental damage was a serious problem, that easy technical fixes were not always available, and that prevention is often wiser and cheaper than repair. No less significantly, the new laws responded to a wave of public concern about environmental abuses. Concerned citizens, often led by public interest advocates and assisted by media attention, drove the process.

This pattern has continued through the evolution of environmental law in Canada. Few innovations in environmental legislation and few major advances before the courts have been the product of government zeal. Virtually all progressive steps in environmental law have required public initiative, public ingenuity, and persistent public pressure.

Not surprisingly, then, Canadian environmental law rests as much on ideas about democracy as on understandings about how to deal with the environment. Two linked aspects of democracy have been particularly important. These are the public welfare role of governments and the importance of citizen participation in policy deliberations. The public welfare idea is that governments in democracies have a responsibility to defend and advance public well-being. Long-recognized priority areas for government action for public welfare include national security, public safety, education, and transportation. Environmental protection became an important item on the list more recently, largely because of public concern and pressure. Environmental law is a response to the emergence of a public consensus that governments need to act on this important but previously neglected area of public interest.

However, getting governments to act on environmental concerns has been only part of the story. The development of environmental law in Canada also reflects an unwillingness merely to trust government officials to do what is necessary. From the late 1960s to the present, Canadian campaigns for stronger environmental laws have also consistently included demands for participative rights—that is, legal requirements for the interested and concerned public to be notified about important findings and initiatives, to have timely and convenient access to information, to have opportunities for effective involvement in deliberations before irrevocable decisions are made, and to be able to enforce environmental laws when governments fail to act. Environmental lawyers acting in the public interest have often used common law principles, as well as available statutory provisions, to assert the legal rights of citizens to participate in environmental regulatory decisions and to stop or delay proposed projects likely to harm the environment. They have also pushed, often successfully, for environmental bills of rights centred on opportunities for effective participation.

Efforts to strengthen environmental protection through regulatory laws—by raising standards, extending the reach of government requirements, and expanding the narrow array of public environmental rights—continue today. But there is now recognition that these approaches have limits and may never be sufficient by themselves. As a result, the public welfare and citizen rights foundations of environmental law are now increasingly being supplemented by efforts to mobilize other players and motivators.

Much of the recent focus of law reform and related environmental initiatives has been on economic tools. While many governments have simply tried to encourage corporations "voluntarily" to exceed regulatory requirements, some have begun to make greater use of law-based economic instruments that give polluters an economic incentive to reduce pollution and waste.

The second set of big ideas underlying environmental law centres on philosophy and ethics. As we noted above, environmental law is not neutral. It has a positive agenda to improve well-being. That is not to say that environmental lawmakers and practitioners always agree on what is required for well-being, or what the priority objectives should be, or even who and what should be included as the intended beneficiaries. But there are some common themes.

Most environmental laws emerged from concerns about threats to human health or other material interests. The initial assumption was that any problems that were serious enough to merit legal attention could be dealt with satisfactorily, one by one, usually through some technological repair, if we put our minds to it. The role of the law was to force attention on the matter where this did not happen automatically. That assumption fit well with the prevailing belief that we could and should dominate nature through applied science, technology, and other servants of economic progress.

But the real world turned out to be inconveniently complicated. The technical fixes did not always work, or they had unsavoury side effects, or they were far too expensive, or the problems came too thick and fast to be manageable. Years of experience gradually taught that prevention was preferable to repair, that considering overall effects was better than dealing with problems one by one, and that we should adopt precautionary approaches because we will never know enough to be able to predict, much less fix, all of the problems we might cause.

Development through economic growth and technological innovation has brought major gains. But it has also begun to eat away at the world's ecological foundations and is digging a dangerously expanding gulf between the rich and poor. In 1987, the World Commission on Environment and Development, convened by the United Nations and chaired by Norwegian Prime Minister Gro Harlem Brundtland, officially declared that the current path was not sustainable and that a substantial shift in agenda was necessary.

Many of the most recent environmental laws have therefore begun to reflect a new understanding of the world and our place in it. That understanding accepts that

- we are permanently dependent on a natural environment made of highly complex and interrelated systems at every level from global climate chemistry to the soil bacteria affecting growth of individual plants;
- we will never control nature in any complete and fully competent way; and
- we must find better ways to live in and with the rest of nature, by establishing better integrated socio-ecological systems that are farsighted, careful, and adaptable enough to serve present needs without sacrificing the prospects of future generations.

In addition, we now face plenty of evidence that human activities are producing significant adverse effects well beyond the national and provincial reach of most environmental law. To deal with greenhouse gas emissions that contribute to global climate change and a host of other transboundary pollution, resource depletion, and ecological damage, we will need also to develop better means of designing and applying international controls.

This new understanding is far from fully accepted or adopted. Its implications are much debated. As well, there is (and perhaps should be) a great diversity of views about how best to express, order, and apply the main principles in corrective action, including correction through environmental law. Some focus on economic tools, while others stress links between social justice and ecological protection or between women and nature. Yet others advocate a less or non-anthropocentric (human-centred) approach that recognizes the intrinsic value of nature and assigns legal rights of some sort to the environment. And there are emerging versions of a sustainability ethics that attempt to pull all of these together in an integrated package.

As we will see in the chapters that follow, little of this is entirely unprecedented. Many old laws include components that anticipate the new understandings. For example, some environmental assessment laws define the environment to encompass humans and their communities and cultures along with biophysical and ecological systems. The objectives of many other environmental statutes extend beyond benefits for humans, and recognize interactions between human beings and natural systems. Humans are sometimes included as merely one category of "living organism."

Many long-standing proposals for the law also anticipate recent ideas. For example, in 1948, Aldo Leopold proposed a "land ethic" that would extend ethical or moral considerations to reflect the interconnections of ecosystems so that soil, plants, and animals, along with humans, would merit moral consideration as important parts of the land on which all live. In a 1972 law journal article, Christopher Stone argued in favour of giving trees standing (capacity) to sue, with the help of human next friends (substitute litigants), to protect themselves and their habitat. And in 1973, Laurence Tribe published a paper entitled "Ways Not to Think About Plastic Trees," in which he proposed moving beyond transcendence (human domination over natural objects) to immanence (respect for natural objects and systems).

Proposals for sustainability ethics also predate the Brundtland commission's introduction of the phrase "sustainable development" into household use. Indeed, the idea that we should integrate moral commitment to environmental protection with advocacy for basic livelihood security, race and gender equality, participative political rights, and other aspects of human justice has a long and distinguished pedigree. Implementation is, however, just beginning. And because of the ambitiousness of the agenda and the extent to which it challenges well-entrenched practices, change in this direction is likely to be slow.

But this is the general nature of the relationship between the law and society, or between environmental law and the world of concerns about human–nature relations. Both the big ideas and their application in law evolve. Law is one field, among many, in which the big ideas of the day are introduced, tested, and adjusted or supplanted by new ideas, ideally better ones that have been built on the lessons learned from past failures as well as past successes.

The Role and Place of Environmental Law

As we have seen, law carries the weight of societal consent and authority. It is composed of the rules and prohibitions that society prescribes through its recognized law-making institutions: the legislatures and the courts. It is not just a set of guidelines, suggestions, or practices that we can choose to follow or not. It lays down requirements that can be enforced through regulatory agencies or the courts.

It is important to keep this mandatory feature of environmental law in mind because so much human activity, including building structures and extracting natural resources, seems to happen under guidelines, codes of practice, and simple convention (or "the way we do this"). But guidelines, codes, and customary practices are only convenient recipes for complying with the basic expectations that underlie or are embedded in environmental (and other) legal requirements.

For example, practitioners of environmental assessment have developed extensive guides and handbooks for doing assessment work. But environmental assessment law, and the regulations and formal decisions made under the law, set the requirements concerning, for example, which proposed undertakings must be assessed, what the scope of the assessment must be, what factors must be considered, how public involvement must be facilitated, what standards must be met, and what follow-up and monitoring must be carried out.

Environmental law is not just about prohibitions and penalties. Many environmental laws are principally devoted to providing legal frameworks for processes that may involve information dissemination, review and research, consultation, planning and actual environmental protection, and remediation actions. Environmental assessment and land use planning laws, for example, centre on establishing structured approaches to decision making that consider specified factors and provide opportunities for participation by interested and affected parties.

We can put environmental laws into two main categories: environmental **laws of general application** and **sectoral laws** (laws dealing with a resource sector such as water or forests, or an industrial sector such as fisheries or waste management) in broadly environmental areas or with substantial sections addressing environmental considerations. Environmental laws of general application are typically devoted to conventional environmental issues such as pollution control and natural resource protection, and they apply to everyone and all activities. Laws focused on the activities of particular industrial sectors may be less obviously environmental but can be just as important. They include the many broadly environmental laws that deal with the allocation and use of natural resources (such as land, water, forests, agriculture, and fisheries) and have significant effects on environmental systems. Other important sectoral laws (such as those governing mining, oil and gas extraction, and nuclear power) may cover a wide range of considerations but include important provisions addressing environmental concerns—for example, concerns about air or water contamination, wildlife habitat damages, human health threats, and maintenance of resources for future generations. As you will see, we have chosen to include overviews of a variety of sectoral laws in chapter 9.

Laws governing activities in particular industrial sectors sometimes appear to overlap or conflict with environmental laws of general application. For example, the federal government's general environmental assessment requirements may apply to energy projects that are also subject to evaluations under federal energy sector law. To deal with some of these situations, the laws may provide for harmonization through joint or substitute procedures. An example is the joint board procedure under Ontario's environmental, water, and municipal planning legislation that allows for a single hearing on matters involving two or more different laws. If there is conflict, disputes are resolved by negotiation or, if necessary, by the courts, which apply general principles of statutory interpretation to decide which law prevails. In such cases, the courts carefully assess the language of each law and the objectives that can be understood by reading each law as a whole. Courts ask themselves whether the legislature intended that the general environmental law—that is, the "law of general application"—should apply, or whether the special sectoral law should apply as an exception to the general requirements.

Both environmental laws of general application and special sectoral laws set out enforceable requirements. The requirements can, however, take various forms, of which the most important are the statutory provisions and regulations discussed in chapter 3. These enforceable requirements can also be supplemented by influential guidance documents covering such matters as desirable and best practice, standard administrative procedures, testing protocols, and enforcement priorities. And they can have a powerful indirect effect in the larger realm of forces pushing for environmental recovery and protection.

Finally, there are many other powerful laws and law-related influences that do not really qualify as environmental law, but that can have sufficiently significant effects on environmental concerns to merit attention here. These include

- liability rules, tax laws, spending powers, and other financial tools that provide the basis for imposing and adjusting incentives for better environmental practices and disincentives for undesirable behaviour;
- general laws ensuring public access to information and other opportunities for effective scrutiny of and participation in important decisions, including environmentally significant ones; and
- the broad law-making power itself, which gives governments the ability to use the plausible threat of new legal obligations to encourage "voluntary" efforts to improve environmental performance.

While we tend to think of particular environmental laws and even categories of environmental laws as individually important, the key consideration is how well the whole suite of laws and related instruments works as an overall regime.

CHAPTER 3

The Canadian Legal Framework

Legal Systems

As we have seen, Canada's basic environmental legal framework consists of statute law and law established through judicial decisions. But there is not just one legal framework. Canada is unique in having two legal systems and two corresponding sets of legal traditions. In Quebec there is a system of **civil law** that dates from the *Quebec Act, 1774*, which was enacted following the British conquest. The rest of Canada is governed by the English common law that was applied in the colonial period and has since been advanced by Canadian courts.

In fact, as professors Lorne Giroux and Paule Halley have pointed out, Quebec has a dual legal system, and this is reflected in Quebec environmental law. The civil law, originally based on the Custom of Paris and later codified using French civil law and the Code Napoléon, applies to private disputes between citizens. But Quebec public law, which governs relations between citizens and government, is based on English law.

So for Quebec environmental law, the civil law concepts "abus de droit" (abuse of right) and "troubles de voisinage" (neighbourhood annoyances) create rights to protect private citizens against personal or property damage that are very similar to, but not the same as, the common law tort (private wrong) of nuisance. Administrative law and regulatory criminal offence concepts, which are based on English law, are relevant to issues that arise under environmental statutes and apply equally in Quebec and the rest of Canada.

The Role of the Constitution

Canada's **constitution** occupies the highest level in our hierarchy of laws. It is the "supreme law" with which all other laws must conform.

The constitutions of many countries include provisions concerning environmental protection and improvement. For example, the constitution of India states:

> Protection and improvement of environment and safeguarding of forests and wild life—The State shall endeavour to protect and improve the environment and to safeguard the forests and wild life of the country.
>
> Fundamental Duties.—It shall be the duty of every citizen of India—...(g) to protect and improve the natural environment including forests, lakes, rivers, and wild life, and to have compassion for living creatures.

Most constitutions established since the United Nations Conference on the Human Environment held in 1972 in Stockholm contain some environmental protection principles. Many older constitutions have been amended to add environmental provisions.

Canada's *Constitution Act, 1867* refers to fisheries and public lands but does not expressly allocate environmental management powers. This has not changed despite determined lobbying by environmental groups and legal professional organizations in the early 1980s, when constitutional changes were discussed before the passage of the *Constitution Act, 1982*, and in 1987, when the proposed Meech Lake Accord on the allocation of federal and provincial powers was being debated. When the Charlottetown Accord was drafted in 1992, the issue of how to deal with the environment was discussed, but none of the proposals fundamentally affected the division of legislative powers.

The Constitutional Division of Powers

Constitutional power to make laws is divided between the federal Parliament and the provincial legislatures. The *Constitution Act, 1867* establishes this division and lists federal and provincial subjects (areas of authority). Certain subjects, such as "seacoast and inland fisheries" on the federal list and "management and sale of public lands" and "property and civil rights" on the provincial list, have obvious environmental significance.

The provinces' constitutional jurisdiction over property and civil rights, local works and undertakings, and the management and sale of public lands in the province meant that it was the provinces that staked out the environmental regulatory field. The federal government's jurisdiction over fisheries supported its *Fisheries*

Act, while other specific federal powers—for example, navigation and shipping, criminal law, federal works and undertakings, and interconnecting undertakings such as railways and pipelines—supported federal environmental legislation over these other subjects.

Environmental Law and Policy and the Division of Powers

The powers in the *Constitution Act, 1867* that are relevant to environmental law and policy are divided as follows:

Provincial powers—sections 92 and 109

- Specific areas where the provinces can make laws:
  - s. 92(5)—management and sale of public lands
  - s. 92(8)—municipal institutions
  - s. 92(13)—property and civil rights
  - s. 92(16)—matters of a local or private nature
- Natural resources
  - s. 92A—the "1982 resources amendment" captures changes in powers to manage and to capture revenues from non-renewable and forestry resources and the generation of electrical energy
- Proprietary interests
  - s. 109—vests public lands, minerals, etc., with the provincial government (unless interests are federally owned or the federal government has authority over them, as in national parks)

Federal powers—section 91

- Specific areas where the federal government can make laws:
  - s. 91(2)—trade and commerce
  - s. 91(3)—taxation power
  - s. 91(10)—navigation
  - s. 91(12)—seacoast and fisheries
  - s. 91(24)—First Nations and Aboriginal interests
  - s. 91(27)—criminal law
- General power—The federal government can also make laws for the "Peace, Order and good Government" of Canada
- Treaty-making power—The federal government can also negotiate internationally, although it cannot implement international agreements without constitutional authority or provincial agreement.

Judicial decisions have reaffirmed existing constitutional provisions or allocated some specific subjects of environmental importance to the federal or provincial governments. Pollution "deleterious" to fish, marine pollution, regulation of highly toxic substances such as PCBs, and environmental assessment of actions related to subjects on the federal list have all been held to be within federal constitutional powers. The control of water pollution (even where fish are present) that results from debris from logging operations in provinces, and the environmental regulation of (otherwise federally regulated) railways in provinces, were ruled to lie within the exclusive powers of the provinces.

The Supreme Court of Canada considers environmental protection not to be a distinct subject for constitutional purposes, but rather to be an aggregate matter, made up of many separate elements. Everything from the licensing of toxic substance discharge and criminal offences (federal subjects) to the regulation of local businesses and provincial property (provincial subjects) falls within the sphere of environmental protection. This being the case, environmental protection cannot be allocated exclusively to the federal government as a matter of "national concern" under the residual "peace, order and good government" power that the courts have identified. The result is that the environment is a shared constitutional subject. Most of its various elements can be the subject of either federal or provincial legislation, or both.

If there is a conflict in the operation of federal and provincial environmental laws dealing in different ways with the same matter, so that complying with one government's statute involves breaching another's, then under the doctrine of paramountcy, the federal statute prevails. But the scope of this potential operational conflict is narrow, and governments are likely to have the skill to craft laws that are capable of operating without conflict. Though there is no explicit judicial decision, it is not likely that different federal and provincial environmental standards applying to a particular person or facility will trigger federal paramountcy. Affected persons do not face a compliance dilemma. They can comply with both laws simply by meeting the higher standard.

The Supreme Court of Canada's 1997 decision in *R v. Hydro-Québec* suggests that the federal criminal law power may potentially support a wide range of federal environmental laws. But this may not be as important as it sounds. It is not clear whether criminal law, with prohibitions and offences at its core, is capable of supporting sophisticated regulatory techniques, including frameworks for market mechanisms such as emission-trading systems.

The result is that federal–provincial agreements and other harmonization techniques have proven very useful. Examples include intergovernmental agreements under the federal *Canadian Environmental Protection Act, 1999* to accept provincial regulations as equivalent and withdraw federal regulations, agreements for joint federal–provincial environmental assessment processes, and the Canada-wide Accord on Environmental Harmonization. The objective of the latter is national harmonization of environmental standards for greater consistency and efficiency. There was considerable criticism of the accord, with some fearing that standards and other environmental measures would lead to the lowest common denominator among the provinces and the federal government. An environmental organization unsuccessfully attempted to challenge the legality of the accord: see *Canadian Environmental Law Association v. Canada (Minister of the Environment)*, 30 CELR (NS) 59 (FCTD); aff'd. 34 CELR (NS) 159 (FCA).

Municipal Jurisdiction

Strictly speaking, municipalities draw their powers to pass **bylaws** on environmental matters from the provincial municipal acts that create them and specify their powers to legislate. But these legislative powers, in many ways, mirror the division of federal and provincial legislative powers under the *Constitution Act, 1867*.

Until recently, municipalities were considered to be legally obliged to remain strictly within their listed bylaw powers. Where it was not clear what a particular power to make bylaws covered, judicial interpretation was formal, with more attention given to the text than the problem it addressed. But the Supreme Court of Canada has now made it clear (in the 2001 *Spraytech* case) that it will use a purposive interpretive approach, analogous to that used for constitutional interpretation. This approach is designed to ensure that municipalities can deal effectively with emergent environmental problems such as regulating pesticide use within their boundaries. It must also be remembered that, in addition to municipalities potentially exceeding their powers under provincial municipal acts, their bylaws may also be outside provincial legislative powers under the *Constitution Act, 1867*. In short, municipalities must act within their powers under municipal acts and under the constitution. For example, a municipality cannot set rules affecting navigation within a harbour because navigation is a federal constitutional responsibility.

Municipalities also deal increasingly with environmental issues in carrying out their traditional functions of land use planning and development control. In addition to being regulators, municipalities are also "corporations" in their functions of developing and managing municipal institutions, facilities, and infrastructure such as roads, bridges, and public transport systems. In this role, they are subject to provincial and federal environmental laws and must behave like good corporate citizens.

Aboriginal Jurisdiction

Self-government institutions that have been established under land claim agreements with First Nations and Inuit peoples represent another group of emerging jurisdictions. These regional jurisdictions are based on the inherent right of self-government that Canada recognizes as an Aboriginal right under section 35 of the *Constitution Act, 1982*. Many land claim agreements are the result of decades of negotiations. They are complex and contain major environmental parts, including entire regimes for wildlife management and environmental impact assessment. When the negotiations are successful, the resulting agreements are ratified by federal statutes and have constitutional authority beyond that of ordinary federal laws.

Land claim agreements typically establish an array of land and renewable resource agencies that regulate and manage water use, wildlife, and land use planning in the different settlement areas. Most such agencies are co-management arrangements with representatives from the Aboriginal organizations and from government departments sharing the responsibilities. The most ambitious creation of a new decision-making regime was the establishment of the territory of Nunavut in 1999, which resulted from the government's 1992 agreement with the Inuit people of the eastern Arctic.

Statutes and Subordinate Legislation

There is a hierarchy of environmental legislation, beginning with the constitution:

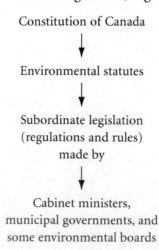

Constitution of Canada

↓

Environmental statutes

↓

Subordinate legislation
(regulations and rules)
made by

↓

Cabinet ministers,
municipal governments, and
some environmental boards

The federal and provincial environmental statutes include powers, usually vested in the **governor in council** or the **lieutenant-governor in council** (the federal or a provincial Cabinet respectively), but sometimes assigned to ministers or boards to make subordinate legislation in the form of regulations and rules. The idea is that the statutes provide the legislative framework. They specify their objectives and purposes and the general scheme by which they are to be accomplished; specify or create the officials or agencies that are responsible for administering and enforcing them; and enable the making of regulations and rules. The regulations and rules make environmental regulatory systems work. They set out the operational details, including particular limits, obligations, and requirements for providing information, applying for approvals, and paying fees.

How Laws Are Made
Statutes

Creation of a statute begins with a government's development of a policy. Processes for enacting statutes by Parliament and by provincial and territorial legislatures are broadly similar. Initial policy development may include preparation of public discussion documents, including green papers, which outline the main options that the government is considering, and white papers, which set out the government's preferred approach. Often, as in the case of the *Canadian Environmental Assessment Act*, enacted in the early 1990s, and the *Canadian Environmental Protection Act, 1999*, a re-enactment of earlier legislation, the government organizes public consultation in the form of public information, hearings, and workshops.

If implementation of the policy is not merely a matter of spending money or issuing public information, for example, it may require legislation. In such cases involving environmental matters, a proposal for legislation is developed by the Department of the Environment or its equivalent. There is legal review at this stage, including assessment of the constitutionality of the proposed legislation and its consistency with statutes of general application such as the *Freedom of Information and Protection of Privacy Act*. At the federal level, the Cabinet Directive on the Environmental Assessment of Policy, Plan and Program Proposals provides for some consideration of the possible environmental effects of proposed legislation. The environment minister then sends the proposal, with the necessary supporting information, to Cabinet, through the provincial Cabinet Secretariat or the federal Privy Council Office.

If, after review, the relevant Cabinet committee approves the proposal, it is sent to the legislative drafters for preparation of a **bill**. Even at this stage of the process, policy development is not necessarily over. Sometimes, a draft bill is used as the basis for public consultation, with the Cabinet committee endorsing this initiative.

This occurred in the early 1990s when Alberta's *Environmental Protection and Enhancement Act* was proposed. A committee, which included non-government members, held a series of public hearings and meetings on a draft bill, then prepared a report for the government and the public. Subsequently, a new bill was drafted, taking into account public feedback and new information. The ultimate draft bill is reviewed by the Cabinet committee on legislation and, when approved, is ready for introduction in the legislature.

The following outline of the federal legislative process also applies, with some modification, to provincial processes:

- *First reading.* The bill is introduced in the House of Commons by the environment minister and given first reading. There is no debate. It is printed and circulated. Sometimes a bill is referred directly to a legislative committee at this stage.
- *Second reading.* The bill is debated, then approved in principle and referred to an all-party parliamentary committee. Usually this is the Standing Committee on Environment and Sustainable Development, but a special committee may be created or the committee may be a committee of the whole House.
- *Committee stage.* If the bill is referred to a committee, the committee studies the bill clause by clause and may hold hearings, at which witnesses may include the minister, departmental officials, experts, and citizens. The committee may draft proposed amendments to the bill.
- *Report stage.* The committee adopts any amendments that receive approval from a majority of the committee members, and submits a report to the House with its findings, including recommended amendments.
- *Third reading.* If the minister and the government accept the committee amendments, they are adopted and the bill is given third and final reading. But not all committee amendments are accepted. When the bill to establish the *Canadian Environmental Assessment Act* was being passed in the early 1990s, the relevant Commons committee was highly influential, recommending important amendments that were accepted and greatly strengthened the law. A decade later, in 2003 when Bill C-9 to amend the *Canadian Environmental Assessment Act* was being debated, a legislative committee held lengthy hearings and only some of its amendments were accepted by the minister.
- *Senate.* Federal bills require a second legislative step. They must clear three readings and committee review in the Senate. The senators may propose amendments, to which the Commons may agree. If not, a conference

process involving representatives of both bodies may be used to try to
resolve differences.

- *Royal assent.* With third reading, the bill has passed the House of Commons.
  But it does not become law until it has received royal assent by the governor
  general (the lieutenant-governor in a province). This is usually just a
  formality.

- *Coming into force.* An additional step is often required to bring the Act into
  force, thereby making it legally enforceable. The Act comes into force when
  its "coming into force" section says it does. This may be on royal assent, on a
  specified date, or upon proclamation (published in the *Canada Gazette*) by
  the governor (or provincial lieutenant-governor) in council. Parts of the Act
  may be proclaimed in force at different times. Often this delay exists to
  permit implementing regulations to be made and administering institutions
  to be established and staffed. Sometimes the delay is measured in years.
  Because of regulatory difficulties and other problems, nearly three years
  passed between the enactment of the *Canadian Environmental Assessment
  Act* and the Alberta *Environmental Protection and Enhancement Act* and the
  date they were finally proclaimed in force.

It is not unusual for parliamentary or legislative sessions to end before a bill makes
it to third reading. If this happens, the bill "dies." It may be reintroduced in the next
session as a new bill, in the same or revised form, or it may never be reintroduced.
You would not be wrong to think that timing of legislative sessions may be used
strategically by legislatures and their members. As legislative sessions unfold, legislators are likely to face pressure from various interests, as well as changing political,
economic, and social conditions, to act more quickly on some matters and to delay
or avoid acting on others. It took over six years and three separate bills before the
federal *Species at Risk Act* was finally passed in 2002.

Regulations

The process for making regulations is broadly similar at the federal and provincial
levels. Here more detail is provided for the federal system.

Initially, policy is developed by government departments or agencies. There may
be formal or informal public information and consultation at this stage, but it is
not legally required. Federal departments and agencies must prepare one-year
reports on plans and priorities, table these in Parliament, and post them on their
websites. A federal regulatory policy emphasizes consultation, considering risks

and benefits, minimizing impacts such as "regulatory burdens" on citizens, and using regulatory resources efficiently.

During the next step, legal drafting specialists draft regulations. Draft federal regulations must be accompanied by a regulatory impact analysis statement. This assesses alternatives, benefits and costs, consultation, proposed compliance and enforcement, and contact with affected interests. Some of this may be done in less formal ways for provincial regulations.

There are four fundamental requirements for making federal and provincial regulations:

- *Legal examination.* Proposed regulations must be reviewed to ensure that they are within the legal authority of the enabling statute, are not unusual or unexpected uses of this statutory authority, are consistent with the *Canadian Charter of Rights and Freedoms*, and are drafted according to established standards.

- *Order-in-council approval.* The federal governor in council or provincial lieutenant-governor in council makes a regulation by issuing an order in council. Sometimes a statute says that regulations can be made by ministers or tribunals. For federal regulations, Cabinet approval occurs after approval by the responsible minister and review by Privy Council Office legal specialists and Treasury Board financial officers.

- *Publication.* The formal announcement of regulatory intent is publication in the *Canada Gazette* (or in a provincial gazette). Interested persons are given a time period (usually 30 days, but longer for technical regulations) to express their views. Publication of the final regulation after order-in-council approval constitutes notice to the public of the regulation's contents. Citizens are legally bound by a regulation only after final publication and registration.

- *Registration.* The federal *Statutory Instruments Act* and the provincial regulations acts require registration to ensure that regulations are accessible to the public. Registration also specifies the date on which the regulation comes into force.

You can see that making regulations is a less open process than enacting statutes. Though there is notice and opportunity for written comment and, sometimes, public involvement at the early stage of regulation making, what is missing is the open public debate and often extensive media attention that characterizes the legislative process. This is significant for environmental law because environmental statutes are usually framework statutes, with critical details including standards and specific requirements left to regulations.

At the federal level, there is scrutiny of regulations by Parliament's Joint Committee on Statutory Instruments (as required by the *Statutory Instruments Act*). There are also regular reports to Parliament. The objective is to identify, publicize, and make recommendations concerning regulations that are overly intrusive or inconsistent with federal legislation or policies.

The Concept of Jurisdiction

As we have discussed earlier, statutes must lie within the **jurisdiction** (power to legislate) of the enacting federal or provincial government under the *Constitution Act, 1867*. Subordinate legislation such as regulations must similarly lie within the legal authority in the empowering statute. Otherwise, the legislation is outside the jurisdiction of the Cabinet, minister, or tribunal that attempted to make it. The same concept applies to municipal councils. Their bylaws must be within their jurisdiction under the authorizing provisions in the provincial government statutes that establish and empower municipal governments.

Determining whether a legislative authority has jurisdiction is not just a technical exercise in reading a statute. Rather, a purposive approach is taken. This involves examining the language of a statutory power within the context of the whole statute and within the external social economic and policy context in which it was enacted. For example, in *114957 Canada Ltée (Spraytech, Société d'arrosage) v. Hudson (Town)*, the town passed a bylaw that restricted application of pesticides within its boundaries. It acted under statutory powers to pass bylaws to regulate for the "peace, order, good government, health and welfare of its citizens." When the bylaw was challenged by a pesticide applicator company, the Supreme Court of Canada refused to follow its own earlier decisions that had taken a narrow technical approach to interpreting municipal enabling powers. Instead, it said that it had to look at the bigger picture of what municipal governments of community representatives should be entitled to do to protect the environment in which their citizens live. It considered the even bigger picture of environmental law, including the idea of "precaution," which is emerging as an international law principle. In this light, the authorizing provision must be given a "benevolent construction." The court found the bylaw to be a valid exercise of the town's jurisdiction.

We have seen that the idea of jurisdiction also applies to the powers of cabinets to make regulations. In this context, particularly where the authorizing provision is more specific than in the *Spraytech* case, the courts take a narrower approach when determining the scope of legislative power. For example, in *Heppner v. Alberta (Minister of the Environment)*, the Alberta legislature, acting under its regulation-making powers set out in the *Environment Conservation Act*, established a restricted development area on the edge of Edmonton for the purpose of an energy transmission and utility corridor. The Alberta Court of Appeal ruled that the legislature lacked the jurisdiction to do this because the purposes for restricted development areas in the authorizing statute listed conservation and pollution control; it did not mention transportation and utility corridors.

Discretionary Decisions and Policies

The concept of jurisdiction also applies to **discretionary decisions** made by authorized tribunals and government officials under powers conferred by environmental statutes. A discretionary decision-making power offers the decision-maker considerable latitude concerning the basis for a particular decision and the factors that can be taken into account in reaching the decision. In such cases, the clauses in the statute describing the official's decision-making power do not place any specific limitations on the scope of the decision or the relevant factors. Rather, they often state, for example, that the decision must be in the "public interest," or may simply state that the decision-maker "may" decide the issue. With a discretionary decision-making power, there is no single decision that is legally the right one.

Discretionary decisions include key regulatory decisions under environmental statutes, such as whether contaminant discharges should be approved or licensed, or whether forestry, mining, or other public natural resource rights should be granted to private developers. Even if the statutory power includes matters that must be considered in making the decision, these matters may be very broad. Consider how wide a discretion is left to a decision-maker empowered to have "regard to economic, social, and environmental effects."

As we will see in chapter 14, even these discretionary decisions may be challenged through judicial review. Courts assess a decision-maker's jurisdiction using a deferential approach. They consider the relevance and purpose of the factors and (sometimes) the specific information that the decision-maker looked at, and the consistency of the decision-maker's reasoning.

Policy decisions cannot usually be challenged on jurisdictional grounds because they do not involve the exercise of a specific statutory decision-making power. They are exercises in setting objectives and planning, under general powers given to ministers by statutes that establish and define the subjects of their government departments. They are decisions about what actions to take and how to take them. It is putting these policies into operation that requires either legislation or decisions under existing statutory powers. For example, a government policy decision to establish a greenhouse gas emission trading system, expressed in a ministerial statement or a government policy paper, cannot be challenged for lack of jurisdiction. But a statute to establish this kind of system can be challenged for lack of constitutional jurisdiction. For example, if the trading system requires specific emission limits for a facility, the federal government would have to establish a constitutional basis to impose such limits. If the trading system is established by means of new regulations under an existing statutory power, it can be challenged for lack of jurisdiction under the existing statute. In this instance, the statute has to give clear authority for Cabinet to pass such regulations. The challenge is not a constitutional one; rather, the challenge would be that the provincial legislation did not contemplate this type of initiative being undertaken under the statute. The question in all cases is one that lawyers ask governments with numbing regularity: What is your authority for that? In other words, where is your jurisdiction?

The Concept of Liability

Liability is a legal term that is surprisingly difficult to define with precision, yet it is fundamental to environmental law. It is essentially about obligation. *Black's Law Dictionary* defines **liability** as "every kind of legal obligation, responsibility, or duty." Legal obligations and responsibilities are enforced through the decisions and orders of courts and regulatory tribunals.

Environmental liability arises from obligations imposed by either

- the general law (codes or common law), or
- specific environmental legislation.

A common example is legislation that establishes liability for personal injury or property damage resulting from breach of a requirement of an environmental statute. Of particular importance is statutory liability for damage caused by contaminant spills, and liability for damage, remediation, and sometimes restoration of contaminated sites.

Liability can be civil, criminal, or administrative. Civil liability produces obligations to take or cease certain actions and to pay compensation to persons who have suffered harm. Criminal liability is penal, involving public sanction for breach of environmental legislation. Administrative liability is enforced through regulatory bodies and officials; it can impose specific abatement requirements, including compensation obligations in some cases.

Major issues concerning environmental liability include

- the kinds of environmental damage that result in liability,
- the classes of persons who can be held responsible,

- establishing through evidence the causal connection between the activity undertaken by one party and the harm endured by another,
- the threshold at which environmental damage entails liability, and
- the standard of care applicable to the obligation to prevent environmental damage.

Liability operates in international as well as in domestic law and, indeed, the major issues with respect to establishing liability under domestic law also apply to the international realm.

CHAPTER 4

Courts, Tribunals, and Dispute Settlement

An Introduction

The Canadian legal system can be a confusing maze of structures and terms. This should not be surprising since the Canadian system emerged from various other legal systems and then has evolved over the past century. This chapter attempts to provide a very basic overview of how Canadian courts and tribunals operate. This introduction is important since it

forms the foundation for an understanding of the following chapters. The courts' application and interpretation of substantive environmental issues are discussed in chapter 13. The functioning of tribunals is elaborated in chapter 14.

Civil Law and Common Law Jurisdictions

As we saw briefly at the beginning of chapter 3, the Canadian legal system is largely based on common law, except in Quebec, where the civil law also applies. Common law is a body of laws or general principles that are declared or applied by the courts. These principles emerged from customary arrangements, have evolved over hundreds of years of court decisions, and continue to evolve as courts deal with new circumstances and new understandings. Common law principles stand as basic tenets of our legal regime, guiding behaviour among us as citizens and neighbours. For example, as discussed in chapter 13, the common law establishes that we cannot undertake activity on our property if that activity unreasonably interferes with our neighbour's use of his property. Such interference constitutes the tort of nuisance. This idea is not written in any statute. Rather, it is a basic principle of common law.

When a court makes a decision applying the common law in a new case, that court sets a precedent. Its decision stands as a firm guide to courts making decisions about similar cases in the future. This principle is called *stare decisis*. As one case builds on another case, a whole body of case law is developed. Reading through the succession of cases that address a particular area of conflict can provide a clear understanding of the state of the law in that area. A higher court, such as a court of appeal, can overrule a lower court and create a new precedent. In Canada, the final say goes to the Supreme Court of Canada.

The role of lawyers is to inform their clients about the state of the law on any given topic. Because of the importance of common law, it is not enough merely to know what is set out in statutes and regulations. Often it is the long succession of common law decisions that is most important. For example, what are the rights of an ardent organic gardener whose neighbours are spraying pesticides on their lawns? Can the gardener argue that the neighbours are violating a common principle of nuisance because the spray appears to be migrating across the property line and into the organic garden?

In such a case, the lawyer for the organic gardener might first look for similar cases that have been decided in the past. Even if there are no cases with identical issues, the lawyer might find analogous cases that show how the common law goals of equity and fairness have been applied in ways that favour protecting the gardener's interests in the present case. Of course, the lawyer for the neighbours would look for precedent-setting cases that favour the lawn sprayers' position. The court would then have to apply the common law and make a decision. This decision would be binding for future cases.

It could, for example, become a precedent in a later case where a family is barbecuing meat every night next door to a vegetarian family. The vegetarians object, saying that the constant smell of burning meat spoils the enjoyment of their patio and that the barbecuers are committing an "unreasonable interference." Perhaps these neighbours can work out their differences. But if the conflict comes to court, and if the earlier decision had favoured the organic farmers over the pesticide sprayers, the vegetarian family could use the decision as a precedent. They could argue that the court should protect their patio enjoyment from barbecue odours just as the earlier court had protected the organic farmer from pesticide spray. The lawyer for the barbecuing family, however, could argue that the precedent does not apply because this case is fundamentally different from the earlier one. While spraying pesticides on a lawn serves only a cosmetic purpose, cooking is an essential human need. Hence, fumes from cooking do not create the unreasonable interference complained of in the lawsuit.

Common law jurisdictions must be distinguished from **civil law jurisdictions**. While most of Europe relies on civil law, only Quebec and Louisiana in North America are civil law jurisdictions. The basic principles and rules of law in civil law jurisdictions are derived from a civil code—le droit civil—that the courts interpret and apply on a case-by-case basis. Unlike common law, civil law does not rely on precedents. There is no doctrine of *stare decisis*. While these are two different theories of law, there are many similarities.

Civil Law and Criminal Law Systems

Although the term "civil law" can refer to civil law jurisdictions like Quebec, it also has another connotation. Even within common law jurisdictions, there is an important distinction between **civil law systems** and **criminal law systems**. In most countries, including Canada, the civil law and criminal law systems work side by side. Civil law cases deal with disputes between parties—that is, between individuals in society, whether someone is collecting on money owed or neighbours are involved in a dispute over a fence. In a civil law case before a court, the party pursuing the claim, usually called the plaintiff, must establish that the defendant committed a wrong. Such a wrong is called a tort in common law jurisdictions and a responsabilité civile under the *Civil Code of Québec*. For example, in the organic farmer versus the pesticide sprayers case described above, the organic farmer (the plaintiff) would bring a claim in the tort of nuisance against the sprayers (the defendants). In chapter 13, we provide more information about environmental claims. If the plaintiff is successful, the court may order the defendants to stop their spraying and/or require them to compensate the plaintiff with a payment of money called **damages** and/or grant some other type of relief.

The criminal law system, in contrast, deals with breaking the laws designed to protect the interests of society in general. If one breaks a criminal law (for example, a federal law against theft) or a quasi-criminal law (for example, a provincial statute against dumping toxic chemicals), then the government (usually the attorney general's office) can prosecute the lawbreaker. The violation of the law is not only a wrong against the victim of the crime, but a wrong against society in general.

A key difference between the civil and criminal law systems involves the standard of proof that has to be met. In a criminal law case, the prosecutor must establish that the accused person is guilty beyond a reasonable doubt. Before convicting the accused person, the court must be satisfied that there are no reasonable grounds for thinking that the accused might not be guilty. In a civil matter, the standard of proof is much less onerous. The plaintiff must prove only that on a balance of probabilities the defendant is in the wrong. In other words, the court decides which party is more likely to be right and gives a judgment in that party's favour. In a criminal case, the accused, if convicted, is subject to incarceration and/or a fine. In a civil suit, the usual remedy is monetary damages.

It is important to re-emphasize that the civil and criminal systems coexist. A person can be charged with a criminal or quasi-criminal offence *and* be subject to a civil lawsuit for damages. A classic example is the O.J. Simpson case in the United States, where a well-known football player was charged with the murder of his wife. At the criminal trial, the accused was found not guilty. However, the family of the deceased brought a civil action against the defendant and won a fairly large damages award. In this case, one can speculate that although the government could not prove "beyond a reasonable doubt" that Simpson caused the death of his wife under criminal law, the plaintiff family could prove that he was liable for her death on a "balance of probabilities."

Courts and Tribunals

Courts may often seem to be the only major decision-making bodies in the Canadian legal system. However, the situation is much more complex, especially in environmental matters.

Courts have long played an adjudicative role in resolving disputes concerning environmental abuses. In fact, cases date back at least to the 1600s, when the courts in England ruled on issues involving contaminated drinking water or neighbourhoods poisoned by air emissions. Most cases today are considerably less dramatic, but the courts are still often called upon to rule on a wide range of environmental matters.

Since the Second World War, however, the courts have increasingly shared adjudicative tasks with other bodies. As a consequence of technological innovations, expanding pressures on limited resources, rising public expectations, and other related factors, environmental problems became more complex. In response, new regulatory regimes were developed, often with specialized **tribunals** established to deal with particular categories of concerns and conflicts. Some of the more important tribunals now carry much of the responsibility for adjudication of disputes in land use planning, sectoral regulation, pollution control, and assessment of new undertakings. While the courts retain advantages in breadth of authority and experience, key features of the tribunals can make them better equipped than courts to oversee and administer complex environmental regimes.

How Courts Work

Courts are an integral part of our democratic system. Their primary functions are to apply the law (for example, by imposing sanctions through the criminal law), to provide a check on the use of government power (for example, by protecting civil rights), and to adjudicate on matters of rights and liabilities (for example, by ruling on disputes over property rights). In short, the courts attempt to deal with disputes in society.

The courts are, by design, adversarial in nature. The underlying theory is that the truth will emerge from the conflict of opposing positions. Accordingly, lawyers for each side are expected to represent their clients' interests fearlessly. Judges are appointed usually through a formal process and given a high degree of independence. In a civil matter, the result of a court case is a judgment in favour of a plaintiff or a defendant. In a criminal matter, the accused is either acquitted or found guilty of committing an offence.

How Tribunals Work

A tribunal is an administrative board, commission, panel, or some other decision-making body. Today there are hundreds of tribunals making decisions ranging from the Canadian Radio-television and Telecommunications Commission granting licences to broadcasters to university adjudication bodies deciding what action to take when a student appeals a course mark.

Many tribunals have been established to implement statutory schemes that involve the granting (and withdrawal) of permits or that provide for hearings in planning or environmental assessment cases. Tribunals are meant to be less formal than courts and thus more accessible to the public. Although tribunal proceedings can be fiercely adversarial, often tribunals encourage the participation of many diverse parties beyond the immediate proponents and critics of the matter in question. Unlike courts, tribunals often take an active inquisitorial role, asking their own questions and perhaps even initiating their own research, rather than relying solely on the emergence of information from opposing positions.

In Canada, many legislated regimes dealing with environmental matters include roles for tribunals. At the federal level, the boards of review can be set up under the *Canadian Environmental Protection Act, 1999* to deal with certain chemical assessments. Panels can also be set up under the *Canadian Environmental Assessment Act* to consider the potential effects and desirability of major proposed projects.

Provincial examples of environmental tribunals include Ontario's Environmental Review Tribunal, which is mandated to examine and rule on undertakings subject to environmental assessment and to hear appeals about administrative orders (for pollution cleanup, for example) or decisions to grant or refuse approvals (for new sources of air or water discharges, for example). Alberta's Environmental Appeals Board is a tribunal that allows Albertans to appeal decisions of Alberta Environment under the *Environmental Protection and Enhancement Act* and the *Water Act* regarding development approvals, water licences, reclamation certificates, and enforcement orders, for example.

Not all tribunals have final decision-making authority. Some (for example, federal environmental assessment panels and water boards in the northern territories) are empowered only to make recommendations to the relevant government minister. And in other cases, a tribunal's ruling (such as a decision of the Joint Board in Ontario) may be appealed to the relevant federal or provincial Cabinet.

	Courts	Tribunals
Purpose	Adjudicating rights among the parties	Overseeing a legislative framework
Mode of operation	Adversarial	Inquisitorial
Participants	• Judge adjudicates • Plaintiff brings action • Defendant defends action	• Tribunal members render decision • Proponent main player has onus to establish statutory tests for approval requested • Government officials may appear • Members of public may intervene
Nature of outcome	Judgment outlining winners and losers	Decision geared to further the public interest in administering the regime

Dispute Resolution

It would be misleading to suggest that all disputes are resolved through the courts or the tribunals. In fact, most matters are resolved through some sort of **alternative dispute resolution (ADR)** mechanism. ADR includes formal or informal negotiation or mediation. It is often difficult to become involved in a court or tribunal process without also becoming involved in an ADR process. Some ADR processes are very formal exercises with professional facilitators. Others rely on less formal negotiations to resolve some or all of the issues before the court or tribunal by mutual agreement among the parties.

CHAPTER 5

The Relationship Between Canadian and International Law

How International Law Works

International law is a collection of rules governing countries. This simple definition should not disguise the complexity of international law. It is somewhat dangerous to compare international and **domestic law** (law within a particular country) because there are so many differences. Unlike domestic law in Canada, international law has no legislature that actually makes law, and it has no police force that can readily enforce the law. In fact, a constant challenge in international law is even identifying the precise obligations that states must fulfill.

The most fundamental precept of international law is that states are sovereign in nature. They can do what they want subject only to limits imposed by international law. In general terms, a state may be bound by conventional law or customary international law. How well this precept will serve in coming years is uncertain, in part because of the expanding challenges of environmental protection on a global scale. Many traditional environmental problems (resource degradation and overuse, habitat destruction, biodiversity loss, and exposure to toxic substances, for example) are now cross-boundary issues and pose international threats to human and ecosystem well-being. Moreover, we now have fully global problems, the most serious of which is probably human-induced climate change. To deal effectively with these concerns, some further strengthening of international environmental law may be needed.

Conventional International Law

Conventional international law is established when two or more countries conclude a **treaty** or an international **convention.** These conventions bind only those countries that have signed them. Essentially, a treaty or convention is like a contract between two people. In a contract, one party agrees to do something (such as paint a house) if the other party agrees to some equally valuable action (such as paying a stated price for the work). Similarly, a country may agree to give up a small portion of its sovereignty on particular matters within specified limits that are defined in the treaty. As might be expected, great efforts are usually made in treaty negotiations to determine precisely what the agreement covers and what obligations are involved.

Most treaties and conventions take a long time to negotiate and implement. The basic steps of this process usually start when an international body (for example, the United Nations Environment Programme) agrees to sponsor the negotiations among countries. If the international negotiating sessions are successful, an agreement is drafted and signed by the participating countries. However, the agreement does not take effect until a defined number of those countries have ratified the agreement within an allotted time.

Ratification simply means agreement to the terms of the convention by the national legislature of the countries signing the convention. On ratification, the agreement comes into effect, although most often there is a multi-year phase-in period. Once the agreement is in effect, the countries meet periodically in "conferences of the parties" to review the progress of the implementation.

A good example is the 2001 Stockholm Convention on Persistent Organic Pollutants, an agreement in which Canada played a major role. The thrust of the convention is to phase out the "dirty dozen" most dangerous toxic substances in the world. Among other things, the Stockholm convention finally put in place a timeline to phase out DDT, which was identified as a damaging persistent toxin by Rachel Carson in her famous book *Silent Spring.* The book appeared in 1962, nearly 40 years before the Stockholm convention finally brought international action on this issue.

Negotiations for the Stockholm convention commenced in 1996 in Montreal. In 2001, after five more negotiation sessions, the parties concluded the convention in Stockholm, Sweden. The convention did not come into force until May 2004, when the last of 50 countries ratified it. One year later, the first conference of the parties was held to review the implementation of the convention.

Generally speaking, international conventions use a standard framework consisting of sections that set out

- the purposes of the convention,
- the general and specific obligations of the parties,

- reporting obligations,
- dispute settlement and compliance mechanisms, and
- review mechanisms for the convention.

There are now hundreds of bilateral and multilateral treaties, conventions, and agreements pertaining to environmental protection and resource management. Hence, the first task in understanding the commitments of a particular state is to list the international agreements to which it is a party, and to understand the precise nature and scope of the obligations it has agreed to in each instrument.

Customary International Law

Customary international law is the set of rules that have evolved over time and been accepted by states as effective law. There are two attributes of customary law. First, states must recognize a particular rule of law to be binding (this doctrine is called *opinio juris*). Second, states must in fact follow the rule.

With respect to the environment, there are a number of important international customs that are relevant, such as the following:

- *The good neighbour rule.* This principle requires a state not to cause damage to the environment of another state. It can be applied in situations such as dumping toxins into the Great Lakes, where a particular neighbour is affected, which is reminiscent of the tort of nuisance. It can also be applied to greenhouse gas emissions, where the scope of the neighbourhood is the entire planet.
- *Duty of equitable utilization.* This principle requires the fair sharing of resources outside national boundaries, such as in international waters. It involves an imperative to preserve and protect these resources with thought to the rights of others who also have the right to use them.
- *Duty to notify and consult.* This principle requires a state that is undertaking an activity that could result in harm to neighbouring nations to notify and consult with the governments of those nations. For example, if radioactive waste is to be shipped in international waters, any countries that could be affected by a spill should be notified in advance.

Relevance to Canadian Environmental Law

The effect of international environmental law on domestic law varies. Arguably, international law influences domestic law by imposing requirements that must be carried out by Canada. However, whether or not these are carried out in practice depends largely on political will, and on the effect of changing governments. For example, Canada signed the United Nations Framework Convention on Climate Change in 1992, promising to stabilize greenhouse gas emissions at 1990 levels by the year 2000. We also signed the Kyoto Protocol in 1997, promising to cut Canadian emissions to 6 percent below our 1990 levels by 2012. But the Canadian Parliament did not formally ratify the Kyoto Protocol until late 2002, and no Canadian government took effective action on the file. In 2005, Canadian greenhouse gas emissions levels were 32.7 percent above 1990 levels and rising. In contrast, the United Nations Convention on Biological Diversity was signed and ratified by Canada in 1992. Ten years later, in 2002, the *Species at Risk Act* was enacted, finally bringing Canada into compliance with its obligations under the convention.

In other cases, Canada has influenced international law. The classic example is the expansion of Canada's rights over the oceans' resources. During the 1960s and early 1970s, Canada unilaterally extended its rights by establishing an exclusive economic zone stretching 200 nautical miles from the coast. This was a new development; previously, states controlled only a very narrow belt of water adjacent to their coasts—approximately 3 to 12 nautical miles. Beyond this belt of **territorial waters**, the ocean was part of the high seas and open to use and exploitation by anyone. Before the new international regime introduced by Canada, two United Nations conferences on the law of the sea were unable to achieve consensus on extending jurisdiction to even a 12-mile limit. Despite this history, Canada's initiative was embraced internationally, and the principle of an exclusive economic zone was accepted as a customary rule of international law. Later it was entrenched in the Law of the Sea Treaty. This treaty now provides all coastal nations with exclusive rights to a very important economic resource, including rich fishing and fossil fuel reserves.

Canada has not been a major player in the international environmental law scene. We have, however, made some significant contributions while at the same time being careful and not always consistent about the obligations we have been willing to take on through the negotiation of international agreements. In fact, at times Canada has been obstructive in achieving more progressive international obligations under international law. For example, Canada has not taken proactive or progressive positions with respect to international negotiations on an international agreement to control mercury or on a proposal to add chrysotile asbestos to the Rotterdam Convention. Although Canada is often considered to be a leading member of the pack, in practice, at the international level, Canada has too often tried to stall positive environmental initiatives.

PART II

The Basics of Environmental Law

CHAPTER 6

The Development of Canadian Environmental Law

Four Evolutionary Phases in Canadian Environmental Law

The four evolutionary phases show Canadian environmental laws addressing a rough succession of increasingly difficult subjects. These four phases are reasonably easy to discern in the overall history of federal and provincial environmental law, but they certainly did not evolve in a tidy sequential arrangement; nor did they evolve at the same time everywhere.

Phase 1: Common Law Rights and Early Statutes

The 1960s were characterized not just by the Beatles, bellbottoms, and rebellions against authority. They are also remembered as the decade when legislators began to give serious attention to the environment. Still, a contemporary environmental lawyer transported back to the 1960s would quickly discover that almost her entire kit of environmental law tools was missing. She would find no regulatory statutes with contaminant discharge limits, no approvals based on these limits, and no civil and criminal penalties for failure to comply.

A bit of legal research (the old-fashioned library kind) would show our environmental lawyer the tools available to her. The federal *Fisheries Act* would be there, as it has been since the 1860s, but it would be limited to blanket prohibitions against discharge of "deleterious substances" in "waters frequented by fish." She would also find public health statutes, a public nuisance offence in the *Criminal Code*, and a scattering of anti-pollution provisions in natural resource development statutes. Courts would not recognize the right of citizens to challenge government statutory decisions (or non-decisions) that resulted in environmental harm, unless the citizens could show direct harm to their persons or property.

The main tools available to an environmentally conscious lawyer in the 1960s were the **causes of action** available under the tort and property law components of the common law (or the *Civil Code of Québec*). The most promising of these would likely involve lawsuits in nuisance and **negligence**. While effective in some circumstances, nuisance and negligence lawsuits were designed to resolve disputes between private parties and compensate persons harmed. As legal tools, they fall well short of providing comprehensive and systematic environmental protection. Private civil actions against polluters that were also important employers and revenue producers, such as natural resource development operations or industrial plants, often ran squarely into unsympathetic judges. But as the 1960s progressed, citizen awareness of environmental problems increased and prompted demands for more effective ways of combatting them.

This is not to stay that civil actions are less important today. In addition, in attempting to recover damages or to halt some action that is harmful or may harm the environment, there are many "test" cases where lawsuits are brought in hope of a decision that breaks new ground in terms of introducing or reinterpreting a principle or interpreting a statute. Sometimes, even if a particular legal action is unsuccessful, it may lay the foundation for a more protective legal regime in the future.

Phase 2: Waste Control and Cleanup Laws

In the late 1960s, citizens and governments awakened to the recognition that concerted and comprehensive environmental protection action was needed. Basic air, water, and land pollution statutes were enacted by the provinces in the late 1960s and 1970s. The federal government broadened its *Fisheries Act*. The essential objective was control of harmful substances that were being deposited on land or discharged into air and water.

Governments established regulatory systems to identify waste sources and require permits to control the quantity and quality of substances discharged. The terms and conditions of permits were often the result of closed negotiations between the industrial applicants and the regulators. Failure to comply with these requirements was an offence punishable on summary conviction (a minor offence) and resulted in modest fines for those found guilty.

The discharge of waste that was likely to harm the environment or human life or health was often established as a general offence. In this context, the "environment" was generally defined as air, water, and land upon which human life depends. Governments only gradually issued regulations specifying requirements for control of particular contaminants.

The new statutes were **cleanup laws**, designed to regulate discharge of human and industrial waste into the environment. Among them were comprehensive statutes dealing with air, water, and land pollution. Examples of these statutes include the Ontario *Environmental Protection Act*, the Quebec *Environment Quality Act*, and the BC *Pollution Control Act*. There were also single-element statutes, such as Alberta's *Clean Water Act*, *Clean Air Act*, and *Land Surface Conservation and Reclamation Act* (these Acts were consolidated in the 1990s into the *Environmental Protection and Enhancement Act*).

The underlying assumption was that the natural environment could be used to dispose of, dilute, and cleanse the waste produced by human activity, as long as sufficiently careful management prevented too much contamination at any one time and place. Legislation was a matter of fairly allocating nature's assimilative capacity. Though these laws have changed significantly, this waste control function still remains at their core.

Waste control laws were administered by environmental departments that were largely technical agencies, staffed by scientific and engineering experts who administered the permit or approval schemes. These departments developed guidelines, rather than enforceable regulations, for "safe" waste discharge. Initially much effort was required simply to bring all waste sources under permit.

Phase 3: Toxics Control Laws

When people think of environmentally harmful chemicals or substances, they may expect that the government can step in and quickly deal with the issue. However, the regulation of toxic chemicals is far more complicated.

Emerging evidence in the 1970s and 1980s indicated that waste control laws aimed at allocating assimilative capacity did not address accumulation in the environment of persistent toxic substances. This realization led to new legislative action. Both levels of government, at least in part, have the authority to regulate the toxic substances. In *R v. Hydro-Québec*, the Supreme Court of Canada recognized the federal government's authority to regulate toxic substances under the criminal law power (see chapter 3).

The major **toxics control laws** are the 1975 federal *Environmental Contaminants Act* and its successor, the *Canadian Environmental Protection Act* (CEPA). CEPA is the primary vehicle for the regulation of both existing and new substances in Canada. It provides a number of processes for assessing substances with respect to their risks to environmental or human health, and imposes information requirements on manufacturers and importers introducing new chemicals to Canada. At present, over 23,000 substances that are made, imported, or used in Canada on a commercial basis have not undergone a full assessment.

Amendments to CEPA in 1999 sought to expedite the assessment process by requiring Health and Environment Canada to categorize or identify certain substances that pose a significant risk, namely, those that

- are inherently toxic (cause toxic effects) and persistent (take a long time to break down);
- are bioaccumulative (collect in living organisms and move up the food chain); or
- have the greatest potential for exposure to individuals.

Under CEPA, existing substances may be subjected to assessment in various ways. Consider the following lists used for categorizing and assessing substances:

1. *Domestic Substances List.* Under the general scheme of the Act, all existing substances are placed on the Domestic Substances List (DSL).

2. *Priority Substances List.* Substances can be placed on the Priority Substances List (PSL) and undergo a rigorous assessment of their risks to the environment and human health. Of the 69 or so substances assessed to date, over 40 have been found to be toxic as defined under CEPA.

3. *Toxic Substances List.* If a substance is found to be toxic as defined under CEPA, it may be placed on the Toxic Substances List (TSL). Once a substance is on the TSL, the federal government has very broad authority to regulate the substance. Dioxins, PCBs, and mercury, to name but a few, are regulated under these provisions.

More about the categorization process can be found at www.ec.gc.ca/CEPARegistry/the_act/guide04/toc.cfm. If a substance meets the criteria, a screening-level risk assessment is undertaken to determine whether the substance is toxic as defined under CEPA. The assessment of substances may also be based on a review of the assessments undertaken in other countries.

A number of other federal statutes deal with potentially harmful substances, such as the *Pest Control Products Act* (PCPA), the *Transportation of Dangerous Goods Act* (and its provincial clones), and the *Hazardous Products Act.* The PCPA regulates products that are used to control pests, insects, and so on (see chapter 9). The *Transportation of Dangerous Goods Act*, as its name suggests, imposes restrictions and safeguards on the transportation of materials and goods that could be dangerous to the public in the event of an accident. The *Hazardous Products Act* regulates products that may contain toxic or dangerous substances.

On April 8, 2008, the federal government introduced Bill C-52, the *Canada Consumer Product Safety Act*, which is intended to replace and update substantial portions of the *Hazardous Products Act* and to respond to growing fears of toxic contamination of consumer products such as children's toys. The proposed legislation would endow the government with new testing powers and the authority to issue mandatory recall orders for unsafe consumer products and to require manufacturers, sellers, and importers to take corrective measures. More about the proposed legislation and related initiatives can be found at www.healthycanadians .ca/pr-rp/action-plan_e.html.

Provincial statutes were tightened with the addition of requirements for the reporting and cleanup of toxic substance spills. Provisions were also added that imposed liability for spills and contaminated sites on landowners and former landowners, and even on manufacturers, sellers, and users of toxic substances.

These laws recognize that environmental protection is a long-term process that must address potential intergenerational effects of environmental damage. Because scientific knowledge about the toxicity of particular substances is continually developing, these laws include protocols and processes for identification and effective control of contaminants. The approach is preventive and anticipatory, not merely reactive.

Also reflected in these statutes is the fact that toxic substances respect neither ecosystem nor political boundaries. Consequently, the laws are outward-looking in their development, implementation, and administration. The federal statutes took into account toxics research and international standards. Both federal and provincial laws began to reflect interprovincial and federal–provincial undertakings and commitments more clearly than before. They were also made more consistent with international conditions and Canada's international obligations. For example, in the 1980s, Ontario stated that it wanted its water quality program to reflect the zero-discharge objectives for control of persistent toxics under the 1978 Great Lakes Water Quality Agreement between Canada and the United States.

Phase 4: Comprehensive Approaches Involving Environmental Assessment and Planning and Management Regimes

During the early period when new waste control and cleanup laws were being introduced, many governments in Canada and elsewhere began to consider more anticipatory and preventive approaches to pollution and other environmental problems. Chief among the anticipatory and preventive tools were **environmental assessment** requirements and **planning and management regimes**. Environmental assessment requirements forced proponents of environmentally significant new projects, such as hydro power stations, airports, mines, roads, and landfills, to predict and evaluate the potential effects of these proposed undertakings. Sometimes comparison with reasonable alternatives was required before approvals were granted.

Assessment requirements were imposed hesitantly in most jurisdictions. The federal government relied on a more or less discretionary policy-based assessment process for two decades before it finally passed legislated requirements. Ontario, which applied a strong assessment law to public sector undertakings beginning in 1975, left the private sector largely free of obligations. But eventually, the federal government, every province and territory, many land claim agreement areas, and a substantial number of municipalities had law-based environmental assessment processes.

Although some Canadian assessment processes remain quite limited in application and ambition, most now go beyond mere evaluation of direct project effects to consider at least some of the following matters:

- cumulative effects (of the project plus other existing and expected activities);
- combinations of ecological, socioeconomic, and cultural effects;
- implications of uncertainties; and
- effects of strategic undertakings (plans, programs, and policies).

Some legal authorities argue that environmental assessment constitutes the only area of environmental law that is unique, and not merely an application of established legal approaches and instruments to environmental issues.

Planning and management regimes have a longer history than environmental assessment. Some law-based processes for decision making, concerning the management of fisheries, forestry operations, protected areas, and other Crown land uses, for example, go back 100 years or more. But most have been strengthened considerably in recent years in response to a variety of concerns that include the following:

- rising pressures on limited resources, such as old-growth forests;
- conflicts among competing uses, such as those that arise between sprawling suburbs and wildlife habitat; and
- evidence of serious management failures, such as that revealed by the destruction of the north Atlantic cod fishery.

Today there are many and various legislated planning and management regimes. They deal with many different resources—for example, forests, fisheries, endangered species, farmlands, and watersheds—and many different sectors—for example, electric power, solid waste, urban growth, and transportation. Not surprisingly, the approaches taken differ in important ways. Even within the same resource or sector, different provinces have adopted different requirements and procedures. This is evident in the field of forest management, for example.

Despite differences, the general trend is toward more comprehensive approaches that recognize numerous influences and complex implications, consider more response options, give greater respect to uncertainty, and include a wider range of interests.

Many of these regimes no longer focus solely on particular resources or environments, but rather on the interrelations and potential conflicts among many objectives and activities. As a result, environmental law as well as broader land use and other planning laws are beginning to be combined in more comprehensive responses to pressing problems. This is evident, for example, in the regional growth management initiatives in the rapidly urbanizing areas of southern British Columbia and southern Ontario.

Five Associated Trends

In the environmental statutes, regulations, and administrative practices introduced since the 1960s, we can see several trends that have affected the laws' core concerns and the roles of various interests in their design and application. While these terms have had different effects in different jurisdictions, each has been or promises to be significant everywhere in Canada.

Regional, Continental, and Global Effects

In the early days, environmental protection efforts focused on the local effects of particular sources and contaminants. As noted above, the popular view was that "dilution is the solution to pollution." Accordingly, when industrial air emissions were causing undeniable damage in the neighbourhood in which a plant was situated, the accepted response was to require construction of a taller emission stack.

This technique was most famously used in Sudbury, where acidifying emissions and other contaminants from the nickel smelters had killed much of the local vegetation and left a moonscape suitable for astronaut training. Construction of a 380-metre (1,250-foot) stack at the Inco smelter in the early 1970s helped reduce local pollution loadings and allow vegetation recovery. But it also spread the acidifying contaminants much farther. By the early 1980s, the long-range atmospheric transport of acidifying pollutants from Sudbury and a host of other major and minor sources was clearly having serious effects on the overall acidity of precipitation across huge areas of North America and Europe.

The **dilution solution** had led to environmental damage on a regional and continental scale. Eventually, environmental authorities in Ontario and other jurisdictions in North America and Europe were moved to rewrite their environmental laws and facility-specific requirements to deal with effects well beyond the local scale.

Today the best-publicized environmental concern is global climate change, which has also resulted from emissions from a multitude of local sources. While responses to this problem are still far from adequate, the planetary scale of the challenge and the need for similarly inclusive action is well recognized.

Transparency and Citizen Participation

In Canada, as in many countries, the initial inclination of government authorities was to deny or minimize environmental problems, and to resist imposing the full costs of environmental protection on corporate or individual taxpayers. In the late 1960s and early 1970s, a wave of public interest environmental groups emerged to challenge government authorities. Through effective collaboration with the news media, environmental groups raised public awareness of environmental problems and pushed governments toward stronger and more comprehensive environmental protection laws.

Unfortunately, the failure of governments to take initiative in acknowledging and addressing environmental problems contributed to public distrust of government authorities on issues of environmental protection. This distrust was deepened by the frequent weakness of government efforts to enforce the new laws and by the common practice of developing pollution abatement requirements through secret negotiations between regulatory authorities and polluting industries.

As a reaction to these frustrations, environmental groups began to push for greater transparency in the decision-making process, including the following:

- timely and convenient access to information,
- opportunities for direct involvement in deliberations leading to new policies,
- regulatory requirements and case-specific decisions, and
- rights to demand action and to participate in or pursue public interest litigation.

While not all of these efforts have been successful, most Canadian jurisdictions now make decisions related to environmental law in a much more transparent and participatory way than they did 30 years ago. The Supreme Court of Canada improved access to justice by removing doctrinal barriers to bringing legal challenges. The court substituted relatively flexible criteria for discretionary public interest standing. (The concept of **standing** in courts is discussed further in chapter 13.) Simply put, the issue is about whether members of the public can challenge the legality of a provision of legislation or a government decision when they may be directly affected by that decision in cases where their property or health may be harmed. The courts have stated that the public can at times bring such lawsuits if certain criteria are met and, most important, if the person bringing the action has a genuine interest in the matter and there is no other way to bring the issues before the court. See: *Minister of Justice v. Borowski*, [1981] 2 SCR 575; *Canadian Council of Churches v. Canada (Minister of Employment and Immigration)*, [1992] 1 SCR 236; and *Finlay v. Canada (Minister of Finance)*, [1986] 2 SCR 607. And many of the newer environmental laws, such as the *Canadian Environmental Protection Act, 1999* and Ontario's *Environmental Bill of Rights, 1993*, encourage public consultation and participation. Residents may even become decision-makers under provisions for mediated negotiation among stakeholders. It is no longer a two-party government–industry negotiation process.

International Influence on Precaution

Modern environmental law in Canada and other nations is increasingly influenced by international law principles and agreements. Below are examples of international agreements explicitly implemented by Canadian environmental laws:

- The Biological Diversity Convention was implemented by the *Species at Risk Act* to protect endangered species.
- The London Dumping Convention was implemented by the *Canadian Environmental Protection Act, 1999* to reduce marine pollution.
- The Montreal Protocol on Substances That Deplete the Ozone Layer was implemented by the *Canadian Environmental Protection Act, 1999* to protect against ozone-depleting substances.

The rising influence of international law results in part from the need for responses to international-scale environmental problems. These problems include climate change, stratospheric ozone depletion, acidic precipitation, biodiversity loss, and trade in toxic substances. Perhaps because of the evident perils involved, international environmental law has also been a forum for significant innovation.

One such innovation that is particularly important is the legal adoption of the precautionary principle, which holds:

> When an activity raises threats of harm to human health or the environment, precautionary measures should be taken even if some cause and effect relationships are not fully established scientifically. In this context the proponent of an activity, rather than the public, should bear the burden of proof.

Essentially, the precautionary principle recognizes that the world of environmental interrelations is extremely complex and that our ability to describe it, much less predict the effects of new interventions, is extremely limited. Uncertainty is therefore always present and often important.

In international law, including multilateral environmental agreements, the precautionary principle is now widely accepted and increasingly applied as customary law. Application in Europe is also extensive. In Canada precaution is frequently advocated in policy statements, sometimes incorporated in statutory objectives and purposes, and often seen in some areas of implementation. Attention to uncertainties, anticipation of worst-case possibilities, and planning for adaptation are now commonly expected in major environmental assessments.

So far, the influence of these precautionary steps on the character of Canadian environmental law and practice has been limited. There is little evidence that the principle is applied rigorously in permit and approval decisions or in enforcement actions. However, in *114957 Canada Ltée (Spraytech, Société d'arrosage) v. Hudson (Town)*, a notable decision in 2001, the Supreme Court of Canada used the precautionary principle in its interpretation of a municipal government statute to decide whether it authorized a municipal bylaw regulating and restricting pesticide use. Justice L'Heureux-Dubé's use of the precautionary principle was based on her assessment that it was, at least arguably, a principle of customary international law.

Effective and Efficient Application of the Law

Especially since the 1990s, the introduction, design, and application of environmental law in Canada have been affected by increased scrutiny of government initiatives. The main factors driving this trend are the following:

- ideological predispositions and corporate interests,
- concerns about the costs of government programs, and
- doubts about effectiveness.

Environmental laws have not been alone in this. But they have received particular attention because industrial interests have associated environmental laws with increased costs. They have also suffered long-term frustration as a result of the great diversity of general approaches and specific environmental requirements imposed by different jurisdictions. In response to concerns about costs and regulatory burdens, some governments have repealed or weakened environmental laws. Witness, for example, the virtual elimination of environmental assessment law in British Columbia. Some governments have also put more emphasis on **voluntary compliance** initiatives.

At the same time, public interest advocates have consistently underlined the continuing failure of current environmental laws and their application to resolve problems in most areas of environmental concern. More positive initiatives include a new generation of environmental statutes with sophisticated enforcement provisions. Environmental laws are now being drafted as broader packages that include legal, economic, educational, and other means to encourage and enforce environmental improvements.

These new approaches give regulators greater flexibility to choose from a broad range of enforcement tools, depending on what is most appropriate in the circumstances. Some such tools include the following:

- tickets for minor offences,
- criminal indictments for endangering life or health,
- mandatory administrative orders,
- administrative penalties, and
- lawsuits.

The broader packages use regulation and the threat of additional regulation along with more general liability provisions, incentives, multi-stakeholder negotiations, and sector-specific "voluntary" programs to push for compliance and performance beyond legal requirements.

To catch the attention of the corporate sector, some jurisdictions have accompanied these more flexible approaches with provisions for large fines and potential imprisonment for serious environmental offences, as well as with provisions for corporate officer and director liability. This has given corporations a strong incentive to review and audit their compliance with environmental requirements, take necessary action, and prepare and implement environmental management policies and plans.

Not all of these flexible approaches are well integrated or consistently applied. Moreover, there is still great variation from one jurisdiction to the next. When something goes wrong, the various environmental agencies may point the finger of responsibility elsewhere. Provinces, for example, may blame federal officials and vice versa. However, most agencies also guard their mandate, authority, and independence tenaciously.

The resulting differences in requirements have frustrated not only many corporate interests that are subject to environmental laws but also environmental advocates who would like to push them all along a little faster. In response, federal and provincial governments, especially through the Canadian Council of Ministers of the Environment, have begun over the past decade to take some steps toward harmonizing environmental law requirements. This too remains a work in progress.

Sustainability Objectives

The final general trend is the continuing spread of official commitments to sustainability or **sustainable development**. The concept of sustainability, popularized by the 1987 report of the World Commission on Environment and Development (the Brundtland commission), has been much debated and often misused. But its essential role has been threefold:

1. to underline the unsustainable character of present inequities and environmental degradation;
2. to recognize the interdependence of social, economic, and ecological well-being; and
3. to encourage attention to the interests of future generations.

In Canada sustainability has been included as a core purpose of most recent federal and provincial environmental statutes. All federal departments and agencies are required to have sustainable development strategies that are regularly reviewed and updated every three years. Manitoba has a *Sustainable Development Act*, which is, among other things, meant to encourage and guide government decision-makers to integrate the broad range of interrelated sustainability considerations into their decision making under existing and future laws, even when these laws have a specific, narrow focus. Several other provinces (including Nova Scotia, Quebec, and British Columbia) have sustainability-centred statutes, plans, ministries, and reporting requirements.

As with the closely associated precautionary principle, the adoption of sustainability objectives is still much stronger in expressed intention than in rigorous application. But there have been important practical applications under environmental law. The sustainability-based provisions of British Columbia's *Growth Management Strategies Act*, for example, have encouraged better integrated and more farsighted approaches to planning in urban regions. The several review panels established under the *Canadian Environmental Assessment Act* have used the law's sustainability purposes as justification for requiring project proponents to show that their proposed undertakings would make a positive contribution to sustainability rather than merely avoid causing significant negative effects.

All of these trends are continuing, and we will return to them at the end of the book, where we consider what may lie ahead for environmental law in Canada. But now, with this brief historical review in hand, we are ready to take a more comprehensive look at the environmental law system.

CHAPTER 7

The Basic Structure of Environmental Regimes

Introduction

The previous chapter outlined the development and evolution of environmental law in Canada from the last century into this century. This chapter outlines the basic structure of environmental law in Canada. Although there are significant differences among the various regimes at both the federal and provincial levels and among the provinces, there is a common framework. We will explore this framework further in chapter 8, where the various regulatory regimes are considered in greater depth.

There are two basic categories of environmental law: private law and public law. **Private law** pertains to the protection or furtherance of personal or individual interests and property. Most environmental law is **public law**—that is, rules made and enforced by the state to protect the public interest and safeguard the public good. Table 7.1 provides a brief overview of the key components of private and public environmental law.

Private Law

Private law rights are the rights of private parties to seek compensation when they are harmed by others. Generally private law rights are thought of as those derived from the common law (or the *Civil Code of Québec*), although various statutes augment the common law rights. Recently the right of stakeholders to participate in the environmental approval process has become an important tool.

Table 7.1   Key Components of Environmental Law

	Private Law	**Public Law**
Description	Individuals exercise rights against others to protect their own property or interests	The state imposes regulatory frameworks that set environmental standards and consequences for non-compliance
Examples	Torts, such as nuisance, Ontario *Environmental Bill of Rights, 1993*	Federal *Environmental Protection Act, 1999* and the regulations passed under it; Ontario *Environmental Protection Act* and the regulations passed under it
Source	Common law and some statutory law	Statutes, regulations, administrative orders and approvals

Common Law Rights

Common law rights, such as nuisance, negligence, trespass, and interference with riparian rights (water rights), allow one party to sue another party, such as a neighbour, for harm caused.

For example, in the old and well-known nuisance case of *Rylands v. Fletcher*, a reservoir burst and water escaped through an underground channel of which the reservoir owner was unaware, damaging a neighbour's property. The rule that arose from *Rylands v. Fletcher* provides that a person who has a dangerous thing on his land is liable for any damage to neighbouring lands caused by the escape of the thing.

A private civil cause of action—the nuisance suit in *Rylands v. Fletcher*, for example—can still be useful in limited circumstances. However, these laws were intended to address specific disputes arising between private parties and to compensate identifiable victims, not to protect the environment generally for the benefit of the public and future generations.

Participation Rights

A new area of interest is the **participation rights** of private citizens in what is essentially a public law process: the granting of environmental approvals. As environmental law evolved over the past half-century, there has been a constant tension regarding the rights of the public to participate directly in environmental decision making.

Historically the legislature, made up of elected representatives of the people, passed statutes and regulations on behalf of the people. Even today the government generally negotiates with the applicant—that is, the person or corporation subject to regulation—for an environmental approval without any public involvement. Not even those residents living beside a factory are consulted, or even informed, about the negotiations. After many decades of effort, the nature, scope, and extent of public participation remains a vigorous point of discussion.

To date, litigation to establish an implied environmental right in the *Canadian Charter of Rights and Freedoms* has not been successful. Moreover, neither any of the provinces nor the federal government has enacted an omnibus law to legally define the rights of the public. In Quebec, however, it has raised the profile and importance of environmental rights by adding such rights to the Quebec *Charter of Human Rights and Freedoms.* As well, some progress has been made to further these rights in environmental decision making. By the early 1990s, numerous provinces enacted either laws or policies that addressed participation rights in some fashion. Some of these initiatives are outlined in chapter 16. Of particular interest is Ontario's *Environmental Bill of Rights, 1993.*

It is difficult to provide an accurate overview of public participation rights in Canada because they vary from province to province. They vary within regulatory sectors. In other words, there are different rights in environmental assessment regimes and pollution approvals even within individual provinces. I. Weidemann and S. Femers thought in terms of a hierarchy, and their ladder of public participation is reproduced below in table 7.2.

Weidemann and Femers's ladder of public participation demonstrates a hierarchy or spectrum of public participation rights. The most basic right is the **right to know**—that is, the right to be informed of what is being proposed. In the early 1990s, the right-to-know concept was used to establish the National Pollutant Release Inventory, a federal databank that outlines the releases and transfers of pollutants of all major facilities in Canada.

Moving up from the right to know, we find the right to comment on and object to proposals. Higher up the ladder is the opportunity to participate more meaningfully in environmental decision making.

Public participation rights are never static. It is sometimes stated that the process of making a decision is just as important as the decision itself. Democracies are not particularly cost-effective, but we are willing to pay the price to have our voices heard. Public participation is essential for ensuring that a wide spectrum of interests and concerns are considered, and to ensure that decisions have an air of legitimacy and are therefore respected by the public, even by those who are in disagreement with the result.

Table 7.2   I. Weidemann and S. Femers's Ladder of Public Participation

Public Participation

Increasing level of participation →	Public participation in final decision
	Public participation in assessing risks, actors, and recommending solutions
	Public participation in defining interests, actors, and determining agenda
	Restricted participation
	Public right to object
	Informing the public
	Public right to know

Source: I, Weidemann and S. Femers, "Public Participation in Waste Management Decision-Making: Analysis and Management of Conflicts" (1993), vol. 33 *Journal of Hazardous Materials* 355-68.

Public Law

Public law consists of regulatory frameworks established by statutes, regulations, and policies. A regulatory framework may pertain to a specific sub-environment, such as air, water, or land. It may apply to a specific sector, such as energy, mining, or agriculture. There are also regulatory frameworks governing planning and management in certain areas, such as urban planning, watershed management, parks, and endangered species. These are explored in chapters 9 and 11.

Because most environmental law is public law, the rest of this chapter focuses on regulatory frameworks. It is difficult to make general statements about how regulatory systems work because the division of powers created by the constitution results in overlapping federal and provincial regimes. Some regulatory frameworks are more focused on one sector than another, and some are more sophisticated than others. However, there are a number of general characteristics or themes that can be discerned from a review of these regimes.

Approval-Based Regimes

While most of the provincial laws governing air, water, and land-based resources are prohibitory in nature, the prohibition is rarely absolute. The legislation may state that "no person shall discharge contaminants into the water" or "no one shall store, deposit, or dispose of wastes" but there is usually a proviso—that is, an "unless" under which an approval may be obtained. The legislation or its regulations usually establish a framework where a person wanting to release pollutants, take minerals or resources, or otherwise use the air, water, or land in a way that could impair the environment must proceed through some process in order to obtain the permission of a designated governmental agency.

Approvals vary significantly both in name and type. They may be called certificates of approval, permits, licences, authorizations, or orders, for example. The nature, scope, and content of the approvals process can get fairly complicated. And these complications explain why helping individuals and companies obtain and maintain their approvals provides the bread and butter of many firms practising environmental law.

Approvals may be very simple, as in the case of permission to store waste containers on an individual's property. They may also be very comprehensive, as in the case of an air pollution approval for a large factory, which could include dozens of conditions dealing with such issues as monitoring, reporting, emission limits, emergency response and notification, and financial assurances. As table 7.3 shows, "approvals" give permission to a facility to do something. The approval is based on the scientific research and policy context within the standard-setting process. Once granted, the approval is enforceable and thus subject to compliance measures.

Standards and the standard-setting process as well as compliance and enforcement are described in detail in chapter 8. It is sufficient at this point to note that standards include regulations, objectives, guidelines, criteria, and other instruments and documents that guide government agencies in drafting approvals.

Generally the regulatory framework is based on legally enforceable requirements, including approvals. Once a government agency grants an approval, the approval becomes as legally binding and enforceable as a provision in a statute. One of the objectives of government agencies is to promote and facilitate compliance with the law. Compliance measures may include consultations with agency staff, financial incentives, and inspections. They may also include enforcement actions or prosecutions if an agency determines these measures to be necessary.

It is important to understand this basic framework of approvals since it is really the foundation for both media-based regimes and sector-based regimes, which are discussed below and in subsequent chapters. Most environmental laws—for

Table 7.3   Component Goals of Environmental Legislation

	Standard Setting	Approvals	Compliance
Goals	Establish reasonable limits and restrictions on environmental harm based on science and policy	Establish the kind of permission required before environmentally risky or damaging actions may be taken	Establish penalties, if any, for non-compliance
Examples	Standards, objectives, guidelines, criteria	Permits, authorizations, licences, approval orders	Prosecutions and fines, voluntary abatement

example, section 9 of the Ontario *Environmental Protection Act*—state that one cannot legally discharge any contaminant into the environmental media of air, water, or land without first seeking an approval from the government. When someone or some organization applies for an approval, the government official designated to issue the approval relies on the regime of regulations, policies, and guidance documents that govern the relevant medium (air, water, or land).

It should be emphasized that there is very broad discretion in granting approvals and the terms and conditions attached to those approvals. Those terms and conditions are based mainly on policies and guidelines that are not in and of themselves binding until they are incorporated into a specific approval. Because an approval makes terms and conditions based on these policies and guidelines enforceable, complex approvals can be like individualized sets of regulations. Once the approval is issued, the person or organization holding the approval can be prosecuted if the terms and conditions of the approval are not met.

By this means, approval-based regimes deploy a media-based approach. Similarly, sector-based regimes, described below and discussed in depth in chapter 9, also involve environmental approvals.

Chapter 8 gives further details on how the basic approvals framework works, particularly for air, water, and waste media. Chapter 9 describes approvals in the context of specific regulatory sectors.

Media-Based Regimes

As the next few chapters illustrate, governments approach the protection of the environment in different ways depending on the situation. Generally speaking, environmental protection regimes focus either on a certain environmental medium—for example, air, water, or land—or on a particular sector—for example, mining or forestry.

Media-based regimes are perhaps the most plentiful. Virtually every province has a specific regime to protect air and water from pollution and to protect land from waste. For example, a factory might be required to comply with the following media-based obligations:

- *Air.* Approval for air emissions.
- *Water.* Approval for discharge to water, approval to take water from a local water body, and compliance with sewer-use bylaws for discharge to sewers.
- *Land.* Approval for waste storage or processing on-site.

Arguably the distinctions among media are artificial. For example, wastes stored on land can leach into ground water, and sulphur emissions into the air cause acid rain and damage lakes. Although statutes with titles such as "Environmental Protection Act" suggest an integrated approach—where air and water emissions, and wastes from a particular facility are reviewed as a whole—the actual mechanics of the legislation continue to separate the environment into separate media. This results in a piecemeal, and at times fragmented, approach to environmental law.

This compartmentalization of the environment has historical roots that are based on the crisis–response development of environmental law. For example, as air pollution became recognized as a problem, legislatures dealt with it through specific legislation. When water became recognized as a problem, legislation was then enacted to address the issues of the day, and so on. Many provinces in the 1960s and 1970s actually had separate air quality, water quality, and waste management statutes. Through the 1970s, the separate statutes were consolidated into environmental legislation statutes, but the legislation was not rewritten based on an integrative approach.

The practical effect of the current system is that one facility may require a whole host of approvals based on different statutes. In Ontario, for example, a facility may need multiple approvals for air emissions and waste disposal under the *Environmental Protection Act* and the *Ontario Water Resources Act* for water quality issues. Different parts of the factory, emitting different contaminants, would require different approvals.

Over the years, pilot projects and experiments have been undertaken, particularly in the United States, to try a more integrative approach to environmental regulation. For example, **whole facility permitting** involves a review of all the environmental exposures from a particular facility taken as a whole. Although some advances have been made toward embracing an integrative approach, most jurisdictions continue to use media-specific legislative frameworks.

The concept of media-based environmental protection applies generally to control of pollution to air, water, and land, although the specific requirements vary. Chapter 8 gives a general overview of media-based regimes but the specifics for air, water, and waste legislation for each province and territory would take up virtually a chapter for each and another for the federal government. Instead, the basic framework is outlined. In addition, the concept is extended to specific sector-based regimes as in the next section and in chapter 9.

Sector-Based Regimes

In addition to media-based regimes, environmental laws also can be categorized into **sector-based regimes**—that is, laws and policies that apply to a particular sector or specific area, such as energy, endangered species, or agriculture. The framework for sector-based regimes is more difficult to describe because of the varied nature of these regimes. Many are similar to media-based regimes that are focused on approvals, but others are more complicated and are customized to the specific area of interest.

More Integrated Environmental Assessment and Planning Approaches

The 1970s witnessed an effort to require developers to assess the possible environmental, social, and physical impacts of development. As a result, a body of laws and policies arose governing environmental assessment and planning. This was an effort to take a more holistic, integrative, and preventive approach to environmental management than had been taken before. Today every province and the federal government have an environmental assessment regime in place.

Overlap with Other Areas of Law

Although there is a recognized legal specialty known as "environmental law," this branch of the law is highly interrelated to other areas. Environmental lawyers are often thought to have many specialties. Some of the areas of law that frequently overlap or connect with environmental law are examined briefly in the following sections.

Administrative Law

Administrative law pertains to the legal rules and processes that govern administrative decision-makers. These decision-makers include tribunals (also called boards, commissions, and panels), which make decisions after a hearing, as well as other administrative decision-makers, which make bureaucratic and ministerial decisions that grant or withhold a benefit without a hearing.

Administrative decisions must be made in conformance with the applicable legislative framework. Courts are empowered to review the decisions of tribunals to ensure that they are acting within the powers granted under the legislation, and to ensure that they respect the common law rules of fairness and natural justice. This process is called **judicial review**.

Criminal Law

Breaches of environmental statutes are **quasi-criminal offences**. They are not technically criminal matters since only the federal government has the constitutional powers to enact criminal law. However, the violation of environmental laws can lead to heavy fines and up to six months in jail. Some provinces also have innovative initiatives that allow courts to order restitution, cleanup, and other alternative measures.

Most environmental approvals are legal instruments. This means that if their terms and conditions are not followed, the relevant environmental enforcement agency can prosecute the violators of those terms and conditions. Hence, there are many prosecutions throughout Canada each year against companies, directors, and other individuals.

Civil Law

In civil law, an individual or corporation known as a **plaintiff** brings an action in court against another individual or corporation known as a **defendant**. The plaintiff claims that the defendant caused harm to the plaintiff's health or property. The 1998 movie *A Civil Action*, starring John Travolta, is a good example of civil litigation in the environmental context. Here neighbouring residents brought a legal action against a company dumping wastes. Many environmental lawyers either practise civil law themselves or, when appropriate, refer their clients to lawyers who practise civil law.

Municipal and Land Use Planning Law

There has always been a close connection between land use planning and environmental concerns. Urban boundaries, densities, and water and sewage infrastructure have a direct impact on the environment. Urban development on agricultural lands, development on wetlands, woodlots, and sensitive cultural or archeological resources have always been the subject of much debate and often litigation before both courts and tribunals.

The redevelopment of brownfields or deindustrialized land has also been the subject of much attention in recent years. The discussion has been driven both by the need to contain residential and commercial development within existing urban boundaries and by the high cost of real estate.

Corporate and Commercial Law

Corporate and commercial law is concerned with matters such as the rights and liabilities of shareholders, bankruptcy and insolvency, and directors' and officers' liability. Issues often arise whether directors and officers are liable for the environmental wrongs of the company. Other issues involve what priority is given to environmental cleanup (as opposed to the interests of creditors) when a company goes bankrupt.

International Law

As explored in chapter 5, many international concepts and principles such as the precautionary principle were first recognized in international law. Slowly they became accepted principles within Canada.

Multidisciplinary Approaches

Historically environmental issues have been associated with upper- and middle-class society attempting to protect their health or property interests. However, over the years it has become apparent that the development and implementation of environmental law and policy are intimately connected to a broad range of other interests and values.

The environmental justice movement emerged in the United States in the 1970s when low-income communities composed predominantly of visible minorities organized and fought against the siting of hazardous landfills and other environmentally risky endeavours in their neighbourhoods. By the early 1990s, the environmental justice movement established that low-income disadvantaged communities were disproportionately affected by environmental stress, such as air and water pollution, and proximity to landfills and incinerators. In 1993 President Clinton issued an executive order requiring every federal agency to

> make achieving environmental justice part of its mission by identifying and addressing, as appropriate, disproportionately high and adverse human health or environmental effects of its programs, policies, and activities on minority populations and low-income populations.

Environmental law is often connected to issues of social justice, public rights, and the protection of the public interest. In Canada these connections also exist. There is a rich body of literature furthering these links and emphasizing, for example, the relationship between disadvantaged communities and environmental risks, and the connection between Aboriginal rights and environmental management. Professor Morgan Gardner puts it this way in her book *Linking Activism: Ecology, Social Justice, and Education for Social Change*:

> Events contributing to this awakening of social justice-ecological linkages in the United States and Canada include the Brundtland Report's call for "sustainable development" and the United Nations conference on Environment and Development in Rio de Janeiro in 1992, the reaction to toxic waste in Love Canal, the rise of ecological feminism and the Fourth World Conference on Women, Equality, Development and Peace in Beijing in 1995, the creation of a Movement for Environmental Justice in the United States, the heated discourse pitting jobs versus the environment, and the continual struggle for justice by First Nations peoples in Canada and the United States. Together these forces are pushing these issues of gender, race, class, labor, health, democracy, geographical location, and North–South world power relations into the arena of environmental debate and concern. Their message is clear: we are not simply in this environmental challenge and solution together, we are also in it differently.

PART III

Regulatory Regimes

CHAPTER 8

Environmental Protection Regimes: Command and Control

Introduction

When governments regulate any sphere of activity, they traditionally employ a powerful one–two punch of state intervention known as **command and control**. Command involves setting rules for human behaviour. Control involves ensuring compliance with these rules. Almost all environmental protection regimes that have been established in Canada over the past 30 years generally follow this command and control structure.

In most environmental protection regimes, statutes that set out general prohibitions against polluting are the primary standard-setting mechanism. Most statutes also empower government officials, usually federal or provincial Cabinets, to establish regulations to set more specific standards for environmental behaviour. Environmental laws also typically give power to enforcement officers to carry out policing functions. Crown attorneys are usually charged with the task of prosecuting individuals and companies that fail to comply with the rules set out in environmental statutes and regulations.

This basic crime-and-punishment approach to environmental protection, however, does not begin to describe the complexities of environmental protection regimes. Many environmental statutes also establish a broad range of management and decision-making powers, which serve the general policy objectives of environmental protection. For example, most environmental statutes provide for the licensing and approval of activities that could pose a risk to the environment.

Licensing and approvals incorporate elements of both command and control. On the command side, individuals and companies are prohibited from carrying out an identified activity unless they are able to obtain approval from a government official. In addition, approvals often contain detailed standards in the form of conditions of approval. The licensing requirement, however, is itself also a control mechanism. It prohibits an individual or company from carrying out an environmentally risky activity unless it can be demonstrated that the impacts of the activity have been carefully studied and mitigated so that the risk of environmental damage is low.

This chapter outlines the inner workings of the command and control structure of environmental protection, and explores other areas of government action that have grown up alongside the basic command and control structure. Specifically, it covers government regulation of environmental planning and management within specific environmental sectors. Taken together, these elements of an environmental protection regime constitute a formidable array of regulatory tools to implement a government's environmental protection objectives.

Command: Setting Standards for Environmental Behaviour

In this section, we explore different instruments used to set standards, such as statutes, regulations, policies, and administrative orders. We also compare various methods of formulating standards.

Setting Standards: The Tool Box

Statutes, regulations, and administrative orders are legally enforceable, while policies and guidelines are not. What role does each play in protecting the environment?

Statutes

The primary tool available to government to command environmentally appropriate behaviour rests with elected officials. Parliament and the provincial legislators, our society's lawmakers, set the framework for the command and control model through the passage of statutes. For example, Ontario's *Environmental Protection Act* establishes the following general prohibition against polluting in section 6(1):

No person shall discharge into the natural environment any contaminant, and no person responsible for a source of contaminant shall permit the discharge into the natural environment of any contaminant from the source of contaminant, in an amount, concentration or level in excess of that prescribed by the regulations.

Of course this provision will have no effect whatsoever unless a regulation has been put in place to prescribe specific standards establishing an unacceptable "amount, concentration or level" for a contaminant.

Regulations

Using our example above, the lieutenant-governor in council is empowered to make such regulations pursuant to section 176(1)(e) of the *Environmental Protection Act* as follows:

The Lieutenant Governor in Council may make regulations ...

(e) prescribing maximum permissible amounts, concentrations or levels of any contaminant or combination of contaminants and any class of either of them.

This section tells us who is responsible for setting the specific standards and regulations. As is common in most legislation, the power is given over to the executive branch of government—that is, the Cabinet.

As we dig deeper into the search for environmental standards, we find that Cabinet has indeed passed regulations setting limits for the "amounts, concentrations and levels" of contaminants under the *Environmental Protection Act*. For example, a review of the listing of regulations shown online at e-Laws, the Ontario government's complete listing of Ontario's laws and regulations, shows numerous regulations passed under the *Environmental Protection Act*.

In addition, there are a host of other specific standards governed by regulations under the *Environmental Protection Act* relating to construction, design, and operation of environmental control equipment; monitoring and cleanup procedures and protocols; and a myriad of other environmental-related rules.

We have now identified two important actors in the field of environmental standard setting: (1) legislatures, which establish general provisions governing environmental conduct; and (2) Cabinets, which can establish more specific rules and standards if granted this power by the legislatures. However, to understand the full range of legally binding standards affecting environmental behaviour, one must look beyond statutes and regulations.

Site-Specific Legal Instruments

Standards are also set on a case-by-case basis using site-specific legal instruments such as **certificates of approval** and **administrative orders**. The *Environmental Protection Act* delegates the power to issue certificates of approval and administrative orders to a government official known as a **director**. As its name implies, a site-specific legal instrument is specific to a particular site, plant, facility, individual, or company. However, it is legally binding in the same manner as a statute or regulation.

CERTIFICATES OF APPROVAL

Certificates of approval are required under the *Environmental Protection Act* in certain circumstances. For example, any person wishing to carry out an enterprise or activity that involves a discharge into the air must first obtain a certificate of approval according to section 9 of the Act. Conditions of approval typically include specific requirements for the construction, operation, monitoring, and performance level of pollution control equipment.

The conditions of approval apply only to the specific individual or company to which the section 9 approval has been issued. For that individual or company, however, the conditions of approval have the force of law, and failure to comply may lead to prosecution.

ADMINISTRATIVE ORDERS

Under the *Environmental Protection Act*, a director may issue an administrative order under certain circumstances. For example, where an investigation indicates that a company is discharging a contaminant, an administrative order, called a control order, may be issued against the company to impose conditions and cleanup requirements. Administrative orders are discussed later in this chapter.

Policies and Guidelines

Government officials may also establish policies and guidelines, which are not legally enforceable. However, policies and guidelines can have a powerful impact on environmental behaviour, as in the case of the Blue Book guidelines.

In the early 1980s, Ontario's Ministry of the Environment established guidelines that set specific limits on discharge to surface water for a long list of contaminants. These guidelines, known informally as "the Blue Book," were developed by ministry scientists and civil servants and were ultimately approved by the minister.

Because they were only guidelines, the Blue Book standards could not be enforced in the typical command and control sense. Charges could not be laid, and a company could not be convicted for failing to meet the Blue Book requirements. However, the Blue Book guidelines did affect environmental conduct in Ontario in two less direct ways. Consider the following:

1. The Blue Book standards were adopted by the director for granting approvals for discharges to surface water under the *Ontario Water Resources Act*. In this way, the unenforceable ministry guidelines were implemented in a very meaningful way.

2. The Blue Book standards were considered by the courts when determining if an alleged offender was guilty of the prohibition against discharge of "a contaminant into the natural environment that causes or is likely to cause an adverse effect."

The Blue Book standards are but one of many examples of how standards established in ministry policies and guidelines may play a powerful role in influencing environmental behaviour.

Approaches to Standard Setting

What choices are available to environmental decision-makers as they set about the task of establishing rules for environmental behaviour? What factors are taken into account in establishing these rules? In this section, some of the basic options available to the rule-makers are described.

Performance Versus Construction Standards

If you were a rule-maker and wanted to control the amount of a particular contaminant entering the environment, you could do so by setting a performance standard or a construction standard.

A **performance standard** is a pollution limit imposed on a polluter. It is the responsibility of each operator to make sure that the standard is met. Using this approach, the rule-maker is unconcerned about how the result is achieved. A company can bring discharge levels into line with an established performance standard in a variety of ways—for example, by installing state-of-the-art pollution control equipment, reducing its rate of production, or making changes to the input chemical materials.

Alternatively, rule-makers may prefer to establish a specific **construction standard**, which requires that only government-approved pollution control systems be used.

In most environmental regimes, both performance and construction standards are employed in different circumstances. In Ontario, for example, performance-based standards have been set for the discharge of specified contaminants to surface water under the *Environmental Protection Act.*

In contrast, the practice has developed in Ontario of the case-by-case approval of air pollution control equipment by the Ministry of the Environment through certificates of approval. Similarly, sewage treatment systems are governed by specific construction standards set out in regulations under the *Building Code Act, 1992.*

Performance-based standards are often supported by industry associations because they give industries the flexibility to find their own solutions to pollution control objectives. Critics also argue that construction standards entrench pollution control approaches and technologies that are not cost-effective and can quickly become obsolete. Performance-based standards encourage research and innovation, and they are more likely than construction standards to advance new, cheaper, and more effective technologies.

In other situations, however, construction-based standards provide some advantages to both government and industry, particularly where the required technology is reliable. For government, such standards may be easier to enforce. Monitoring requirements can focus on ensuring that the required pollution control equipment has been properly installed and maintained. For industry, there may be less worry about the need to make operational changes to meet evolving, more restrictive performance-based standards.

Establishing Specific Limits

The task of establishing specific limits for discharge or emission of contaminants into the environment may seem as though it should be an objective scientific process. In practice, however, the process of setting such standards requires a complex balance of scientific and non-scientific factors. It requires consideration of societal goals and objectives, economic constraints, and occasionally controversial assumptions about the short- and long-term health, safety, and environmental consequences of industrial practices.

ENVIRONMENTAL QUALITY-BASED STANDARDS

The traditional approach to standard setting has been to base standards on societal objectives for environmental quality. Franson, Franson, and Lucas, in their book *Environmental Standards*, have described this as the five-step process set out below:

- *Step 1.* Identify the objectives for pollution control, including the uses of the environmental resources to be protected.
- *Step 2.* Formulate specific criteria for meeting these objectives by collecting scientific information to answer questions such as "Is this water safe to drink?" or "Is this air safe to breathe?"

- *Step 3.* Based on these criteria, formulate specific ambient quality standards—that is, the quality of the air or water that is deemed necessary to achieve the desired objectives.
- *Step 4.* Translate the desired ambient quality standards into specific emission or effluent limits that are designed to control the amount of contaminants entering the environment.
- *Step 5.* Develop monitoring and other information-gathering programs to provide feedback on whether the environmental objectives are being met.

Establishing standards using this approach has proven to be a contentious, lengthy, and expensive process. When we consider the room for disagreement and political and/or scientific judgments that need to be made at each stage of this process, we can begin to understand why.

Another type of environmental quality-based standard is the **health risk assessment standards**, which involve linking the standard under consideration to the health risks posed. This approach requires the use of risk assessment to determine the health risks associated with the level and duration of exposure to a contaminant.

A health risk assessment attempts to examine two controversial scientific relationships:

- the relationship between the release of a contaminant into the environment and the subsequent level of exposure to an individual, and
- the relationship between the release of a contaminant into the environment and the potential for health-related effects resulting from varying levels of exposure to the contaminant.

This analysis then leads to a risk calculation intended to determine the acceptable level of chemical exposure.

This approach to setting standards presents a number of problems. Because gathering health risk assessment information is expensive, there is little hard data available on the long-term health impact of many known contaminants. Scientists often suspect health effects that they are unable to prove because of a lack of information. In addition, long-term risks are difficult to identify because of the time it takes for the effects to manifest themselves.

Many environmental scientists suspect that the health risk assessments will underestimate the real health costs. With persistent toxic contaminants, risks increase over time because these contaminants do not break down but bioaccumulate. These complicating factors mean that appropriate environmental standards for dangerous contaminants are rejected because time and resources are insufficient to draw the link between the contaminant and harm to health.

These problems suggest to some that a new approach is needed. Many scientists, environmental advocacy groups, and other stakeholders argue that the onus should be reversed. Pollutants should not be assumed innocent until proven guilty. Individuals and companies proposing to release a contaminant into the environment should be required to demonstrate that the contaminant will not cause an adverse effect before any release is permitted. This approach reflects the **precautionary principle**.

The precautionary principle is only starting to find its way into the standard-setting process in environmental protection regimes in Canada. This may well change, however, as public awareness and concern about the long-term environmental health risks of industrial activity increase.

TECHNOLOGY-BASED STANDARDS

This standard-setting approach sidesteps many of the problems associated with developing environmental quality-based standards by asking a simple question: what is the best available technology currently available for controlling the particular pollutant? If agreement can be reached on the answer to this question, it is a simple matter to impose a specific limit for this pollutant based on what the best available technology can achieve.

This approach has one obvious advantage: it removes many of the controversial political and scientific judgments that need to be made when establishing standards based on environmental objectives. Instead, the focus is on what limits to polluting are technologically possible.

Critics identify at least two important problems with technology-based standards. First, standards are developed without considering the needs of the environment. If a particular contaminant is having a catastrophic impact on unlimited environmental resources, why should a limit be based solely on current technology? Second, the approach entrenches prescribed technology and therefore discourages technological innovation to meet tougher standards linked to environmental quality-based objectives.

Practical experience with technology-based standards has led to mixed reviews. In 1986 the Ontario government initiated an ambitious technology-based standard-setting program for nine industrial sectors that discharge directly to surface water. The government initially focused on technology-based standards in the hope of gaining consensus among the industrial sectors on sector-wide effluent limits.

The program, known as the municipal–industrial strategy for abatement (MISA), created nine separate industry–government working groups to develop standards using the criteria of "best available technology economically achievable." Over the next four years, the program established specific effluent standards for all nine sectors. For the first time in the history of the province, Ontario had clear limits on specific pollutants on a province-wide basis.

However, the MISA process was slow and expensive. Representatives of industrial sectors and government officials debated for many months in an attempt to reach agreement on what "best available technology" and "economically achievable" should mean in a particular sector. The process demonstrated one of the problems with the technology-based approach: it opens the door to bargaining between industry and the standard-setting authority over what is practical, feasible, and "economically achievable." After spending so much time and effort to reach consensus on these standards, the provincial government appears to have little stomach for reviewing and updating these standards to reflect technological advancement. As a consequence, the hard-won MISA effluent limit standard, based on late 1980s pollution control technologies, remains entrenched in Ontario almost 20 years later.

POINT OF IMPINGEMENT VERSUS CONTROL AT SOURCE

Another decision faced by environmental rule-makers is where to draw the spatial boundary for meeting discharge standards. Many environmental standards are still based on the human-centred principle that pollution is not significant until it crosses property boundaries. Air pollution standards are often based on **point of impingement** models that attempt to predict the impact of a pollutant at a property's boundaries, rather than at the end of the stack. For example, Ontario's general air pollution regulation requires companies to apply a computer model that predicts the concentration of a contaminant at its property boundaries based on information about discharge levels from the facility and weather data.

The flaw in this approach, of course, is that pollution does not respect property boundaries. Pollutants begin to have negative effects as soon as they are released into the environment. It is almost universally acknowledged that environmental contaminants must be controlled at their source. Point of impingement standards remain in place in Ontario, and many other jurisdictions, despite an overwhelming consensus that the approach is out of date and fundamentally flawed.

Pollution Prevention

Since the early 1990s, a new type of standard setting, called **pollution prevention**, has been recognized and applauded, but formal acceptance and implementation have been slow. This approach changes the focus from *control* of the quantities of pollution at the end of the pipe to *prevention* of the use of potentially harmful substances in the first place. Pollution prevention involves avoiding the generation of pollution through techniques and methods such as the following:

- changes to manufacturing or production processes,
- product reformulation or substitution, and
- chemical substitution.

Pollution prevention is not about reducing levels of pollution; it is about examining why waste is being created in the first place and seeking to avoid it. Consider the example of a company that is discharging a problematic chemical. The traditional approach is to ask how much of the chemical the company can be allowed to discharge while still protecting human health and the environment. Pollution control equipment is then installed to meet the discharge or effluent requirements. Pollution prevention, on the other hand, requires an examination of the company's manufacturing process and asks why that chemical is being used or generated. Can the process be changed so that it will not be used or generated?

Some American states, such as Massachusetts, have enacted progressive and successful pollution prevention laws, which are called toxic use reduction laws. In Canada there is considerable support for the principle, although implementation has been slow.

The Canadian Council of Ministers of the Environment (CCME) formally committed to pollution prevention in 1993 and in 1996 released the document *A Strategy to Fulfil the CCME Commitment to Pollution Prevention.* It works in conjunction with the Canadian Centre for Pollution Prevention. Ontario has committed to introducing a comprehensive pollution prevention regime by late 2008.

Control: Compliance and Enforcement

We now turn to the "control" part of the command and control strategy of environmental protection. In this section, we examine the tools available to governments for ensuring that environmental protection rules and standards (the commands) are followed.

Enforcing Standards: The Control Tool Box

One can imagine a full spectrum of enforcement tools ranging from the carrot of positive incentives to the most puwnishing of sticks—that is, an aggressive policing approach with high fines and even jail terms for offences against the environment. The range of options is summarized in table 8.1.

Table 8.1   Control Tool Box

Tools	Key Players
Incentives/assistance	• Environmental abatement officers • Research and funding agencies
Licences/approvals	• Government environment officials • Hearings tribunals
Administrative orders	• Enforcement officers • Government environment officials • Hearings tribunals
Prosecutions	• Enforcement officers • Prosecutors • Criminal courts

Incentives and Financial Assistance

Incentives and financial assistance are the least intrusive ways of encouraging good environmental behaviour. They involve establishing government programs to assist potential polluters in meeting government pollution control standards. This may entail setting aside public funds as grants for individuals and companies to assist them in upgrading their pollution control equipment and production processes.

However, governments may have a hard time explaining to their constituents why tax dollars should be spent subsidizing businesses. If producing a particular product requires expenditure of funds to protect the environment, why should those costs not be borne directly by the company and, ultimately, the consumers of the goods that are creating the risk to the environment? Grants are generally more popular with voters when they are directed toward the public at large, as when recycling containers are provided free of charge or rebates are available to offset the cost of making homes more energy efficient.

A less direct means of providing encouragement is the use of tax incentives, which reward companies for good environmental behaviour through reduction in taxes. However, tax incentives are a close cousin of direct subsidies and, for the reasons cited above, are unpopular with voters. There are only a few examples where tax breaks have been allocated to give "green" companies an advantage over companies using older and dirtier pollution control technology.

Governments' taxing powers are more commonly used as a stick than a carrot. For example, in the United States, a special tax is imposed on chemical producers and tied into the volume of chemicals generated. This creates an incentive to reduce reliance on persistent toxins in production processes.

Another form of government incentive involves sharing expertise and research to assist industries in improving their environmental performance. In the early 1980s, for example, the Ontario Ministry of the Environment established the position of abatement officer. This government employee's sole function was to work with industries to develop programs to reduce the amount of pollution that they generated. Abatement officers would meet with plant managers, inspect their operations, and provide them with information and advice on how their companies could improve their environmental performance. Many governments make an effort to share research and to fund and share industry research on improving pollution control and production process methods. International treaties such as the Kyoto Protocol to the United Nations Framework Convention on Climate Change, described in chapter 9, have motivated governments to fund this type of research.

Licences and Approvals

Licences and **approvals** are another important compliance tool available to government. The licensing of various types of facilities and projects that have potential environmental impacts combines both the carrot and the stick approach. On the carrot side, a particular environmental activity cannot proceed until an approval is granted. The approval authority must be satisfied that the project has been appropriately planned and studied, and that environmental risks are minimized. This gives proponents of these projects the incentive to ensure minimal environmental impact.

On the stick side, most environmental approvals come with conditions attached. These conditions can spell out exactly how a facility must operate, setting out certain performance standards that must be met during the operating life of the facility. If these standards are not met, environmental officials usually have the power to take both administrative and enforcement action. Most environmental statutes give these officials enforcement options: the power to issue orders, and the power to commence prosecutions against companies that do not comply with conditions of approval.

Consider a chemical plant that obtains a licence to discharge treated waste water into a local stream. The conditions of approval may set standards for the quality of the water being discharged. It may also require ongoing self-monitoring and reporting to a regulatory authority such as the Ministry of the Environment. If the monitoring results show that discharge standards are not being met, the operator will be required to take certain actions. Some approval instruments even specify the particular remedial action that the company must take. If the specified action is not taken, charges can be laid, or an order can be issued requiring the company to shut down until the environmental problem is corrected. In this way, environmental approvals may be converted into direct and powerful enforcement tools.

As with all command and control mechanisms, there is a price tag attached to the tool's effectiveness. In many jurisdictions, including Ontario, there are insufficient resources for proactive monitoring by the ministry. A great deal of reliance is placed on the operator to self-monitor, to report, and to address environmental issues before they become compliance problems.

In some cases, the final decision on environmental approvals and conditions of approval is made by a tribunal. With the care that these tribunals take in imposing conditions of approval, they can play an important role in addressing future potential compliance issues.

Administrative Orders

Administrative orders are directives issued by government officials; they impose legal requirements on individuals or companies to take specific action to control pollution discharges, investigate and/or clean up environmental problems, repair damage caused to the environment, or take action to avoid future pollution problems.

Administrative orders can sometimes be more punishing for an individual or company than a conviction for an environmental offence. For example, an environmental administrative order could require a company to carry out extensive investigative and cleanup work that costs millions of dollars. Alternatively, an order could require a company to shut down operations until pollution control is brought into compliance with standards. Such an order could shut down a company for months, or even permanently, if a feasible solution cannot be found.

If convicted of an environmental offence, the offender eventually will have to pay a fine, but will not have any obligation to address the environmental problem unless ordered to do so by a court. In contrast, administrative orders are focused not on punishing offenders but rather on solving problems. An environmental order compels immediate direct and specific action to prevent spills or to clean up an environmental mess. Administrative orders may not carry the same stigma as a conviction for a crime against the environment but, as noted above, they may pack a financial punch. The cost of complying with an order could be as much of a deterrent as a conviction for an environmental offence. In many cases, orders and prosecutions are pursued concurrently.

INVESTIGATION AND REPORT

The process of issuing provincial orders starts in a manner similar to the investigation of any environmental offence. An enforcement officer is dispatched to the scene of a complaint or an environmental problem. The **provincial officer (PO)** then begins to gather evidence about the incident. Once sufficient evidence is obtained, the officer prepares a report, which provides sufficient information to conclude that an environmental offence has occurred.

Given the potential consequences, it is easy to understand why the making of administrative orders must begin with an investigation and a report. For example, in Ontario POs have the power to issue **provincial officers' orders (POOs)**, which compel the individual or company receiving the order to carry out certain specified actions to prevent or respond to an environmental problem. These orders are accompanied by a PO's report, which provides a summary of the PO's rationale for the issuance of the order. In the case of most administrative orders, the PO must have "reasonable and probable grounds" to believe that an adverse environmental effect is associated with a particular undertaking or activity before the officer can issue the order.

TYPES OF ORDERS

In Ontario, there are two categories of environmental orders: POOs and director's orders. The actions that may be required by an administrative order are broad ranging and potentially extremely onerous.

POOs may be issued more quickly and with less administrative process than director's orders; they are therefore more common. They may demand a broad range of actions including the following:

- taking steps to stop contamination from entering the environment,
- removing waste material from a site,
- repairing injury from damage to the environment,
- providing alternative water supplies,
- submitting a plan to achieve compliance, and
- taking a range of preventive measures to prevent an adverse impact on the environment.

POs have slightly less latitude than the director in issuing orders. POOs may be issued under the *Environmental Protection Act* if a PO has "reason to believe that the person is contravening a provision of the act or regulations, an existing administrative order, or the terms or conditions of an environmental approval." POOs are also subject to review by directors.

Director's orders are typically, though not always, used for complex large-scale environmental issues that require a more detailed and nuanced approach. The four types of director's orders specified under the *Environmental Protection Act* are listed below.

1. *Control orders.* These orders are issued when a contaminant is being discharged into the natural environment, and there is a need for the person responsible for the source of the contamination to take steps to control it through improved pollution control measures.

2. *Stop orders.* These orders are issued in the more unusual and serious circumstance where a particular source is discharging a contaminant that the director believes constitutes an immediate danger to "human life, the health of any persons, or to property." In this case, the director may issue an order requiring the discharge to stop entirely.

3. *Remedial orders.* These orders require the subject of the order to take action to repair or to prevent injury or damage to the environment.

4. *Orders for preventive measures.* These orders are issued when there are "reasonable and probable grounds" to form the opinion that preventive measures are necessary in order to prevent or reduce the risk of an impact on the environment.

What do all of these kinds of administrative orders have in common? They all start with an investigation by an enforcement officer; they all involve tailored administrative responses to a particular environmental problem; and they all are based on evidence of a breach of an environmental law or regulation.

Administrative orders can have a broad scope. Before 1989, orders could be imposed only on the current owners of the source of a contaminant. This issue was debated at the Ontario Court of Appeal in *C.N. Railways Co. et al. v. Ontario (EPA Director)*. In this case, the ministry issued an order to investigate and clean up a serious environmental problem created by the manufacturing of railway ties. This process involved the use of creosote, a highly toxic preservative. The creosote plant was sold in 1982, and there was evidence of widespread off-site contamination of groundwater. The director issued an order not only against the current owner of the plant but also against the previous owner and Canadian National Railway.

When the order was challenged, the court found that the present owner was liable, leaving the former owner of the plant—that is, the company largely responsible for the pollution—with no liability. This decision triggered action by the provincial government. In 1989, amendments were made to Ontario's *Environmental Protection Act* that gave the director discretion to issue orders to previous or current owners of the property, and to previous or current persons in charge of management or control of a source of a contaminant.

Because of the serious consequences that may result from an order, most environmental legislation provides an avenue for appeal. In Ontario, a director's order, as well as POOs that have been reviewed by a director, may be appealed to the Environmental Review Tribunal. The tribunal then stands in place of the director to determine whether the issuance of the order was warranted.

Finally, to avoid the possibility that an appeal may be used as a stalling tactic to dodge cleanup responsibilities, many jurisdictions including Ontario have specifically provided that launching an appeal does not automatically trigger a **stay** of an order. In other words, while an appeal is in progress, there is an obligation to carry out the terms of the order, unless a motion is successfully brought for a stay.

Prosecutions

When it comes to controlling the behaviour of potential polluters, prosecution and financial incentives lie at opposite ends of the spectrum. Prosecution employs the full weight of government power to compel acceptable environmental behaviour. Unique among compliance tools, successful prosecutions cast a negative moral judgment on a particular environmental action or inaction by giving it a criminal connotation. Individuals and companies are effectively being told that, in the opinion of the prosecuting authority, their behaviour has run afoul of accepted societal standards.

If a decision is made by the enforcement branch of a Ministry of the Environment to prosecute an alleged environmental offence, the matter is turned over to a Crown counsel. His job is to build a case that will lead to a conviction by a criminal court.

Considering the advantages of administrative orders, why would a decision be made to prosecute, particularly given that prosecutions are expensive and require a significant investment of public resources? There are at least two persuasive reasons:

1. *Specific deterrence.* A company that has been embarrassed by a public prosecution and conviction for violating environmental standards may be less likely to risk further damage to its reputation by offending again.

2. *General deterrence.* By prosecuting an individual or company that has caused environmental harm, the government makes a public statement that this behaviour will not be tolerated. Most companies are sensitive to public image. The message to potential polluters is that they risk public humiliation and financial consequences if they pollute.

Since the mid-1980s, the concept of treating breaches of environmental standards in the same way as any other alleged criminal activity has gained credence among government regulators. By associating harmful environmental behaviour with criminality, the government has an opportunity to send the message that polluting is not just a cost of doing business. Fines or penalties, without a criminal association, are simply another production expense that gets passed on to consumers. Once government becomes successful at branding a polluting company as a societal wrongdoer, it creates a much larger customer/consumer relations problem that can potentially threaten that company's economic viability.

In most Canadian jurisdictions, governments have established the equivalent of environmental police forces with a mandate to investigate potential violations of environmental standards and lay charges. Ontario led the way in 1986 with the establishment of its Investigations and Enforcement Branch, a centralized agency within the Ministry of the Environment, charged with the responsibility of carrying out high-profile investigations of potential polluters.

POs are Ontario's "green cops" whose responsibility is to investigate potential environmental offences. These officers have been given significant powers, equivalent to those of police officers, to investigate alleged environmental violations and gather evidence in preparation for prosecutions.

INSPECTIONS AND SEARCHES

In Ontario the *Environmental Protection Act* gives POs a broad range of powers to help in an investigation, including the power to act in the following ways:

- Without a warrant or court order, a PO may enter private property or any other place where she has reason to believe that the environment may be adversely affected by an activity.
- During an inspection, a PO may carry out a range of activities, including excavating soils, requiring machinery to be operated under certain conditions, taking samples for analysis, conducting any tests or taking measurements, examining or copying any documents of data, taking photographs or video recordings or other visual recordings, requiring production of any documents or data and removing such documentation for copying, and making "reasonable inquiries of any person either orally or in writing."
- By special order, a PO may protect the scene of a potential environmental offence by prohibiting entry onto public or private property, and by prohibiting the use of, interference with, destruction of, or disruption of anything during an inspection or during the time required to obtain a warrant.

A PO also has specific powers to carry out a search, without a search warrant, of any place that is not a room used as a dwelling if the PO has reason to believe that

- an offence has been committed,
- the place to be searched will provide evidence of the offence, and
- it is impractical to obtain a search warrant.

SEIZING EVIDENCE

A PO has the power to seize anything found in an inspection or search without a warrant under certain conditions. In the case of an inspection, the PO may seize anything that is produced to her or that is in plain view under any of the following conditions, which are set out in section 160 of the *Environmental Protection Act*:

- the thing could be used as evidence of an offence,
- the thing is being used in connection with the commission of an offence, or
- the thing is discharging or likely to discharge a contaminant into the natural environment.

In a case of a search, a PO may seize anything without a warrant or court order under the following conditions:

- the provincial officer reasonably believes that the thing could be used as evidence of an offence, or
- the thing is being used in connection with a commission of an offence and seizure is necessary to prevent the continuation of the offence.

Like police officers, environmental POs often go to court to obtain search warrants or court orders to carry out an investigation, search, or seizure. In some cases, it is safer for a PO to obtain court sanction for a search in this way. The alternative is to risk a challenge launched on the basis that the investigation, search, or seizure violated the rights of the company or individual being investigated. If such a challenge is successful, a court could dismiss the pollution charges against the accused without having even considered the merits of the charges themselves.

GATHERING EVIDENCE

The gathering of evidence for an environmental offence can be a highly technical exercise that requires scientific knowledge. Environmental enforcement officers usually require technical support from other experts and specialists in chemistry, air quality, or other disciplines. Four practical steps that enforcement officers must follow to gather sufficient and accurate evidence to support a prosecution are set out below.

- *Step 1.* Take careful notes of observations during any inspection or search.
- *Step 2.* Take photographs, noting the time, date, and precise location of each picture. Videotapes may also be useful.
- *Step 3.* Take water, air, and soil samples based on established protocol and procedure, labelling them with the time, date, and precise location, and sealing the evidence and storing it properly. As in any criminal investigation, officers must be meticulous in cataloguing the chain of custody of samples from the moment they are obtained to their delivery to an accredited laboratory for analysis.
- *Step 4.* To prove the source of pollution, obtain comparative samples. For example, take water samples and visual evidence upstream and downstream of a release of effluent in water, or air samples upwind and downwind of a release into the air.

Cases are won or lost on the basis of whether or not these critically important steps are followed.

STANDARD OF PROOF

The prosecutor of any offence must prove the offence beyond a reasonable doubt. This **standard of proof** applies to *Criminal Code* offences, traffic violations, and environmental offences. It is a much heavier burden than the civil standard of proof—a **balance of probabilities**, which applies in civil cases, such as tort and contract lawsuits.

In civil cases, the intention of the law is to make things right between the parties, so the court rules in favour of the party with the stronger case. For example, if a person sues a neighbour for the loss of a tree allegedly caused by the neighbour's overuse of winter salt, he must prove the elements of the tort of nuisance on a balance of probabilities. This means that he must prove that his version of events is more probable than his neighbour's version.

However, when a prosecutor is proving the elements of an offence against a defendant, the intention of the law is to punish an offender and to avoid convicting and punishing an innocent individual or corporation. Therefore, it is not enough for the prosecutor to prove that the defendant is probably guilty; rather, it is necessary to prove that the defendant is guilty **beyond a reasonable doubt**.

STRICT LIABILITY OFFENCES

Although all offences must be proven beyond a reasonable doubt, the elements of an offence that must be proven by the prosecutor vary in accordance with the type of offence. Environmental offences are strict liability offences. To understand what this means, it is necessary to understand the meaning of criminal liability offences and absolute liability offences for the purpose of comparison.

The most serious offences under the *Criminal Code*—murder, for example—are known as **criminal liability offences**, and are viewed by society most severely. The penal consequences are serious and include incarceration. The prosecutor must prove not only that an illegal action (the *actus reus*) occurred but also that a mental element (the *mens rea*) or guilty mind existed at the time of the crime. *Mens rea* reflects moral culpability on the part of the accused.

At the opposite end of the spectrum from criminal liability offences are the least serious offences, which are known as **absolute liability offences**. The prosecutor need only demonstrate that a particular illegal act occurred. The intention of the offender is not relevant. The consequences for the defendant on conviction are relatively minor: small fines or demerit points.

Environmental offences fall into a middle category known as **strict liability offences**. In these cases, the prosecutor's burden is greater than it is in an absolute liability offence but not as great as it is in a criminal liability offence. As is the case when prosecuting absolute liability offences, the prosecutor need not prove *mens rea*. Once the *actus reus* is proven—that is, once the prosecutor proves that the offence occurred and the defendant was responsible—the burden of proof shifts to the defendant. The defendant now carries the burden of proving that she took "all reasonable care" to prevent the offence. To escape liability, the defendant must prove **due diligence**—that is, the defendant must prove that she made serious efforts to become aware of the environmental risks and to prevent harm from occurring. The shift of the burden of proof to the defendant is necessary. Without it, the Crown would be put in the almost impossible position of trying to prove a negative: that the defendant did not take the reasonable steps needed to prevent the offence from occurring. Also, this shift of burden recognizes the reality that the defendant, not the Crown, is the party that has direct access to the evidence (if it exists) demonstrating that the defendant took "all reasonable care." The defendant must meet the less civil standard of proof: due diligence/reasonable care must be proven on a balance of probabilities rather than beyond a reasonable doubt.

Due diligence is a critically important concept in environmental law because it provides a significant incentive to businesses to use studies and regular monitoring to become aware of the potential environmental harm they may cause. It also encourages businesses to be proactive and focused on prevention in order to limit their exposure to prosecution.

CHAPTER 9

Sectoral Regulatory Regimes

Introduction

This chapter examines the regulatory regimes governing several important sectors: fossil fuels, nuclear energy, mining, agriculture, aquaculture, pesticides, and biotechnology. The governance of a single sector often involves the overlapping jurisdictions of international law, federal law, provincial law, and municipal law. Even within a jurisdiction, there may be several statutes and numerous regulations that apply to each regime.

Fossil Fuels

Fossil fuels include oil, natural gas, and coal, all of which contain **hydrocarbons**, the organic compound of hydrogen and carbon atoms, which produces energy when burned.

Located mainly in western Canada and the Atlantic offshore region, the fossil fuel exploration and extraction industries are Canada's largest private sector investors. The trade surplus in fossil fuels represents 45 percent of Canada's trade balance, according to statistics from the Canadian Association of Petroleum Producers. Nearly all trade is with the United States, for which Canada is the largest supplier of natural gas and the third largest supplier of crude oil.

Oil and gas revenues have fuelled economies in western and Atlantic Canada and in the Arctic, where a major natural gas pipeline is proposed. Coal is also important, accounting for nearly 20 percent of Canadian electricity generation, mainly in Alberta and Ontario. The tar sands of Alberta may be the largest remaining source of fossil fuels in North America, and their importance to Canada's economy is likely to become momentous as other fossil fuel sources are depleted.

Unfortunately, the environmental impacts of fossil fuel operations are significant. Consider the following:

- Exploration, development, and production, often in remote areas, are major land uses. They have the potential to create serious impacts on land, wildlife, air, water, local communities, and Aboriginal peoples.
- There are environmental and human health risks from the development of "sour" natural gas—that is, gas that has a high sulphur content.
- The oil and gas industry produces 20 percent of Canadian greenhouse gas emissions, a 47 percent increase over 1990.
- With the decline in conventional oil and gas reserves, recent industry developments, particularly oil sands and coal-bed methane in western Canada, have resulted in new land use effects and environmental risks.
- Emissions from coal-fired electricity generation are a major problem in Alberta and Ontario.

To complicate matters, the environmental regulation of fossil fuels occurs primarily at the provincial level of government. The effects of exploration, development, production, and initial transportation within the provinces are regulated by both provincial environment departments and regulators of energy and natural resources.

Direct federal environmental regulation of oil and gas activities within provinces is limited to interprovincial and export pipelines. There is full exploratory and developmental regulation in the northern territories. In the Atlantic offshore area, federal and provincial environmental regulation is harmonized through the Canada–Nova Scotia Offshore Petroleum Board and the Canada–Newfoundland and Labrador Offshore Petroleum Board. There are federal and provincial moratoria on West Coast offshore hydrocarbon activities that date from the 1970s. Though British Columbia is anxious to develop offshore resources, constitutional jurisdiction over the most promising area remains uncertain.

The most sophisticated hydrocarbon regulator is Alberta's Energy Resources Conservation Board (ERCB). This board is an independent government agency responsible for protecting the public interest and ensuring fairness in the exploration, development, and delivery of Alberta's energy resources. There are analogous oil and gas agencies in British Columbia and Saskatchewan.

The ERCB applies environmental criteria in licensing the following:

- oil and gas wells;
- facilities such as natural gas processing plants, oil sands mines, and upgrading plants;
- provincial pipelines; and
- coal mines.

The criteria used by the ERCB are elaborated in the relevant statutes: the Alberta *Oil and Gas Conservation Act*, the *Oil Sands Conservation Act*, the *Pipeline Act*, and the *Coal Conservation Act*. These criteria are also found in the regulations under these Acts.

In Alberta licensing of approvals involves a coordinated process with Alberta Environment for environmental impact assessment under the *Environmental Protection and Enhancement Act*. If an approval application goes to a hearing because objections are filed, the environmental assessment reports and studies are part of the evidence before the ERCB. The board and Alberta Environment cooperate in setting terms of reference and reviewing the environmental assessment documents.

For applications that require ERCB approval and also approval for contaminant discharge under the *Environmental Protection and Enhancement Act*, the ERCB and Alberta Environment operate together as a "single window" under a memorandum of understanding. Reviews of applications are coordinated, and an Alberta Environment official may sit as an acting ERCB member. Section 2 of the *Energy Resources Conservation Act*, the board's empowering statute, gives the ERCB a discretionary power to determine whether a proposed development is in the public interest, having regard to its economic, social, and environmental effects. The *Oil and Gas Conservation Act* provides for ERCB approvals, including environmental conditions imposed by Alberta Environment.

Oil and Gas

There are specific prohibitions against hydrocarbon releases to land, water, and air, including detailed performance standards for natural gas flaring from oil and gas facilities. In Alberta the ERCB enforces these requirements through an **enforcement ladder system** of inspections and progressively more serious warnings, monetary penalties, shutdowns, and prosecutions.

In Alberta the licensing of wells for waste disposal and oil and gas wells and the approval of processing plants, pipelines, and storage facilities involve the coordinated process described above.

Special attention is given to proposed wells in the sensitive montane region of the Rocky Mountains' eastern slopes, and to proposed sour gas wells. Sour gas wells produce gas that is high in sulphur and that contains hydrogen sulphide (H_2S), a gas that can be lethal even in small doses. Detailed emergency response plans must be prepared by companies proposing to drill for sour gas. There are minimum distance requirements for the placement of sour gas pipelines in relation to human settlement.

The ERCB also regulates contaminated oil and gas sites, including reclamation of **orphaned sites**—that is, wells and other facilities abandoned by oil and gas operators. There is an orphan well program, which manages a fund generated by means of a levy on well operators and well licence fees for new companies. Companies pay sums based on their proportionate share of estimated liability compared with total industry liability. This program is now operated by a non-profit orphan well association as an authorized delegate of the ERCB.

There is also a complex **liability rating system**, which compares the assets of a company proposing to acquire a licence for a facility it wants to buy with the estimated risk that the company will incur contamination liability. The result may be denial of the licence transfer application or the imposition of an increased performance bond requirement.

Oil Sands

Another special subject of ERCB regulation is oil sands development. The **oil sands** are crude bitumen deposits found in an area of northern Alberta and a small area of Saskatchewan that is approximately the size of New Brunswick. Production occurs by means of large-scale mining of surface deposits and in-site thermal recovery through wells for deeper deposits. When oil sands are taken into account, Canadian oil reserves rank second only to those of Saudi Arabia. Production from oil sands has passed 1.1 million barrels per day. During the next decade, it is expected that over $60 billion will be invested in oil sands development.

Environmental impacts of oil sands development are significant. They include vast surface disturbances, water use, pollution, and air emissions, including major greenhouse gas release. Oil sands mining and in-site development are regulated by the ERCB, primarily under the *Oil Sands Conservation Act* and the *Oil Sands Conservation Regulation*. The cooperative arrangements with Alberta Environment, which are described above, apply to oil sands development. Alberta Environment also administers the *Water Act*, which is significant because of the large quantities of water required for oil sands upgrading. It is also responsible for the *Climate Change and Emissions Management Act* and the *Specified Gas Emitters Regulation*.

Under these regulations, major emitters—including oil sands plants—must meet emission intensity reduction limits based on emissions per unit of production, not firm emission limits.

The pace of oil sands exploitation highlights several concerns that need to be addressed, including the following:

- lack of comprehensive planning for oil sands development,
- jurisdictional and regulatory complexity,
- lack of transparency, and
- limited opportunities for public participation.

There is much work to be done if Canada is to optimize the economic benefits while minimizing the environmental harm, both of which are inherent in this significant resource.

Coal

Though regulatory regimes for coal development vary across the provinces and territories, there are common features and issues. Provision is always made for required reclamation of surface-mined land. Containment or treatment of acidic drainage is required. Coal used for electricity generation is a major source of air emissions. Standards are enforced for air contaminants, particularly SO_2. Federal intensity-based greenhouse gas emission targets for large emitters, including coal-fired electricity generation plants, are under development.

In Alberta, where coal-fired plants produce approximately 47 percent of provincial greenhouse gas emissions, limits are set under the *Climate Change and Emissions Management Act*. Though some provinces have reduced or plan to reduce coal-fired generation, Alberta continues to rely on coal for approximately 80 percent of its electricity generation. The ERCB regulates both mines and generating plants in collaboration with Alberta Environment, as outlined earlier in this chapter.

Federal Energy Regulation

There are a number of federal statutes, with accompanying regulations, that affect fossil fuel exploration and development. Consider the following:

- Under the federal *National Energy Board Act*, the National Energy Board (NEB) considers potential environmental effects in certificate applications for major interprovincial and international pipelines, and regulates the direct environmental effects of operating pipelines.

- The *Fisheries Act* prohibits discharge of "deleterious substances" in "waters frequented by fish."
- The *Canadian Environmental Protection Act, 1999* imposes pollution prevention plan requirements.
- The *Canadian Environmental Assessment Act* requires environmental assessments of oil and gas facilities that are located on federal lands or that need an approval under a federal statutory power listed in the regulations. This includes activities in the northern territories and offshore, as well as major interprovincial and international pipelines.
- Environmental effects directly related to a proposed export of natural gas that requires NEB approval must be assessed as a result of *Quebec (Attorney General) v. Canada (National Energy Board)*, a 1994 decision of the Supreme Court of Canada.

In addition, federal and provincial statutes that provide for joint environmental processes often apply to oil, gas, and coal activities. The major program involves a joint environmental assessment panel. Under this program, joint panels of Alberta ERCB members and representatives of the Canadian Environmental Assessment Agency review and assess major proposed oil sands facilities and coal mines. It is likely that some form of joint or cooperative process will be established under proposed federal greenhouse gas legislation for "large final emitters," a high percentage of which are hydrocarbon sector companies.

Climate Change

"The fight against climate change [is] perhaps the biggest threat to confront the future of humanity today," said Prime Minister Stephen Harper in a speech at the G8 Summit in June 2007. This remark was in response to mounting scientific evidence of rapid global warming caused primarily by the carbon dioxide released when fossil fuels are burned.

Carbon dioxide levels in the global atmosphere are at their highest levels in 400,000 years. They have increased 31 percent in the last 100 years. Consequences are likely to include a rise in the sea level, desertification, and extreme weather events. In its four assessment reports since 1990, the Intergovernmental Panel on Climate Change (IPCC) found considerable evidence that most of the recent warming is attributable to human activities. The IPPC's fourth report, issued in April 2007, is particularly clear about the human impact on climate change.

By ratifying the international Kyoto Protocol to the United Nations Framework Convention on Climate Change in 2002, Canada committed itself to a target of reducing its total greenhouse gas emissions 6 percent below 1990 levels by the 2008-2012 Kyoto Protocol commitment period. In April 2007, with emissions approximately 33 percent above this target, the federal government and some provinces announced that compliance with the Kyoto targets is impossible without an economic meltdown.

The federal government introduced a "made in Canada" approach intended to reduce emissions to a lesser degree than the Kyoto requirements. The plan called for **emissions intensity reduction**. This plan requires reductions relative to production that do not include caps or absolute limits on emissions. The emissions intensity reductions are applied sector by sector on the basis of 2006 emissions; implementation is scheduled for 2010. Sectors affected by emissions intensity reduction include the following:

- thermal electricity;
- oil and gas;
- forest products;
- smelting and refining;
- iron and steel;
- some mining; and
- cement, lime, and chemicals.

The government expects a 2 percent annual emission intensity level reduction until 2020, which will result in an absolute emissions reduction of 20 percent. Plans call for a legal framework to be created by amendments to the *Canadian Environmental Protection Act, 1999*. These amendments, dubbed "Canada's Clean Air Act," were introduced in Parliament in late 2006 as Bill C-30. They have been undergoing review by parliamentary committee, and Bill C-30 is on the 2008 parliamentary agenda, with implementation anticipated in 2010.

Meanwhile, several of the provinces have developed climate change policies and passed their own statutes. Alberta, first among provincial greenhouse gas emitters— mainly because of its energy and coal-fired electricity activities—passed its *Climate Change and Emissions Management Act* in 2003. Like the federal scheme, it provides for emission intensity-based greenhouse gas reduction targets for large emitters that are linked to the provincial gross domestic product.

The Alberta targets are intended to reduce emissions per unit of production by 50 percent below 2005 levels by 2050. Under this "intensity-based" approach, while emissions from specific sources should decrease, economic growth in the province, particularly projected oil sands development, is likely to result in increased total emissions. Nevertheless, the Alberta government projects real reductions of 14 percent below 2005 levels by 2050. Included in the Act is the structure for an emissions-trading system, mandatory emissions reporting, and a climate change fund. Property rights in **carbon sinks**—which are created by "sequestering" carbon by growing trees, reducing soil tillage, and injecting CO_2 into depleted hydrocarbon formations—can be traded as **carbon offsets**. Compliance options include the following:

- emissions offsets, representing real, quantifiable, and measurable emissions reduction beyond legal requirements;
- emissions credits from money payments by emitters to the climate change fund, used to fund research and technological innovation; and
- emissions performance credits, purchased from other polluters that have reduced their emissions below targets.

The Alberta system is sensitive to potential developments in federal law and makes provision for agreements with other jurisdictions. British Columbia has also passed the *Greenhouse Gas Reduction Targets Act*, a reasonably comprehensive piece of legislation.

Nuclear Energy

Nuclear power regulation is complex and controversial, perhaps not surprisingly in light of the history of the technology. Originating in the Second World War, it was developed throughout the Cold War. Subsequent events, such as the Chernobyl reactor accident in 1986 and the attacks on the United States on September 11, 2001, have prompted many commentators to raise questions about the safety and security of nuclear power sources. Nuclear power as a technology differs markedly from other forms of power generation in terms of the types of accidents that may occur, the longevity of the hazardous radioactive wastes generated, and the potential for use in weapons.

Many special rules and approaches have developed to enable and continue the use of nuclear power. The presence of these rules sets nuclear energy apart from natural gas, coal, hydroelectricity, wind, solar, geothermal, and other sources of power. The adequacy of these rules is constantly being tested and questioned, and this situation will continue as long as nuclear power forms a substantial portion of electricity supply in parts of Canada.

Canada plays a highly significant role in nuclear power generation internationally. It is the world's largest uranium exporter, providing just over a quarter of the global supply. Canada exports almost 80 percent of its uranium production, currently from mines in northern Saskatchewan. As of 2004, nuclear power accounted for 12 to 14 percent of actual electrical power generated in Canada. The largest user of nuclear energy is Ontario, where nuclear power constitutes up to 40 percent of the total power used in the province.

In the 1950s and 1960s, Canada developed the CANDU nuclear power generation technology. This technology is used in Ontario, Quebec, and New Brunswick; it is exported to India, Pakistan, China, South Korea, Argentina, and Romania for power generation. **CANDU technology** uses heavy water to moderate the uranium fuel fusion reaction and requires fast, redundant shutdown systems to be available in various events. This fusion reaction produces large amounts of energy, which is harnessed through steam to power large turbines for power generation. Nuclear power plants must be located on large bodies of water, which play a role in thermal cooling and provide an outlet for the emissions from the plants.

Nuclear facilities involve an immense capital cost. For example, $14.4 billion was spent building the Darlington nuclear generating station, Ontario's newest plant, between 1981 and 1993. The Ontario government has estimated that $40 billion will be required between 2018 and 2043 if the existing Ontario plants are to be refurbished and operational to 2043. The Ontario government is now proposing to build new nuclear generation plants and as of June 2008 has announced that new units will be built at the Darlington nuclear generation site. If approved and built, these would be the first new nuclear plants ordered in Ontario in decades. There are many federal and provincial approvals still required before construction could proceed at that location.

There are four main areas of concern articulated in the debate about continued nuclear power generation in Canada:

- the enormous financial cost of nuclear-generated power;
- the risks of a nuclear power plant accident;
- the long-term disposal of nuclear wastes, which are highly radioactive and hazardous, and continue to be toxic for hundreds of thousands of years; and
- the risk of nuclear weapons proliferation and other human and national security risks such as terrorist attacks on nuclear plants.

In addition, there has been longstanding debate with respect to the location of nuclear power generation plants and other facilities, such as low-level, medium-level, and high-level radioactive waste disposal sites; the transportation of radioactive fuel and waste; and the importing of used fuel, including plutonium fuel, from countries such as Russia and the United States.

International Law

The United Nations Atomic Energy Commission was established in 1946 to recommend the use of nuclear energy for peaceful purposes. Eventually, it formed the International Atomic Energy Agency in 1957. One of its first accomplishments was the imposition of safeguards for a Canadian supply of uranium to Japan in 1959.

Around the same time, EURATOM was established in Europe. EURATOM regulated all non-military nuclear activities of the member states, including France and Britain, and theoretically provided for collective ownership of nuclear materials by member states.

In 1968 the Treaty on the Non-Proliferation of Nuclear Weapons was signed by the United Kingdom, the United States, and the Soviet Union. Now all members of the United Nations are signatories except for India, Pakistan, Israel, and Cuba. The treaty attempts to limit the further development of nuclear weapons by additional states.

International treaties that play a significant role in Canadian nuclear regulatory obligations arose as a consequence of events such as the development of nuclear power production and the capacity of various countries for nuclear technology. The various stages of the Cold War and the occurrence of serious accidents, such as the tragedy at Chernobyl in 1986, have also resulted in the adoption of international nuclear treaties. Canada is a signatory to international agreements on the following subjects:

- nuclear safety (1986);
- safety of spent fuel management and radioactive waste management, including transboundary movement of these materials (1997 and 1990);
- third-party liability, civil liability, and supplementary compensation for nuclear damage (various conventions, annexes, amendments, and supplements adopted in 1960, 1963, 1964, 1982, 1997, and 1998);
- physical protection of nuclear material (1979);
- early notification of nuclear accidents (1986);
- assistance in the event of nuclear accident and radiological emergency (1986); and
- prevention of nuclear explosions or disposal of nuclear waste in Antarctica (1959).

Despite being a signatory, Canada is not always in compliance with these international agreements—for example, Canada has so far failed to comply with the treaties covering nuclear liability in the event of an accident.

Federal Regulation

Jurisdiction over nuclear power and activities is primarily federal. The Canadian *Nuclear Safety and Control Act* sets out obligations that are overseen by the Canadian Nuclear Safety Commission (CNSC), which reports to the minister of natural resources. To carry out activities pertaining to the use of nuclear technology in

Canada, applicants must obtain a licence from the CNSC. Separate licences are required for various activities, including uranium exploration, uranium mine development and operation, siting of power plants, construction of plants, operation of plants, research facilities, medical facilities, and production of products using radioactive materials.

The CNSC may take different approaches when determining the level of safety and safeguards that the applicant must meet to obtain a licence. The industry approach, traditionally adopted by the CNSC, has been to reduce risks to a level "as low as reasonably achievable"; this approach is commonly known by the acronym **ALARA**. The approach has been controversial in Canada. Recent initiatives by the regulator to develop criteria for decisions regarding the siting of new nuclear power plants and design standards are subjecting this approach to public scrutiny.

In the past few decades, applicants have been asked to anticipate a wide range of potential multiple failures of components and safety systems, and to build safety redundancy into their systems. The federal auditor general noted that the CNSC has not made the progress it had planned in developing risk-based approaches to nuclear power plant licensing. Other pressures arose as a result of the attacks against the United States on September 11, 2001. Nuclear power plant licensing and safety measures regarding various aspects of public infrastructure in the United States have begun to undergo radical reconsideration because of the 9/11 tragedy and the possible risks that it calls to mind. Any similar changes in Canadian regulation are yet to be determined.

Consider other federal governance affecting nuclear activities:

- Health Canada maintains a registry to monitor the lifelong radiation doses of all workers exposed to radioactive materials.
- A federal–provincial–territorial radiation committee makes recommendations to governments on practices and standards regarding radiation exposure in Canada.
- The *Transportation of Dangerous Goods Regulations* control the transport of radioactive materials in Canada. They incorporate the technical instructions of the Convention on International Civil Aviation for air transport, including provisions pertaining to the specifications of packages and labelling.
- The federal government provides national drinking water guidelines, which most provinces use as standards in their respective drinking water legislation. In Ontario public attention to the issue of appropriate standards for tritium in drinking water has resulted in some reduction in the allowable amount.
- The 1976 federal *Nuclear Liability Act* exempts nuclear power generators and suppliers from the normal rules of civil liability by capping liability at $75

million in the event of a serious accident. This exemption is controversial because it is a significant subsidy that is not available to generators of other types of electrical power.

Provincial Regulation

Each province has jurisdiction over the mixture of electricity sources within the province. For example, the Ontario Energy Board reviews Ontario's long-term electricity supply plan under the recently amended *Electricity Act*. This Act also empowers the Ontario minister of energy to issue directives to the recently established Ontario Power Authority that require it to arrange for electricity supply contracts from particular types of power generators.

Some provinces, such as Saskatchewan and Quebec, also apply their provincial environmental assessment legislation to the nuclear industry within the province. While Ontario is less involved in regulating nuclear power sources than other provinces, matters of general application may apply to the nuclear industry—for example, the need for a permit before withdrawing water from ground or surface water sources.

In addition, the provinces have a voice when considering whether or not to allow the creation of new nuclear power plants within their borders. In Ontario a process is under way for determining whether to select CANDU or non-CANDU nuclear generation technology.

Mining and Aggregates
Mining

Canada is one of the most mineral-rich countries in the world, and mining these resources has always been important to Canada's economy. Non-metal mining (for salt and quartzite) and energy-related mining for coal are also significant industries. Canada's mining and mineral-processing industries contributed $41.8 billion to the economy in 2004; this represents 4 percent of Canada's gross domestic product. In total, these mining-related industries employed 369,000 people in 2004.

Despite its economic benefits, mining causes severe environmental effects that may damage and pollute the landscape for years after a mining activity concludes. The following are typical effects of mining on the environment:

- obliteration of the natural habitat of wildlife and fish;
- generation of large amounts of waste, noise, and dust;

Table 9.1   Jurisdiction Over Mining

Federal Jurisdiction	Provincial Jurisdiction
All mines on federal lands	All mines on provincial lands except uranium mines
All uranium mines	

- contamination of water, land, and air with organic chemicals, cyanide, and heavy metal that leach from acid mine drainage; and
- continued pollution of the environment for decades after a mine closes, if it is not properly rehabilitated.

The federal government is responsible for mines on federal lands, as well as uranium mining regardless of where it is undertaken. Provincial governments are responsible for all other types of mines on provincial lands. Table 9.1 sets out federal and provincial jurisdiction over various types of mines.

Different rules and requirements are triggered at each stage of the mining process; these stages include the following:

- mineral exploration and prospecting,
- claim staking,
- environmental assessment and approvals,
- waste management, and
- monitoring and closure.

The first stage in the mining process is the staking of a mining claim, which is required in order to explore for mineral deposits. A mining claim gives a prospector the exclusive right to conduct an exploration in a specific area, and exploration work must actually be carried out to maintain the claim.

A prospector is allowed only to explore for minerals under a mining claim, and may not extract minerals. In Ontario the *Mining Act* allows for staking of mining claims and exploring on land where the Crown owns the subsurface mineral rights, even though in many cases another person may own the rights to the surface land. This leaves a great deal of land available for mineral extraction, while environmental concerns are rarely considered.

When exploration leads to the discovery of valuable mineral deposits, mining almost always goes ahead. To proceed with mining, the holder of a mining claim must negotiate a mining lease with the provincial government and pay annual rent. Once a mining lease has been granted, the claim holder must follow the requirements of the *Mining Act* and other relevant laws. Although a mine may be designated for environmental assessment in Ontario, mining is not otherwise subject to environmental assessment in the province.

Under the *Mining Act*, a mine closure plan must be prepared. The plan must explain how the mine will be rehabilitated and how environmental problems will be addressed when the mine is eventually closed. The mining company must also offer some financial assurance to cover future costs of mine rehabilitation. In the past, many mines were abandoned and required rehabilitation at public expense.

Aggregates

Aggregates include sand, gravel, and crushed stone, and are extracted from pits and quarries in areas that contain these natural resources. Aggregates are used in highway construction, in building dams and airports, and in some manufactured products. While new aggregates are often used in these projects, it is possible to recycle and reuse aggregate products in order to better conserve existing aggregate resources.

The provinces are responsible for regulating aggregate pits and quarries; in Ontario, an aggregate operator must obtain a licence under the *Aggregate Resources Act*, and this process requires consideration of environmental effects. However, applications for new and expanded aggregate operations are usually successful despite concerns about environmental impacts. Approvals are also required under the *Planning Act* to address land use planning issues.

Many of the best-quality aggregate deposits are located in areas that are ecologically unique and important, such as the Niagara Escarpment and the Oak Ridges Moraine in the Greenbelt of Ontario, and aggregate operations are often permitted in sensitive areas like wetlands, raising issues related to source water protection. Many are calling for new processes that better balance environmental protection with aggregate extraction.

The Ontario government has addressed the problem of rehabilitating pits and quarries differently than it has the rehabilitation of mines. All aggregate operators must contribute money to both their own site-specific fund that serves as financial assurance for the site and a common fund that may be used to rehabilitate orphan sites.

Fisheries

The role of the fisheries in Canada is substantial. According to statistics from Fisheries and Oceans Canada, the value of the commercial catch in Canada was over $2 billion in 2005; this figure excludes the value of **aquaculture**, which exceeded

$700 million. Recreational fisheries exist throughout Canada and also have economic and social significance.

The importance of Canadian fisheries is not limited to coastal communities. The per capita consumption of fish products in Canada in 2001 was 9.57 kilograms. The exploitation of these fisheries has a direct effect on the environment within Canada, as well as neighbouring countries and international waters. This is evident in the near-daily appearance of fishery-related stories in Canada's national newspapers.

Many of Canada's laws that monitor the management and conservation of fisheries derive from international obligations. An example of such a law is the *Coastal Fisheries Protection Act*. The following observations provide further examples of Canada's international obligations.

- Federal law regarding pollution of the marine environment in the **exclusive economic zone** is based on the United Nations Convention on the Law of the Sea. This convention contains a variety of articles relating to conservation and management—for example, articles 60 to 70 and 116 to 120 as well as part XII, which covers the protection and preservation of the marine environment. It also gives coastal states jurisdiction over the marine environment in the exclusive economic zone.
- Federal provisions relating to conservation and management of fisheries are implemented through an agreement generally known as "the United Nations fishing agreement." The agreement creates regional organizations to manage and protect straddling and migratory stocks of marine species both within and beyond the exclusive economic zone.
- Conservation and management measures are also evident in the Convention on Future Multilateral Co-operation in the Northwest Atlantic Fisheries. This convention, which was signed in Ottawa on October 24, 1978, is the governing convention for the Northwest Atlantic Fisheries Organization. Pursuant to this convention, Canada's portion of the northwest Atlantic Ocean is subject to a fisheries management regime.
- Article 3(1)(a) of the Agreement to Promote Compliance with International Conservation and Management Measures by Fishing Vessels on the High Seas and article 18(1) of the United Nations fishing agreement both require Canada to take measures necessary to ensure that fishing boats comply with international conservation and management measures.

The federal government has primary jurisdiction over both seacoast and inland fisheries in Canada, although it interacts closely with the provinces on many matters. The provinces may dispose of the fisheries they own, but may not trespass on the federal power to regulate fisheries. This jurisdictional decision was reached in 1914 in the case of *Attorney General of British Columbia v. Attorney General of Canada.*

Federal jurisdiction creates no right of property, but confers the exclusive right to impose restrictions or limitations to control public fishing. Thus, the statutory conservation obligations rest with the federal government.

The primary legislation that governs fisheries law in Canada is the *Fisheries Act.* The Act applies to all waters in the fishing zones of Canada, all waters in the territorial seas of Canada, and all internal waters of Canada.

The habitat protection and pollution prevention provisions of the *Fisheries Act*, combined with the Act's broad application to internal waters—including rivers and streams—make the *Fisheries Act* a frequent choice for prosecution of environmental offences. Section 35 provides that "no person shall carry on any work or undertaking that results in the harmful alteration, disruption or destruction of fish habitat"; however, these works and undertakings can be conducted if a permit or authorization is issued in advance. Many activities have the potential to affect fish habitat. Builders and others involved in construction are well advised to review sites for streams or other areas of potential fish habitat. Section 20 of the Act authorizes the minister to require the construction of "fishways" around obstacles.

Decisions to grant permits or authorization pursuant to the *Fisheries Act* can trigger a requirement for an environmental assessment pursuant to the *Canadian Environmental Assessment Act.* An environmental assessment is required if a permit is issued or an approval is granted for a project; this includes permits or approvals issued by the minister of fisheries and oceans.

Section 36(3) of the *Fisheries Act* provides that "no person shall deposit or permit the deposit of a deleterious substance of any type in water frequented by fish or in any place under any conditions where the deleterious substance or any other deleterious substance that results from the deposit of the deleterious substance may enter any such water." The phrase "deleterious substance" is defined broadly and includes most substances that would degrade or alter the quality of water, making it deleterious to fish. In *Fletcher v. Kingston (City)*, the Ontario Court of Appeal held that this section does not require actual harm. In other words, the potential of a deleterious substance to cause harm to fish once discharged may be sufficient without proof that the substance actually caused harm to the fish. Section 38 of the Act provides broad powers for inspectors. Section 40 provides that offences are punishable by fines of up to $1 million and imprisonment for up to three years.

Some provincial legislation governs aspects of the fisheries, predominantly licensing and management. There are also limited environmental provisions in certain provincial legislation—for example, section 28 of the British Columbia *Fisheries Act*, which requires the installation of fish-protective devices around dams or hydraulic projects. The federal government has entered into memoranda of understanding with provinces regarding management of aquaculture; this has resulted in various provincial statutes on this subject—for example, the Nova Scotia *Fisheries and Coastal Resources Act.*

Agriculture and Aquaculture

Agriculture and aquaculture—that is, the farming of fish and aquatic plants—have long been important industries and ways of life in Canada. Both continue to be significant to our economy and livelihoods. In 2005 Canada's agriculture system contributed about $86 billion to the national economy and provided work for approximately 2.1 million Canadians. Although agriculture and aquaculture provide many benefits, they can also damage biodiversity and contaminate air, water, soil, and sediment quality.

Agriculture

A major trend in agriculture in recent years has been the growth of intensive **industrial farming**. In the past 50 years, the size of the average Canadian farm has tripled but, at the same time, the number of farms in Canada has steadily declined. Much larger numbers of livestock, particularly pigs, are being kept close together on much smaller areas of land than were traditionally used to farm livestock. By 2006, average pig herd sizes on Canadian farms had increased by 150 percent over the previous 10 years.

Manure

Besides creating increased odour problems, intensive farming of livestock has caused other major impacts on the environment. The ever-growing quantities of manure produced by intensive livestock operations must be disposed of. Farmers have usually disposed of manure by spreading it as fertilizer on farm fields. However, if manure is not properly handled, stored, and distributed, it can harm the air, soil, and water. Too much manure may run off into nearby streams or leach through the soil into groundwater, causing contamination and infections such as E. coli poisoning. This can result in surface water that is not safe for drinking or swimming, and in groundwater that is unsafe to drink. In May 2000, such a situation led to the deaths of seven people and made many others seriously ill in Walkerton, Ontario.

It has been difficult in the past to address some of these environmental impacts because of the economic importance of agriculture. For example, Ontario's *Farming and Food Production Protection Act* notes that intensive agriculture may cause "discomfort and inconveniences" to others and purports to balance agriculture with concerns about health, safety, and the environment. It protects farmers from legal liability for nuisances, such as odour, dust, flies, and noise, caused by standard farming practices.

The federal and provincial governments share responsibility for the regulation of agriculture. The federal government has developed programs to address the environmental impacts of pig farming in particular. However, in 2005 the federal commissioner of the environment and sustainable development noted that the government was not yet certain about whether these programs were successfully reducing problems or not.

Following the tragedy in Walkerton, the Ontario government developed new laws to better protect water from intensive agricultural practices. In 2002 the *Nutrient Management Act* established provincial rules for the appropriate application of manure to help ensure both sustainable agriculture and environmental protection. The *Clean Water Act* was passed in 2006 to assist communities in developing plans to protect their watersheds from threats to drinking water, including potential threats from agriculture.

Other Issues

There are many other environmental issues that relate to agriculture, including the following:

- The use of chemical pesticides is a concern managed by both the federal and the provincial governments. Pesticides are assessed and approved before they are used in Canada, but questions about their effects on environmental and human health persist. Pesticide regulation is discussed in detail later in this chapter.
- Many concerns have also been raised about the use of genetically modified organisms (GMOs) in agricultural production. The use of GMOs is not heavily regulated, and there is no requirement that products containing GMOs be labelled.
- The routine feeding of antibiotics to pigs, cows, and chickens, and the feeding of growth-promoting hormones to beef cattle pose a threat to human health. Contaminants in pharmaceuticals excreted by farm animals are often carried into water through runoff from manure; this may also have harmful effects on the environment, including wildlife.
- Laws have been used to protect prime agricultural lands from residential and commercial development. British Columbia established a special land use zone known as the "agricultural land reserve" in 1973 to protect agricul-

tural land from increasing development. In 2005 the Ontario government enacted the *Greenbelt Act* to protect agricultural land and rural communities around the rapidly growing Toronto area from urban development and sprawl. However, the loss of natural habitat to the initial conversion to agriculture was likely the greatest source of harm.

Aquaculture

Aquaculture may contribute to a range of harmful environmental effects, including the following:

- water and sediment pollution by nutrients from fecal material and waste feed,
- depletion of wild fish as a result of diseases such as fish lice that escape into the wild population,
- depletion of wild fish that are caught to feed farmed fish, and
- negative impacts on biodiversity when a non-native species escapes from an aquaculture cage in open water.

Like Canadian laws governing agriculture, laws governing aquaculture in Canada attempt to balance the economic value of the fisheries industry with the need to protect the environment. The federal and provincial governments share regulatory responsibility for aquaculture, but gaps in regulation remain. The federal government is involved in aquaculture management planning throughout Canada. Provincial governments may require that licences be obtained before an applicant engages in aquaculture; both Ontario and British Columbia have licensing procedures. It is important that all licensing decisions be made with possible environmental impacts in mind.

In 2004 the commissioner of the environment and sustainable development reported on gaps in program coordination between the federal and provincial governments concerning salmon aquaculture. The commissioner also highlighted gaps in scientific knowledge about potential environmental effects that need to be addressed.

Pesticides

The term **pesticide** covers a range of products that have in common the control of living organisms. These products function by means of a variety of mechanisms and are commonly categorized according to the pest that they target. They are known, for example, as insecticides, fungicides, herbicides, and rodenticides. Some pesticides work by killing the target organism by affecting its nervous system; some work by affecting the organism's ability to reproduce; some work as predators of the target organism; others affect living conditions to make the area less attractive for the target pest.

Pesticides are used for a variety of reasons. The most popular uses are for crop and forestry production. They are also used in an attempt to protect property such as wood structures. They may be employed for esthetic reasons—for example, to maintain a weed- or grub-free lawn. Pesticides may be synthetic or natural in origin, and may be contained in the form of a powder, liquid, or spray, or may be a living creature such as a nematode.

A number of pesticides historically manufactured in Canada and elsewhere were found in the 1960s to be persistent in the environment and to be causing population impacts and declines in wildlife. A group of one dozen such chemicals were termed **persistent organic pollutants (POPs)** because of their long-lasting toxicity. POPs were the subject of debate and discussion in Canada and internationally; they were eventually banned for use in many countries, including Canada.

As a result of these efforts, contamination levels of some pesticides have declined. Benefits include the recovery of the bald eagle and peregrine falcon populations in the Great Lakes lowlands, where these species had become nearly extinct. Because of this experience, pesticide accumulation, persistence, and magnification in the food chain is now examined when registration of a new pesticide is considered.

The law regulating the manufacture and use of pesticides comes from a variety of sources: international law, federal law, provincial law, and municipal law. Each source is examined separately below.

International Regulation

There are a number of international instruments, statements, declarations, and initiatives to which Canada is a party. These documents are relevant to Canada's approach to pesticide regulation:

- The Commission for Environmental Cooperation (CEC) is an international organization created by Canada, Mexico, and the United States under the North American Agreement on Environmental Cooperation. The CEC is intended to prevent trade and environmental conflicts and to promote the effective enforcement of environmental law.
- The precautionary principle, which is embodied in the Bergen Ministerial Declaration on Sustainable Development of 1990, states: "Where there are threats of serious or irreversible damage, lack of full scientific certainty

should not be used as a reason for postponing measures to prevent environmental degradation." This principle is referenced in federal pesticides legislation and in judgment of the Supreme Court of Canada pertaining to municipal pesticides regulation.

- The Stockholm Convention on Persistent Organic Pollutants (POP) was signed by nearly 200 countries and came into force in 2004. Since that time, various provinces, including Ontario, recalled POP pesticides and buried them in bulk in landfill locations.
- The Organisation for Economic Co-operation and Development (OECD) brings together the governments of free-market democracies to share information and expertise for common purposes such as sustainable economic growth. The OECD created its pesticides program in 1992 to improve the efficiency and effectiveness of pesticide regulation by such means as harmonization.

In addition, Canada's pesticide registration agency, the Pest Management Regulatory Agency, has developed a policy of harmonizing some of its pesticide re-evaluations with the US *Food Quality Protection Act*, following the same timelines, and using the same information base that is used in the United States. Pesticide re-evaluations are critical because so many pesticides in use in Canada and elsewhere were used or approved long ago on the basis of erroneous risk assessment criteria; under recent amendments to the *Pest Control Products Act*, they must now be re-evaluated to determine whether they meet today's standards.

Federal Regulation

In order for a pest control product to be used in Canada, it must be registered by the minister of health through the federal Pest Management Regulatory Agency. In response to public pressure and a report of the Standing Committee on Environment and Sustainable Development, the new *Pest Control Products Act* was enacted in 2002. This legislation allows the minister to register a pesticide in Canada if the following features are demonstrated:

- the pesticide is of value and effective, and
- requirements to safeguard health are met.

An important component of the pesticides registration process is re-evaluation of already-registered pesticides. Unfortunately, there is an enormous backlog of older pesticides that were never considered under present-day registration standards. So far, many of the pesticides that have undergone the re-evaluation process have had stringent restrictions imposed on their use, or have been withdrawn from use altogether. Re-evaluation of older pesticides is therefore a high priority. Despite the recent amendments and improvements to the *Pest Control Products Act*, there are still some pesticides registered for uses in Canada that are not allowed in other OECD countries.

There are important opportunities for public participation in the pesticides registration, re-evaluation, and other processes under the *Pest Control Products Act*. Members of the public are invited to participate in the following ways:

- review notices of applications for registration,
- comment on proposals,
- review lists of substances undergoing re-evaluation,
- seek special review, and
- review studies and data in special reading rooms.

Registration, if granted, is conditional on compliance with labelling requirements. Labels must clearly outline the proper use of the pesticide, including restrictions on its use, and requirements for protective gear, such as masks and gloves. Pursuant to the federal *Pest Control Products Act* as well as the *Competition Act*, manufacturers, distributors, and retailers must be careful not to misrepresent the health and safety risks involved in the use of their pesticides.

Provincial Regulation

In addition to the federal registration requirement, there are provincial requirements in most provinces and territories—for example, those legislated under Ontario's *Pesticides Act* and Quebec's *Pesticides Act*. The requirements and provisions vary among the provinces, and many contain the following:

- a classification system for pesticides;
- training and licensing requirements for vendors;
- provisions regarding the sale of certain classes of pesticides; and
- training and licensing requirements for agriculture, forestry, and commercial pesticide applicators.

Additional requirements may be specified for some pesticides. Examples include storage requirements when pesticides are included within certain classes of toxicity and signage requirements when commercial applicators apply the pesticides. In 2008, Ontario passed legislation that will allow for a province-wide ban on listed cosmetic pesticides. Once in place, this provincial standard will displace municipal bylaws restricting cosmetic pesticides.

Municipal Regulation

Beginning with a few Quebec communities in the early 1990s, a growing number of municipalities in Canada have passed bylaws to control and reduce the use of pesticides within their boundaries. Most of these bylaws have been directed at the non-essential or esthetic use of pesticides—for example, use in lawns and gardens.

The municipal jurisdiction to pass pesticide control bylaws was unsuccessfully challenged by the pesticide and applicator industries in Hudson, Quebec. All three levels of courts within Quebec and the Supreme Court of Canada upheld the bylaw and the municipality's authority to pass it under the Quebec *Cities and Towns Act*. The City of Toronto passed a similar bylaw, which was also unsuccessfully challenged by an industry organization. The courts have agreed that municipalities have an important role to play in environmental regulation and are trustees of our local environment. The Supreme Court of Canada has also confirmed that Canada's international commitments to the precautionary principle are to be respected in municipal rule making as well as in federal and provincial decisions.

Biotechnology and Genetic Engineering

Biotechnology is commonly defined as the use of living organisms for the production of goods and services. Biotechnology is not a new phenomenon. Fermentation in the making of beer and bread, selective breeding of farm animals to increase certain traits, and the biological processes used in sewage treatment plant all fall within the definition. However, modern biotechnology focuses on **genetic engineering**, which is genetic modification of a microbe, plant, or animal to serve a new or enhanced purpose.

DNA (deoxyribonucleic acid), the genetic code of all livings things, is what makes each species, and each member of each species, unique. For decades, scientists have been able to take genetic material from one species and implant it into another for the purpose of adding very specific characteristics or traits to plants and animals. This genetic engineering can, in effect, create a new life form that can then pass these characteristics on to its offspring.

Applications of Genetic Engineering

There are many different applications of genetic engineering. Consider the following examples:

- *Transgenic crops.* Perhaps the best-known examples of genetic engineering are **transgenic crops**, which have been given specific characteristics to improve taste, appearance, nutritional value, and rate of growth. Some plants are engineered to increase resistance to specific pesticides and herbicides, so that these pesticides and herbicides can be used to kill weeds around the transgenic crops.
- *Microbes.* **Microbes** are single-celled organisms such as bacteria, algae, and fungi. Genetically modified microbes can be sprayed on temperature-sensitive plants and crops to aid in preventing frost damage, which allows for a longer growing season. Genetically altered microbes are also being developed in the mining industry to assist in leaching minerals from ores and tailings. In addition, they are being used in the cleanup of spills and the detoxification of wastes. Microbes also facilitate the efficient degradation of sludges from sewage treatment processes, and serve many other purposes.
- *Hormones.* Hormones have been developed to enhance growth or prevent disease and to substantially increase the milk production of cows.

There are probably hundreds, if not thousands, of biotechnology products existing or under development around the world. Over a quarter of Canada's biotechnology companies focus on the development of agriculture and agri-food products. Although there are many environmental and human health benefits from biotechnology, there are also concerns about the risks posed by products created by means of new biotechnology.

Risks

Concerns about new biotechnology generally reflect the fact that there is seldom enough information to understand how a new life form will interact in the natural environment. It is difficult to evaluate all the contingencies involved in putting the new technologies into use. As is suggested in a 2001 expert panel report on the future of food biotechnology, the "potential risk is most often stated to be of a 'low probability, high consequence risk.' In other words, although the chance of something going wrong may be very slight, if something does go wrong, the ecological consequences may be tremendous."

Consider the following risks:

- *Promotion of monocultures.* A **monoculture** is the production of a single species or genetic variant crop in a particular area. This can result in a crop's vulnerability to disease or infestation, as occurred in the potato famine in mid-19th century Ireland. In Ireland at that time, the particular variety of potato grown was susceptible to potato blight, and the entire crop failed. As new GMOs are introduced, there is a risk that the biodiversity in a particular ecosystem will be reduced by promoting monocultures and uniformity in the breeding of plants and animals.
- *Disruption of the food chain.* When a new invasive or exotic species is introduced from one ecosystem into another, it can have devastating effects by disrupting the food chain. This problem occurred with the introduction of the lamprey, the zebra mussel, and the goby from European waters into the Great Lakes system. With no natural predators in the new environment, the population of any new species may grow unchecked and consume the food supply relied on by native species.
- *Competitive advantage.* Similarly, there is concern that GMOs could expand beyond their niche to disrupt the natural ecological balance. This could happen if they are resistant to certain diseases and thus establish a competitive advantage over natural species.
- *Uncontrolled reproduction.* GMOs may survive and reproduce after the completion of their intended use. Once they are let loose in the environment, it is nearly impossible to contain them.
- *Cross-pollination.* **Transgenes**—that is, genetically modified genes—may find their way into wild plant populations as a result of pollination with genetically engineered plants. The results are unpredictable.

The concerns listed above raise an important question: are all biotechnological applications and products appropriate, or should ethical and policy issues be raised and discussed before new technologies or products are developed and introduced?

The Legal Framework

The federal government's 1983 national biotechnology strategy determined that biotechnology would be governed within the existing framework of legislation and regulatory agencies. During the late 1990s, a consultation process was held to renew the strategy, which is now called the Canadian biotechnology strategy. However,

Table 9.2   Overview of Federal Laws and Agencies Regulating Biotechnology

Nature of Product	Statute and Regulations	Agency
Food and food additives	*Food and Drugs Act* and regulations	Health Canada
Pest control agents	*Pest Control Products Act* and regulations	Health Canada
Feeds and feed additives	*Feeds Act* and regulations	CFIA
Plants and seeds	*Seeds Act* and regulations	CFIA
Plant pests	*Plant Protection Act* and regulations	CFIA
Chemical products	*Canadian Environmental Protection Act, 1999* and Health Canada regulations	Environment Canada

Source: Adapted from Table 1: An Overview of Federal Laws and Agencies for Biotechnology in Expert Panel Report on the Future of Food Biotechnology prepared by the Royal Society of Canada at the request of Health Canada, Canadian Food Inspection Agency and Environment Canada, Elements of Precaution: Recommendations for the Regulation of Food.

the regulatory framework for biotechnology continues to be a patchwork of regimes that are based on the nature of the products involved.

The rationale is that regulatory agencies—such as Health Canada, the Canadian Food Inspection Agency (CFIA), and Environment Canada—have acquired expertise in their respective product areas; they therefore are well suited to expand their safety mandate to assess the risks of bioengineered products. An overview of the legal framework governing biotechnology is provided in table 9.2.

Consider the functions of the following agencies:

- *The CFIA.* The CFIA is the lead agency responsible for agricultural products, including seeds, plants, animal fertilizers, and feeds. The agency enforces the food safety and nutritional quality standards that are set by Health Canada. It also carries out inspections and enforces standards for animal health and plant protection. As part of these functions, the CFIA assesses new products to ensure that they meet the applicable standards under the relevant legislation, such as the *Seeds Act* and the *Feeds Act.* Information that must be provided by the person or business seeking to introduce a new product into Canada includes the nature and type of the new product, test data with respect to environmental and human health risks, mitigation measures, and contingency plans. The assessment is the same regardless of whether or not the product is bioengineered.

- *Health Canada.* Health Canada is the lead agency responsible for traditional and novel foods under the *Food and Drugs Act*, including genetically modified food sold in Canada. Novel foods are dealt with under a separate section of the *Food and Drugs Regulations.* In a manner that resembles the CFIA process, persons wanting to introduce novel foods into the Canadian market must provide information to Health Canada, including data establishing that the food is safe for consumption. Once Health Canada is satisfied that it has sufficient information, it then determines whether the food may be sold.

- *Environment Canada.* Environment Canada is charged with certain responsibilities regarding biotechnology under the *Canadian Environmental Protection Act, 1999.* The Act and its *New Substances Notification Regulations* ensure that no product escapes assessment by requiring an assessment of any biotechnology product that is not regulated by other legislation.

The three agencies listed above are responsible for assessing all new or novel products within their areas of expertise.

Novelty Threshold

A seed, animal feed, human food, or similar product is subject to an assessment if it is considered novel. The novelty test applies to all products regardless of whether or not they are genetically modified. A **novel product** is a product that has an intentionally selected characteristic that is "not substantially equivalent" to an existing organism in terms of its specific use and safety with respect to human health and the environment.

The *Seeds Act* and its regulations apply to plants with "novel traits" that are intended for release into the environment. The *Feeds Act* and its regulations deal with livestock feeds, including novel feeds.

The assessment of all new or novel products in the same way, regardless of whether they result from cross-breeding or from genetic modification, is a controversial matter. Many experts suggest that there should be a separate and more robust review of biotechnological products. A 2001 Royal Society of Canada report concluded that the use of "substantial equivalence" as the threshold to exempt genetically modified agricultural products from a more rigorous scientific assessment was scientifically unjustifiable and inconsistent with the precautionary regulation of technology. The panel recommended a four-stage diagnostic assessment of transgenic crops and foods to replace the substantial equivalence exemption.

Ontario and a number of other provinces have addressed certain issues related to biotechnology or have regulated certain applications of biotechnological products.

PART IV

Integrated Approaches in Environmental Law

CHAPTER 10

Environmental Assessment

Introduction

The regulatory regimes discussed in chapters 8 and 9 have played an important role in limiting environmental damage and forcing corrective action. They protect the air, water, and soil against specific anticipated threats from particular activities and certain sectors. This protection is crucial and will remain so. However, regulatory regimes are not now, and never will be, sufficient guardians of the environment.

That is because standard regulatory approaches work best on problems that are basically simple and many of our most significant environmental challenges are profoundly complex. They could be adequate guardians of the environment only if the world were simpler than it actually is, and if regulators could see into the future with accuracy.

To be convenient for regulatory purposes, all environmental threats would have to be separate, measurable, and targeted at individual receptors. The economy would have to be divided tidily into well-defined sectors, all engaging in predictable activities with specific and well-known environmental effects. The effects would have to be either clearly bad or cheerfully benign, and the detrimental effects would have to be correctable with available technology and finances.

For better or worse, the real world is not like this. It is complicated, variable, full of tangled interconnections, ever changing, and often puzzling. Circumstances—such as ecosystems, community needs, cultural preferences, and economic conditions—are often very different from one place to the next.

Environmental effects also tend to mix with one another, as in the case of chemical soups of air pollutants, and to mix with other factors, as in the case of poor communities economically dependent on a polluting employer. These combinations tend to make decisions challenging. And when environmental damage is done, it is often very difficult and very costly to repair, if repair is possible at all.

This is not a new insight. At least since the 1960s, jurisdictions in Canada and most other industrialized countries have seen the limitations of conventional regulatory regimes and have been gradually adjusting and supplementing them, using a variety of tools. Very generally, this evolution of environmental regulation has centred on the following themes:

- recognition of the complexity of environmental threats,
- awareness of and respect for the diversity of circumstances,
- facilitation of a larger public voice in decision making, and
- emphasis on anticipation and prevention rather than on crisis management.

Initial steps taken to further these objectives have included the introduction of certificates of approval for new emission or discharge sources, site-specific requirements for particular polluters, and anticipatory protection of vulnerable areas. Also important have been broader planning efforts, provision of public access to environmental information, granting of environmental rights, and the use of public hearings. Perhaps the most significant advance was the introduction and gradual expansion of environmental assessment law.

Basic Principles and Evolution

Environmental assessment law began as an attempt to prevent, or at least minimize, environmental damage by changing the nature of project planning, design, and implementation. The central idea was that the proponents of environmentally significant undertakings should take environmental considerations into account in the same way as they already took financial and technical matters into account.

Clearly this was not happening. Private sector proponents, such as corporations developing new industrial facilities, tended to see environmental protection as a cost to be avoided if possible. Similarly, public sector proponents, such as transportation departments planning new highways or municipal officials seeking new landfill sites, tended to focus on their immediate mandate. Sometimes a particularly enlightened proponent would worry about liability for environmental damage, possible costs of cleanup, or loss of public trust. However, enlightenment was not common or reliable enough to ensure careful attention to environmental factors in project decision making. A formalized system for considering these factors and imposing obligations was needed.

The first step was taken in the United States. The *National Environmental Policy Act of 1969* (NEPA) included a short section requiring proponents of environmentally significant new undertakings to carry out environmental assessments before finalizing decisions to proceed. These assessments were to centre on anticipatory prediction of environmental impacts and identification of various means of mitigating or avoiding significant adverse effects.

Unlike traditional regulatory approaches, the assessments were to cover a wide range of environmental considerations, including social as well as biophysical effects, in an integrated way. The predicted effects of the favoured project proposal were to be compared with those of alternatives—such as different landfill sites, recycling, or waste diversion—and other ways of dealing with too much garbage. The assessment findings were to be reported in a publicly available document, and failures to do the work properly could be challenged in court.

The requirements of the *National Environmental Policy Act of 1969* proved to be powerful and controversial. In part because the legal provisions were brief and general, some years and many court cases were needed to clarify the obligations. This made authorities in other jurisdictions nervous. The Canadian government, for example, was under considerable public pressure to establish its own environmental assessment process but did not want to have its decision-making authority constrained by law or subject to litigation.

Canada tried to have its cake and eat it too by deciding in 1972 to introduce a policy-based assessment process. All federal departments and agencies would be required to undertake environmental assessments of new projects that might have significant effects, but implementation was left largely to the discretion of the relevant authorities. There were no penalties for non-compliance and, not surprisingly, there was next to no compliance.

Over the years, the federal environmental assessment and review process (EARP) was gradually clarified and strengthened. But few federal departments took steps to ensure effective implementation. Even the major early cases that proceeded to public hearings before specially appointed review panels revealed the weakness of the federal commitment. In the first EARP review, which examined the proposed Point Lepreau nuclear power station in New Brunswick, assessment requirements were watered down to avoid conflict with the project's financing and construction schedules. The second EARP review involved a more thorough consideration of the Wreck Cove hydroelectric power project in Nova Scotia, but it was not initiated until after the project had been approved. By the time the review findings were available, a good portion of the project work had already been completed.

An internal government audit in 1982, 10 years after the government's initial policy commitment, found continuing disregard for environmental assessment obligations in many departments and agencies. In response, the government issued what it thought was merely a stronger policy statement. The 1984 EARP guidelines order under the *Government Organization Act* was an awkward creation designed to serve conflicting objectives. The government wanted to give the appearance of strengthening a notoriously weak assessment process. However, at the same time, it wished to retain flexibility and avoid imposing difficult obligations on itself. The resulting guidelines order was self-contradictory—guidelines are discretionary, while orders are mandatory.

In 1989 an unexpected court decision changed all that. It established that the guidelines order had the force of law. In the Rafferty-Alameda case, involving a controversial water management undertaking in southern Saskatchewan, lawyers for the Canadian Wildlife Federation argued that federal authorities were legally obliged to apply the guidelines order. To the surprise of many, Justice Cullen of the Federal Court of Canada agreed. His April 1989 ruling that the guidelines order is legally binding essentially meant that the noun prevailed over the adjective: an order was an order. The ruling was upheld by the Federal Court of Appeal in 1990 in *Canadian Wildlife Federation Inc. v. Canada (Minister of the Environment)*. It was confirmed by the Supreme Court of Canada in 1992 in *Friends of the Oldman River Society v. Canada (Minister of Transport)*, a case involving the Oldman River dam proposal in Alberta.

After the Rafferty-Alameda decision, federal authorities immediately began to draft a legislated process. A bill to establish a *Canadian Environmental Assessment Act* was introduced in 1990, strengthened through amendments in 1992, and amended further by a new government in 1994. It was finally proclaimed in force along with a set of key regulations in 1995, a quarter of a century after the US *National Environmental Policy Act of 1969*.

The move to legislation was quicker in other Canadian jurisdictions. Ontario's *Environmental Assessment Act*, passed in 1975, was based on the NEPA model used in the *National Environmental Policy Act of 1969* but was in some ways stronger. Most significantly, its process led to an enforceable decision.

Under the *National Environmental Policy Act of 1969*, proponents doing assessments were required to identify purposes and alternatives, predict environmental effects, consider mitigation options, and justify the preferred alternative in an assessment document subject to public review. But although addressing these matters was mandatory, the work was intended to inform government decisions, not be an approval process. The findings were merely to be taken into account in final decisions and implementation. Under Ontario's 1975 law, in contrast, assessments led to a rejection or approval of the proposed undertaking, and approvals were typically accompanied by formal terms and conditions, with possible fines for non-compliance.

Gradually over the following years, many environmental assessment processes were put in place. Law-based environmental assessment processes have now been established by every province and territory in Canada. The following examples illustrate the variety of processes now in place:

- Provisions in land claim agreements with First Nations and Inuit groups have introduced environmental assessment processes. This began with traditional Cree and Inuit territories in Quebec under the *James Bay and Northern Québec Agreement and Complementary Agreements* of 1975, and led most recently to the *Yukon Environmental and Socio-economic Assessment Act* of 2003, which satisfied a commitment in the 1993 umbrella final agreement with the Council of Yukon Indians.
- The official planning processes of many municipalities include environmental assessment as a requirement.
- Expansions of sectoral regulatory regimes—mining in Ontario and nuclear power facilities under federal jurisdiction, for example—often incorporate environmental assessment processes.
- Laws establishing or guiding specific agencies—for example, the law governing the activities of Export Development Canada—also often include an environmental assessment process tailored to the work of the agency.

No two environmental assessment processes are identical, and the overall variation is great. Indeed the variety and inconsistency of assessment requirements in Canada have been a continuing aggravation for project proponents and others responsible for making the processes work. Nevertheless, environmental assessment regimes in Canada and elsewhere reflect the acceptance and adoption of environmental assessments as a standard basic framework.

The Basic Framework

Environmental assessment is essentially a form of logical step-by-step deliberation and decision making that investigates the likely environmental effects of a proposal. It also tries to ensure that the knowledge gained is incorporated effectively into the selection, design, and implementation of the proposal. Accordingly, laws establishing assessment processes set out the logical decision-making steps in ways that try to ensure that environmental considerations get serious attention and that the results are integrated into overall planning and approvals.

Most assessment processes require the proponent of the undertaking to do the bulk of the assessment work. This is done because the proponent is best placed to integrate the findings into the consideration of technical, financial, and perhaps political factors in the overall planning. Because proponents have rarely done this voluntarily, the law must impose clear obligations to do serious assessments and to apply the findings.

A fundamental difficulty with the proponent-centred approach is that proponents tend to be biased in favour of their established ways of doing things, and this bias may undermine the quality of their assessment work. It is therefore necessary for environmental assessment laws to ensure that the proponent's work is checked by government agencies with environmental mandates and by public interest organizations and individuals who have some motivation for careful and critical review.

Recognizing these basic considerations, assessment laws are generally built around a framework for addressing four key questions:

- What undertakings will be subject to assessment obligations?
- What is the nature and scope of factors that must be addressed?
- How will effective government and public review of the assessment findings be ensured?
- How will the results influence decision making on final design, approval, and implementation?

In addition, all assessment laws define administrative mandates, set out process procedures, and provide for details to be specified in regulations.

Virtually all processes include different streams: relatively quick assessments with minimal reviews for undertakings that are unlikely to pose significant environmental threats, and more demanding obligations and review procedures for undertakings with potentially serious effects.

All processes require the assessment work to be completed before irrevocable decisions are made. They are centred on the submission and review of a formal assessment report that precedes a decision on whether to proceed with the undertaking. Nevertheless, most processes at least suggest that environmental assessment should be seen as a series of deliberations and decisions through the full life of an undertaking from initial conception to final decommissioning.

Beyond these common elements, actual assessment requirements as well as review and approval provisions vary considerably. Most laws apply only to physical projects, but some also provide for assessment of plans, programs, and policies. Some laws require integrated assessment of social, economic, and cultural, as well as ecological and biophysical, effects. Others limit attention to the "natural environment."

In some cases, proponents are encouraged to identify the best option by considering needs, purposes, and reasonable alternative approaches to meeting these needs and purposes. In other cases, proponents are required only to assess their preferred option. Assessment laws also differ on whether to

- require consideration of cumulative effects;
- draw attention to uncertainties;
- foster enhancement of positive effects as well as mitigation of adverse ones;
- facilitate public consultation throughout the process;
- provide for formal public hearings with funding for intervenors; or
- require implementation, monitoring, and decommissioning plans.

The most basic assessment processes in Canada represent only a small improvement over the old regulatory approaches. They are a little more anticipatory, a little more comprehensive, and a little more open to public scrutiny. But the key question is whether the proposed undertaking is "acceptable."

Because there is no set standard that defines an acceptable undertaking, the decisions typically turn on whether "significant" adverse effects are anticipated and, if so, whether these effects can be justified. As might be expected, a good deal of scientific and judicial deliberation has therefore gone into clarifying what should and should not qualify as significant. Determining when significant adverse effects may be justified has involved profound difficulties.

The defining acceptability problem is partially resolved in more advanced and ambitious assessment processes, which centre on a comparative evaluation of the reasonable alternative ways of meeting a public interest, need, or purpose. This approach requires a broad scope and integrated consideration of potential effects—including social, economic, and cultural effects—but it also sets a higher standard than merely requiring an acceptable undertaking. The comparative approach seeks to identify the option that promises the greatest overall contribution to the long-term public interest, including the avoidance of adverse environmental effects.

The key differences between environmental assessment law provisions that aim for acceptability and those that seek the best alternative are set out in table 10.1.

Of course, the existing processes in Canada do not fall neatly into the two general categories above. Nor are the most recent laws necessarily the most advanced. Globally and in Canada, there has been a general evolution of environmental assessment toward adoption of the more advanced and ambitious components, but most existing processes are hybrids of one sort or another.

The Canadian federal process under the *Canadian Environmental Assessment Act* and the Ontario process under the *Environmental Assessment Act* provide illustrative examples.

Table 10.1   The Components of Basic and Advanced Assessments

Component	Basic Assessment	Additions in Advanced Assessments
Threshold for approval	Show that the proposed undertaking is acceptable	Show that the most beneficial option, with the greatest contribution to sustainability, has been selected
Application rules	Specify the sorts of undertakings that are subject to assessment requirements so that planners and proponents know from the outset that they will have to address environmental considerations	Ensure assessment of all undertakings—including policies, programs, plans, and capital projects—that might have significant environmental effects
Levels of assessment	Provisions for more and less demanding assessment streams (for more and less significant kinds of undertakings), with suitable guidance and procedures for determining the level of assessment and review required in particular cases	Requirement that the broader public interest is served by the undertaking
Environmental considerations	Definition of the range of environmental considerations to be addressed, preferably including socioeconomic and cultural as well as biophysical factors	Adoption of a broad conception of the environment as a complex system with intertwined social, economic, cultural, and biophysical/ecological factors and multiple scales
Breadth of analysis	Requirements to identify and evaluate the potentially significant effects of proposed undertakings in light of existing environmental conditions, pressures, and trends	Requirements to identify and compare the reasonable alternatives—including different general approaches and different designs—for serving the established purpose, with justification for selection of the preferred alternative as the proposed undertaking
Scope	Provisions for setting reasonable boundaries and focusing assessment work on the most important issues	Requirements for integrated consideration of related undertakings and of cumulative effects of existing, proposed, and reasonably anticipated undertakings

Table 10.1   Continued

Component	Basic Assessment	Additions in Advanced Assessments
Negative and positive effects	Requirements to identify and evaluate means of avoiding or mitigating predicted negative effects	Requirements to identify means of enhancing positive effects
Evaluation of predicted effects	Overall evaluation of the effects of the proposed undertaking with chosen mitigation measures, with particular attention to any residual significant adverse environmental effects	Requirements to identify and evaluate the significance of uncertainties (about effect predictions, mitigation, and enhancement effectiveness) and associated risks
Public participation	Provisions for public and technical review of the proposed undertaking and the assessment work to evaluate both the proposed undertaking and the adequacy of efforts to incorporate attention to environmental considerations in developing the proposal, including review through public hearings in especially significant cases	Provisions, including funding support, to ensure effective public as well as technical notification and consultation at significant points throughout the proposal development and assessment process, and in the implementation follow-up of approved undertakings
Compliance and follow-up	Means of ensuring that assessment and review findings are incorporated in approvals and permits, and in provisions for monitoring and compliance with approval conditions	Enforceable decisions requiring compliance with conditions, monitoring of actual effects, and adaptive management
Broader links	Encouragement of monitoring to check effect predictions and to encourage learning from experience	Provisions for integrating assessment work, including monitoring, into a broader regime for setting, pursuing, and re-evaluating public objectives and guiding future undertakings

Federal Process

The *Canadian Environmental Assessment Act* came into effect in 1995. It requires environmental screening, or more demanding "comprehensive" assessment, of specified categories of projects. The law applies to projects that are proposed or funded by federal authorities, or that use federal lands, or that require certain federal regulatory approvals. Determination of what projects are subject to the law and its screening or comprehensive study requirements is guided by specific regulations. The overwhelming majority of projects are subject only to screening.

Mandatory assessment work centres on prediction and evaluation of biophysical and related socioeconomic effects, and identification of appropriate mitigation measures. The law provides for public involvement, especially in comprehensive study cases, and establishes mediation and public panel review mechanisms for cases of major conflict or controversy. The panel reviews centre on informal hearings and panel reports. Like all assessment findings in the federal process, panel review conclusions are treated as recommendations for inclusion in approval decisions.

In 1990 the federal government also introduced a non-legislated process for strategic level assessment of government policy, plan, and program proposals, where ministerial or Cabinet approval is required and environmental effects may be significant. The Cabinet directive on strategic assessment requires integration of environmental assessment findings in broader evaluations of strategic options and is framed as a tool to contribute to sustainable development. However, there is no assurance of public involvement or even public access to assessment reports. In 2004, 14 years after the first strategic assessment directive was issued, the federal commissioner of the environment and sustainable development reported limited compliance with the official requirements and a low level of commitment on the part of those responsible for implementation.

Ontario Process

The first environmental assessment law in Canada was passed by the province of Ontario in 1975 and amended in 1996. It applies automatically to undertakings—including both plans and projects—of the provincial and municipal governments. It can also be applied to private sector undertakings, though this has been common only for waste disposal and electricity projects.

Under the Ontario law, "environment" is broadly defined to include biophysical, social, economic, and cultural factors and their interrelations. Proponents are generally required to justify their purposes and carry out a comparative evaluation of alternatives to establish that their proposed activity is environmentally preferable to other reasonable options. Since 1996, however, proponents have been allowed to propose narrower terms of reference for "scoped" assessments that avoid some of the general requirements.

Submitted assessments are subject to public as well as government reviews, which may be followed by formal quasi-judicial hearings before a decision-making board. In every case, a decision is rendered under the environmental assessment law, and approvals are typically subject to enforceable terms and conditions.

Ontario uses a more streamlined **class environmental assessment process** for various categories of mostly moderately significant, repetitive undertakings, including municipal road and sewer projects and flood protection work by watershed-based conservation authorities. The class processes, which guide the vast majority of assessments in the province, require proponents to go through the basic series of logical assessment steps as follows:

- *Step 1.* Identify purposes and alternatives.
- *Step 2.* Select a preferred alternative on the basis of an initial review of potential effects.
- *Step 3.* Carry out detailed design incorporating measures to mitigate possible negative effects.
- *Step 4.* Prepare a report on the process, findings, and conclusions.

Public notices and opportunities for comment are provided at key points. Those with continuing serious concerns after the report is issued may request a minister's order to "bump up" the case to full assessment, though these requests are almost never granted. Unless a "bump-up" is ordered, the proposed undertaking is approved once the final public comment period is over.

The Future of Environmental Assessment

Over nearly 40 years, environmental assessment has been maturing and changing, largely for the better. There have been backward steps in some jurisdictions and few of the positive changes have been fully adopted anywhere. Generally, however, environmental assessment laws and processes have been moving to adopt and strengthen the following characteristics:

- *Mandatory and codified obligations,* reflected in increased adoption of law-based processes, further specification of requirements, and reduction of discretionary provisions.
- *Wide application,* covering small as well as large capital projects, continuing activities as well as new initiatives, developments in whole sectors and

regions as well as single proposals, and strategic as well as project-level undertakings.

- *Initiation early in planning,* beginning with purposes and broad alternatives for action and sometimes starting even earlier with the driving policies, programs, and plans.
- *Open and participatory process,* involving not just proponents, government officials, and technical experts, but also communities, public interest organizations, and interested residents.
- *Comprehensive attention to all environmental concerns,* including socioeconomic, cultural, and community effects, biophysical and ecological effects, and regional and global as well as local effects.
- *Integrative approach,* considering cumulative and systemic effects rather than just individual impacts.
- *Acceptance of different kinds of knowledge and analysis,* including informal, traditional, and Aboriginal knowledge as well as conventional science, and public preferences as well as "facts."
- *Close monitoring,* with courts reviewing application of the law, informed civil society bodies and government auditors checking compliance with assessment obligations, and scientists and stakeholders comparing assessment predictions with the actual effects of approved undertakings.
- *Humility,* recognizing needs to respect and address uncertainties, and to adopt precautionary approaches.
- *Sensitivity to efficiency concerns,* considering how best to focus resources, avoid unnecessary delays, and build mutually strengthening relations with other evaluation and decision-making processes.
- *Adoption beyond formal environmental assessment regimes,* through laws for particular resources and industrial sectors, land use planning, and market-driven corporate initiatives.
- *Ambitious criteria for evaluations,* aiming for overall biophysical and socioeconomic gains and net contributions to sustainability, rather than just individually "acceptable" undertakings with mitigation of significant negative effects.

Improvements in all of these areas persist today and are likely to continue into the future. They have generally made environmental assessments more realistic, useful, and widely applied. Moreover, environmental assessment practice is becoming more and more entrenched internationally. It is increasingly demanded by citizens and civil society bodies that are now much more effectively linked—often through the Internet, with similar organizations in other countries—and that share a broad distrust of government and corporate assurances.

Accordingly, the more advanced forms of environmental assessment are increasingly incorporated in the practices of lending agencies and private corporations as well as governments. They are being merged with related processes in urban planning and resource management, and in more open and comprehensive approaches to sectoral regulation and policy development.

At the same time, expanded emphasis on environmental assessment processes has presented serious challenges. Few environmental assessment processes are well designed for the bigger roles they are being asked to play and this has stirred concerns, especially among proponents and governments, about how to keep the processes manageable, timely, and affordable.

Efficiency and Harmonization

Over the past decade or so, fear of constraints on economic growth led some jurisdictions—notably Ontario and British Columbia—to weaken their environmental assessment legislation or sharply restrict its application. Governments with longer-term economic, as well as environmental, perspectives have continued to value and strengthen environmental assessment. They have also taken administrative and other steps to enhance process efficiency. They have tried to clarify and sometimes to simplify obligations, to minimize application to less significant undertakings and issues, and to set firmer timelines for process steps.

These efforts have limited potential, given the great diversity of cases and contexts for environmental assessment work and the resulting unpredictability of important considerations (for example, how best to ensure effective citizen engagement, what range of possibly reasonable alternatives to consider, and what social and ecological systems to examine most closely). But work to focus attention on the most crucial matters and to avoid unnecessary delays will almost certainly remain a priority for environmental assessment law and practice everywhere.

Efficiency concerns may also encourage more attention to the still-expanding diversity of processes in Canada and elsewhere, and the call for harmonization. Efforts to harmonize the multiple processes have enjoyed a few successes so far. Several jurisdictions allow consolidation of hearings when a proposed undertaking is subject to two or more laws with environmental hearing provisions. The federal government has negotiated harmonization agreements with several provinces to provide for joint federal–provincial hearings in cases where both federal and provincial assessment requirements apply. However, only a tiny fraction of assessed undertakings proceed to a public hearing.

Lack of harmonization results in inequity and unnecessary confusion. Expertise that should be devoted to improving our understanding of environmental effects and deciding how to incorporate them in decision making is instead occupied in wrestling with the divergent details of many different processes. The adoption of a common high standard (with the advanced and ambitious components listed above) would be the most desirable solution.

The danger, however, is that harmonization badly done could favour least demanding requirements and weaken assessment practice. An effort by the Canadian Standards Association to win agreement on a best practices guide, as a basis for harmonization, failed in the late 1990s, in part because of proponent resistance to high standards. It seems unlikely that Canadian jurisdictions will agree soon to a common high standard for environmental assessment, but the need remains.

Sustainability-Based Assessments

Perhaps the most promising examples of positive harmonization come from a series of cases involving environmental assessment review panels jointly established by some combination of federal, provincial, territorial, and Aboriginal authorities. In each case, the joint panels applied a contribution-to-sustainability test requiring a comprehensive assessment of the positive and negative effects and the long-term legacy of the proposed undertakings. Typically, environmental assessment decision-makers have aimed only to ensure that the proponents took environmental effects issues into account and avoided or mitigated any serious predicted damages. As we noted earlier in this chapter, some regimes have gone further by requiring comparative evaluation of alternatives and justification for the selection of one option as the preferred alternative. In theory, that should lead to the best option, not just mitigation of the most serious adverse effects. But in practice, most assessment work has focused on mitigation, not on how to enhance the benefits.

The contribution-to-sustainability test requires lasting net gains. In 1997, in the first explicit application of this higher test in a Canadian environmental assessment, the joint panel examining the proposed Voisey's Bay Nickel Mine and Mill on the north coast of Labrador stated that it wanted to know "the extent to which the Undertaking may make a positive overall contribution towards the attainment of ecological and community sustainability, both at the local and regional levels."

Similar expectations have since been imposed by several other assessment panels. In 2007, two joint federal–provincial panels—one reviewing a proposed quarry and marine terminal at White's Point in Nova Scotia and the other reviewing the Kemess North copper-gold mine case in British Columbia—applied the sustainability test and recommended against approval of the proposed projects because they would not provide lasting net gains.

It is not yet clear how soon this more demanding approach will be broadly applied in Canada. Sustainability-based assessment processes are spreading quickly around the world, however, and it is reasonable to expect further applications here too.

Strategic Level Assessments

Some of the difficulties arising from environmental assessments result from their role as a key venue for public debate and conflict involving matters of great public controversy. Recent assessments in Canada have dealt with uranium mining, a huge pork-packing plant, open-pit coal mining beside a national park, salmon aquaculture, hydrocarbon exploration on important fishing grounds, and highways through a world biosphere reserve. All such undertakings raise big policy issues as well as immediate project-specific concerns, and environmental assessment processes serve an important function when they facilitate appropriately open and credibly impartial deliberation about these issues.

Project-centred environmental assessment processes are generally not equipped to handle these broader-based issues well, and a new kind of assessment—the strategic level assessment—now occupies the liveliest area of environmental assessment theory and practice internationally. Strategic level assessment requirements apply to policies, plans, programs, and other broad-scale initiatives. The Canadian government's formal approach to strategic environmental assessment remains weak—it is based only in policy, has very limited public involvement, and has apparently inspired little effort to ensure compliance. However, practical Canadian experience with strategic level assessments is surprisingly extensive.

Some of the past efforts have emerged under legislated environmental assessment processes. Both British Columbia's assessment of salmon aquaculture regulation and Ontario's class environmental assessment of timber management were major public strategic assessments. There have also been many strategic assessments under other titles and mandates including the following:

- the work of the federal–provincial review panel that examined the moratorium on hydrocarbon exploration on Georges Bank; and
- the growth management strategy development work undertaken by several regional municipalities in British Columbia, including the Capital Regional District (Victoria and area).

Both of these were major public policy and planning exercises that involved careful evaluation of alternatives and considered a well-integrated set of ecological as well as social and economic factors.

Strategic assessment is thus both an expansion of environmental assessment practice and a link with similar public deliberations with different roots and legislative mandates. In this it is like several of the other trends in environmental assessment listed above. Expanding awareness of uncertainty and precautionary needs; greater acceptance of diverse sources of knowledge; increasing focus on integration of social, economic, and ecological analyses; and deeper worries about cumulative and synergistic effects—globally as well as regionally—all reflect an evolution of understanding and concern that extends well beyond environmental assessment law and practice. We will see many of the same themes in chapter 11, where we examine resource management and environmental planning.

Planning and Management Regimes

Introduction

Planning and management regimes are important where long-term planning is needed to preserve, renew, or manage an important resource—such as timber, fish, or electricity—and to consider all competing interests and needs.

As discussed in chapter 9, the sectoral approach continues to dominate the regulatory landscape. However, there is a slow but steady transition toward a more comprehensive and integrated approach to planning and management.

Crown Land Management

Crown land management is the management of land owned by the federal and provincial governments. Governments, particularly provincial governments, have often relied heavily on revenues from the sale and development of public lands. Not surprisingly, financial priorities centred on revenues from major economic uses, such as timber harvesting, have tended to take priority over less economically rewarding land uses.

Crown Land

Crown land, also called public land, is land owned by a provincial or federal government, which controls its use and sale. All land that has not been legally granted to private persons is Crown land; it includes the vegetation, soil, and minerals on and under the surface of the land. Much of Canada's wilderness is Crown land—for example, 87 percent of Ontario remains Crown land.

The Canadian constitution divides Crown land between the federal government and the provincial governments. Provinces generally own public land within their boundaries, with the exception of a few areas specially designated as federal land. Examples of federal land include national parks, harbours, defence properties, First Nations lands, and coastal marine belts.

The northern territories are subject to federal jurisdiction, except to the extent that responsibilities have been delegated to territorial governments or allocated to First Nations under land settlement agreements. There are also areas that are subject to unresolved native claims, where title to the lands is in dispute.

Sectoral Resource Development Law

Legislation concerning public lands has largely taken the form of sectoral natural resource development laws. Sectors include the following:

- forestry,
- minerals,
- water,
- grazing, and
- wildlife (hunting and fishing).

Each sector provides a stage for the recurring drama of development versus protection. This conflict is played out in a variety of different ways as a result of the competing values and interests affected by decisions concerning public land and resource use.

The historical focus on sectoral natural resource development has resulted in several major problems. Consider the following:

- *Fragmented decision making.* Separate legal frameworks for particular sectors—such as minerals, forestry, and recreation—have resulted in fragmented decision making that does not take cross-purposes into account. For example, the noise and pollution caused by mining may interfere with and fail to accommodate nearby camping or skiing uses.

- *Incrementalism.* Decision making on a project-by-project basis without a clear consideration of long-term objectives can send us down an undesirable path. Each additional undertaking continues the development momentum and sets a new baseline level of disturbance and expectation. The succession of individual approvals sooner or later degrades vulnerable lands, eliminates opportunities for non-exploitive land uses, undermines ecological functions, and reduces the environmental legacy of future generations.
- *Pre-emption effect.* When a project such as a mine is proposed, roads and power lines may be built before the environmental assessment process begins. Building of this nature may raise a community's expectations regarding employment and other economic benefits; this situation creates a strong economic imperative that is likely to influence the approval decision. Once a project is approved, the resulting public land allocation, infrastructure construction, and development initiatives establish an irreversible commitment to more of the same kind of economic activity. Thus, one development opens the door for other similar or related public land uses in the area.
- *Cumulative impacts.* The combined effects of multiple land uses and developments are not anticipated and therefore not considered by decision-makers. The cumulative result is often negative, unexpected, and irreversible.

Because of these serious problems inherent in sectoral natural resource development law, the trend in law-making is toward a more forward-looking and comprehensive approach.

Public Land Planning and Management

Comprehensive public land planning and management takes into account the many competing demands and long-term possibilities for public land use. Environmental assessments are a first step, but they are largely project-specific. Assessments of cumulative effects are sometimes performed. However, they are severely limited by a lack of information and an inability to deal with individually innocuous, but cumulatively significant, actions. Cumulative-effects assessments also suffer from a failure to establish workable and generally accepted significance criteria.

Some jurisdictions, such as British Columbia, have initiated a variety of high-profile regional and sub-regional land use planning processes that bring together representatives of the main land use interests and attempt to forge a consensus on land allocations and management principles. If the parties reach a consensus, their consensus can then help guide particular decisions under sectoral legislation.

In other cases, sectoral laws may be used to accommodate attention to competing land uses. Ontario, for example, uses the class assessment provisions of its *Environmental Assessment Act* in combination with its *Crown Forest Sustainability Act, 1994* to provide a framework for forest management planning that includes public consultation. The planners are required to "have regard for" a broad range of social, economic, and ecological values beyond the interests of the forest products industry. Whether non-timber values are given adequate attention and whether the practices resulting from the decisions are sustainable remain subjects of debate. However, Ontario's forest management regime is clearly a step toward a more comprehensive approach.

Public Engagement

Planning and managing public lands is unavoidably difficult. Huge areas are involved, with many different resources, ecosystems, exploitive and non-exploitive users, cultures, and livelihoods. As the competing pressures on public lands and their resources increase, there are growing political tensions and higher expectations for transparent, participative, and fair decision making. It also becomes harder to find ways of satisfying present demands without undermining future opportunities. The gradual development of public land planning practices has been toward more comprehensive and better-integrated means of wrestling with these challenges, though not all attempts have been entirely successful.

In the 1990s, British Columbia's Commission on Resources and Environment (CORE) integrated public land and resource management policy and law with an open and extremely inclusive public process to develop plans for contested public regions of the province. A regional stakeholder negotiation process was created to empower interested parties, and to formulate recommendations on legislation, policies, and practices. CORE's work provided a valuable base for the subsequent sub-regional land resource management planning processes in several areas, and some of CORE's recommendations were implemented. However, major recommendations—such as the enactment of a sustainability statute—were never put into practice, and regional land and resource management plan development and implementation remained incomplete.

As noted above, the Ontario forest management process is also consultative, through less ambitiously so than CORE's, and it became more firmly established and authoritative. However, it too failed to eliminate tensions and doubts about the sustainability of its results. Experience elsewhere confirms that public engagement provides no miracle solution. Competing interests do not easily reach consensus. In some circumstances—for example, when joint management bodies are composed of government officials and indigenous people—there may be a wide gulf to bridge in terms of culture, language, and worldview.

Nevertheless, from these cases and others, it has become clear that land use management is more likely to be accepted as legitimate and potentially trustworthy if it includes direct engagement of the relevant interests. Even if all parties do not reach agreement in the end, they at least gain some understanding of each other's positions and concerns.

Complexity

The second major lesson to emerge from public land planning and management experience centres on the challenges of working in complex systems. The ecologies and socioeconomic activities on public lands are intricately interwoven and constantly changing. Well-informed management decisions need to be based on a solid understanding of these interrelationships and the factors that influence them. But any such understanding is always highly imperfect and must be continuously renewed and reconsidered.

The modern science of complex dynamic systems suggests that wise management must accept uncertainty and anticipate surprise. It must recognize that human well-being depends on ecosystem services, which in turn depend on maintenance of the ability of ecosystems to deal with stresses (most human economic activities) and catastrophes (major forest fires, for example).

Because we cannot know enough about these systems to predict the effects of our activities very accurately, it is important to take a precautionary approach, rather than try to identify the point of maximum sustainable yield. The key is to ensure that our activities do not undermine the resilience of ecosystems and linked socioeconomic systems. If we are to preserve these systems' ability to accommodate and recover from disturbance, we must favour small-scale, diverse, and adjustable activities, rather than single, big, inflexible ones. It also means combining planning and management with monitoring and adaptation.

Public land planning and management that applies this type of thinking is not yet common, but it is increasingly influential. It is perhaps best demonstrated in park management under the *Canada National Parks Act*, which sets maintenance of ecological integrity as the key management objective. It also informs some management practices in the Ontario forestry regime discussed above and under New Brunswick's *Crown Lands and Forests Act*.

Remaining Challenges

If public land law is to incorporate public involvement and an understanding of complex systems more fully into an integrated package, the following actions are essential:

- Include a legislated set of clear purposes and decision criteria that are centred on sustainability objectives and precaution, and that recognize the importance of maintaining the integrity of ecosystems and the socio-economic systems that depend on them.
- Address the full range of potentially competing land values and uses, including social, cultural, ecological, and economic uses.
- Combine the engagement of the many concerned parties with a means of representing and protecting the broader public interest in ecosystem integrity and the well-being of future generations.
- Impose direct requirements for specific decisions—under sectoral laws and in environmental assessments and approvals of individual projects, for example—that comply with overall planning guidance.
- Link the application of the sustainability objectives achieved through consultative planning to continuous monitoring, regular review, and adaptive management.

Endangered Species

The plight of endangered species across the world is well publicized. Current rates of extinction are much higher than historical natural rates of extinction. In response to the endangered species crisis, various international, national, and provincial systems have been created, with varying degrees of effectiveness.

Species at Risk

Canada has close to 600 officially recognized **species at risk**. This collective term includes the five categories used by the scientific body known as the Committee on the Status of Endangered Wildlife in Canada (COSEWIC):

1. *Extinct.* Extinct species no longer exist. For example, the passenger pigeon, which was once North America's most common bird, is now considered extinct.

2. *Extirpated.* A species is extirpated when it no longer exists in the wild in Canada but still exists elsewhere—in a zoo, for example.

3. *Endangered.* A species is endangered if it is facing imminent extirpation or extinction.

4. *Threatened.* A species is threatened when it is likely to become endangered if nothing is done to reverse the factors leading to its extirpation or extinction.

5. *Special concern.* Special concern status is given to a species that may become threatened or endangered because of a combination of biological characteristics and identified threats.

In a non-technical sense, extirpated, endangered, threatened, and special concern species are collectively known as endangered species. As more studies are undertaken and more types of species are assessed, and as more threats to species and habitats manifest themselves, Canada's list of species at risk grows longer.

In order to address the fact that protecting endangered species requires cooperation among governments, a national accord was signed in 1996. This accord committed Canada's governments to establishing complementary legislation and programs that provide for effective protection of species at risk throughout Canada. Implementation of the accord has been inconsistent across Canada. Some provinces (for example, Ontario) have developed new legislation and programs to reflect the commitments in the accord, while others have not done so (for example, Alberta).

Despite the disturbing trend faced by Canada's endangered species as a whole, certain species have benefited greatly from species protection and recovery efforts. The white pelican, for example, has been removed from COSEWIC's official endangered species list. Unfortunately, over 30 Canadian species have already been found by COSEWIC to be extinct or extirpated.

International Trade

The international trade in endangered species, such as wild parrots, and products derived from endangered species, such as ivory, has long been a concern to the international community. Canada is a party to the 1973 Convention on International Trade in Endangered Species of Wild Fauna and Flora (CITES). This convention seeks to ensure that international trade in specimens of wild animals and plants does not threaten their survival.

To implement CITES, Canada passed the *Wild Animal and Plant Protection and Regulation of International and Interprovincial Trade Act.* This Act aims to protect Canadian and foreign species of animals and plants that may be at risk of exploitation because of illegal trade. It controls the international trade and interprovincial transport of listed endangered species and their derivatives through various restrictions and permit requirements.

Habitat Loss

While international trade is a threat to many well-known species across the world, by far the greatest modern threat to biological diversity in Canada, and in many other countries, is habitat loss. Simply put, without the places they call home, species cannot survive.

The decline of biological diversity from habitat loss is partly addressed in the 1992 United Nations Convention on Biological Diversity. It calls on countries to pass laws to better protect threatened species. Canada has attempted to address threats to endangered species within its borders, including some aspects of habitat loss, through the *Species at Risk Act*. This Act addresses those aspects of endangered species protection and recovery that are within federal jurisdiction.

By virtue of their constitutional powers, Canada's provinces have a significant role to play in protecting and restoring the habitat of endangered species. Many provinces have passed endangered species acts (ESAs). The approaches they use vary widely. Some provinces leave the decision to list species for protection to politicians, while others employ independent scientists to create the list. Some make habitat protection mandatory, while others leave this critical issue to government discretion. Some ESAs provide assistance to private landowners to protect habitat, while others focus on a regulatory approach. Very few ESAs include all the elements necessary to provide effective legal protection for endangered species.

Ontario's recent *Endangered Species Act, 2007*, which replaced its 1971 predecessor, is the first Canadian legislation to include both scientific listing and mandatory habitat protection. It also includes important provisions for recovering endangered and threatened species, addressing Aboriginal concerns, and promoting habitat stewardship. Like most environmental laws, however, it still leaves room for the government to create exemptions from the general protections offered to endangered species. No matter how strongly any ESA is worded, the real test is whether it is implemented in such a way that existing endangered species recover and that new species do not become endangered. Judged against this standard, all ESAs have yet to accomplish their lofty objectives.

By their very nature, ESAs often focus on the urgent measures required to bring individual species back from the brink of extinction. Nonetheless, the shortcomings of the typical single-species management approach of current ESAs are well known to conservation biologists. Often the endangerment of a single species is simply an early warning sign that an entire natural community or ecosystem is under threat. To be effective in the long term, ESAs will need to go beyond addressing the loss of biological diversity at the species, subspecies, or population level. Certain ESAs, including the Ontario and federal Act, offer some opportunities for implementing multi-species and ecosystem approaches, and the use of these approaches may increase in the future.

Climate Change

Endangered species protection regimes largely predated attempts to address climate change. Consequently, the ability of ESAs, as currently written, to provide for the long-term protection of biological diversity in the face of large-scale climate change is questionable. As with many areas of environmental law, the successful accomplishment of the goals of ESAs will require effective action in many areas not typically covered within the four corners of endangered species legislation.

Parks and Other Protected Areas

The establishment and maintenance of parks and other protected areas are among the most well-known means of protecting natural habitats and scenic areas. While the word "park" denotes the most well-known type of protected area, there are many other terms used to signify a degree of protection from incompatible uses, including the following:

- reserves,
- sanctuaries,
- wildlife or wilderness areas, and
- conservation lands.

The degree of protection offered in various protected areas may differ widely.

International Law

At the international level, the International Union for Conservation of Nature sets out six categories of protected areas that range from strictly protected areas in category 1 (examples include designated wilderness areas and nature reserves) to sustainable use areas in category 6. Two of the key international agreements that address protected areas are the following:

- the United Nations Convention on Biological Diversity, which encourages parties to establish protected area systems to conserve biological diversity; and
- the United Nations World Heritage Convention, which addresses some of the most important cultural and ecological sites on the planet.

Canada harbours over a dozen world heritage sites, such as the parks in the Rocky Mountains of British Columbia and Alberta; Gros Morne National Park in Newfoundland; and Wood Buffalo National Park in Alberta and the Northwest Territories.

Federal Parks

Canada's protected areas system is subject to a long list of laws and regulations. At the federal level, national parks are the cornerstone of the system. They typically protect representative natural areas of Canadian significance.

The *Canada National Parks Act*, which sets aside parks for public benefit, appreciation, and enjoyment, requires that the parks be maintained in an unimpaired state for future generations. Some of Canada's oldest national parks—Banff, for example—date back to the late 1800s. National parks include landscapes and the resident wildlife that constitute iconic symbols of Canada itself.

In the most recent amendments to the *Canada National Parks Act*, the emerging concept of **ecological integrity** was adopted as the guiding vision for Canada's national parks. Managing for ecological integrity essentially involves considering the needs of nature as the first priority. This approach differs from other approaches that put the human use of parks above the needs of the park's natural inhabitants.

With the authority of the *Canada National Parks Act* and its regulations, national parks prohibit most large-scale extractive uses, such as commercial forestry, mining, and hydroelectric development. Other federal designations, such as migratory bird sanctuaries and national wildlife areas, also offer some protection for natural areas.

Provincial Parks

The national parks of Canada are a key component of Canada's protected areas system; however, other types of protected areas, many of which are administered by the provinces and territories, actually account for more protected land area than the national parks system. Perhaps the best-known and most widely used designation is the provincial park. Like national parks, provincial parks have a long history. For example, Ontario's Algonquin Provincial Park originated in the late 1800s, the same era in which Banff National Park was founded.

Ontario's recent parks and conservation reserves legislation, which covers hundreds of protected areas, embraces ecological integrity as a guiding principle. Like the *Canada National Parks Act*, Ontario's parks legislation and that of many other jurisdictions excludes large-scale industrial uses, subject to certain exceptions.

Aboriginal Partnerships

In recent years, there has been a much greater emphasis on Aboriginal involvement in the creation and management of protected areas. Indeed, entirely new protected area designations and systems are arising from partnerships between Aboriginal governments and federal, provincial, and territorial governments. These approaches can help to maintain natural values and traditional activities, while prohibiting industrial activities.

Private Landowners

Private landowners, such as the Nature Conservancy of Canada, contribute to Canada's system of protected areas as well. Privately owned and managed areas may not be covered by legislated designations such as parks; however, legislative provisions that offer significant incentives to private stewardship often facilitate the creation of these areas. Legislated tax incentives, exceptions, and rebates—as well as innovative legal tools such as **conservation easements**—are among the many means that are used to encourage the protection of privately owned natural habitats.

Marine Areas

While terrestrial, or land-based, protected areas are the most well known, a great deal of recent attention has been placed on marine protected areas. The federal government has set aside some marine parks or conservation areas and has committed itself to creating new marine protected areas in the future. Some provinces have also begun work on systems of water-based protected areas.

Remaining Challenges

Parks and protected areas, especially those offering the highest degree of protection from harmful activities, are a key part of biodiversity conservation. These areas typically maintain the integrity of the natural environment in areas that would otherwise have been subjected to extractive uses or other types of development. While they are often considered to be the backbone of landscape-level protection, it is important to note that they typically occupy only a small percentage of the total land base. It is therefore imperative that the so-called working landscape outside the protected areas be managed sustainably so that the protected areas do not become isolated islands of green in an otherwise degraded environment.

Watershed Planning

A **watershed** is an area of land from which all water drains into a common body of water, such as a lake or river. **Watershed planning** refers to a scale of planning that is based on natural watershed boundaries and hence extends beyond political boundaries.

The alternative to watershed planning is piecemeal or patchwork planning on a municipality-by-municipality basis. The piecemeal alternative involves each city setting its own water and land use practices through its official plan and zoning bylaws, subject to any constraints that exist within provincial or federal environmental legislation. The advantage of this approach is that it is convenient and time-efficient for each municipality to conduct its affairs independently and irrespectively of what neighbouring municipalities are doing. However, the disadvantage is that water does not respect political boundaries and when individual municipalities make decisions in isolation, they are unable to factor in the needs of the watershed as a whole, or the needs of neighbouring municipalities.

For example, if upstream Town A is experiencing a rapid growth in its economy and population, its heavy water usage and growing tendency to pollute may endanger Town B downstream. The situation will continue to degenerate unless the two towns can enter into a joint planning structure whereby they become aware of, and take into account, the effects of their actions on each other and the environment as a whole. If watershed planning were put into practice, the two towns would benefit by

- sharing the information and expertise necessary to assess the overall health of, and broader impacts on, the watershed; and
- gaining access to a planning structure in which the towns' councils could work collaboratively with other councils and stakeholders to develop appropriate land use policies and controls, taking into account not only their own needs, but also the ecological needs of the watershed itself.

Since the effects of human consumption and pollution are experienced across the whole watershed, it makes sense that the planning process should be conducted on the same scale. Additionally, if the ecological integrity of key watershed features—such as wetlands, forests, and shorelines—falters, the water resource is threatened.

The Walkerton Tragedy

In 2000 the contamination of drinking water in Walkerton, Ontario stunned the province and devastated the small town, which suffered the death of 7 residents and the illness of 2,300. The source of the problem was E. coli contamination that originated from manure spread on farmland mere feet from a municipal well. The owner of the farm, who followed best management practices, was unaware that the municipal well was situated so close to his property.

Shortly after the tragedy, Justice Dennis O'Connor was appointed commissioner of the Walkerton inquiry. Following an in-depth investigation of the incident, Justice O'Connor released a two-volume report containing 128 recommendations. The report criticized the weak environmental laws that had allowed the municipality's source of drinking water to become contaminated. One of Justice O'Connor's primary recommendations was that "[d]rinking water sources should be protected by developing watershed-based source protection plans. Source protection plans should be required for all watersheds in Ontario."

Over the next six years, the Ontario government began the daunting task of implementing Justice O'Connor's recommendations. The initial changes dealt with the treatment of drinking water and concentrated on operator licensing and training, laboratory requirements, and standards for drinking water quality. However, it was not until 2006 that one of the final (and potentially most important) pieces of legislation was passed: the Ontario *Clean Water Act*, which was designed to protect the *sources* of drinking water on a watershed scale.

Ontario's Clean Water Act

Ontario's *Clean Water Act* introduced a process for assessing threats to drinking water sources and, where necessary, reducing these threats through risk management policies set out in "source protection plans." The process is guided by multi-stakeholder "source protection committees," composed of representatives from municipalities; the agricultural, commercial, and industrial sectors; and other interests such as environmental groups; health groups; and the general public.

Since the government wanted the committees to be arranged on a watershed-planning scale, it roughly adhered to the existing watershed-based boundaries of the province's conservation authorities. Conservation Ontario defines **conservation authorities** as "local, watershed management agencies that deliver services and programs that protect and manage water and other natural resources in partnership with government, landowners and other organizations."

Conservation authorities have an important role to play throughout the source protection process, beginning with the establishment of source protection committees. They also provide scientific and administrative support and resources, and they ensure that documents are made available to the public. Although it made sense to use the existing boundaries of the conservation authorities as a foundation for the source protection regions, these authorities cover only southern Ontario and select parts of central and northern Ontario. Accordingly, the *Clean Water Act* is unevenly applied across the province; many parts of central and northern Ontario do not enjoy the legislative protection that is available in southern Ontario.

The *Clean Water Act* also omits First Nations and private well owners from the scope of its protective measures. Unless the option to nominate additional systems is exercised, the Act does not encompass First Nations water systems or non-municipal water systems. Under the Act, a First Nations band council can request Cabinet that its system be included and a non-municipal water system can be included by a resolution of a municipal council or a ministerial amendment.

Remaining Challenges

The *Clean Water Act* is a groundbreaking piece of legislation because it brings together stakeholders, conducts assessments, and plans responses on a watershed scale. It also provides municipalities with the additional powers needed to implement a range of risk management measures to reduce significant threats.

However, the approach of the *Clean Water Act* falls short of true watershed planning on three primary fronts:

1. The assessment and risk-management measures do not focus on ecosystem considerations, but rather on the needs of human populations.

2. Not all watersheds across the province are included; those in the north, for example, escape protection.

3. Not all drinking water systems within a watershed are covered; for example, many First Nations and non-municipal water systems are excluded.

Watershed planning is becoming an increasingly popular approach to water protection. Although Ontario is considered to be a leader in source water protection, other jurisdictions are progressing toward watershed planning in a variety of areas.

For example, work groups charged with reviewing aspects of the Great Lakes Water Quality Agreement created a subgroup to address watershed planning and land use. This subgroup recognized the challenges that are inherent in implementing watershed planning in the Great Lakes, given the disconnect that exists between local governments (which are typically responsible for land use planning) and federal governments (which are parties to the Great Lakes Water Quality Agreement). One of the subgroup's recommendations is set out below.

Canada and the U.S. should cooperate to address the issue by pursuing policies and common goals that improve the consistency of watershed planning across the Basin, and by increasing the role that watershed planning can have on local development decisions, on watersheds, and, ultimately, on the water quality of the Great Lakes.

Urban Planning, Growth Management, and Brownfields

Human decisions about the use made of land occupied by many species are fundamental to environmental integrity. Inappropriate use can lead to the physical destruction of the natural environment, the wasteful consumption of agricultural land, the loss of habitat for native species, and the contamination of air, land, and water. Therefore, land use planning regimes, with their control of urban planning, growth management, and brownfield redevelopment, serve a critical role in environmental protection.

Land Use Planning

Municipalities have primary responsibility for land use decision making in most Canadian jurisdictions. In Ontario, for example, the *Planning Act* confers a number of powers on municipal governments for controlling the use of land, including approval of official plans, zoning bylaws, subdivision control, site plan control, and demolition.

The Ontario government has responsibility for matters considered of "provincial interest." The *Planning Act* empowers Cabinet, through the Ministry of Municipal Affairs, to establish provincial policies that are intended to guide all planning decisions made by municipalities. All land use planning decisions must be "consistent with" any provincial policies that are approved by the province.

Land use planning involves the use of a set of assessment tools for making decisions about land use. Professional planners gather information and apply certain principles to make recommendations about how land should be used and where certain types of uses should be located. However, this description makes the procedure sound like a scientific exercise, and it presents only part of the picture.

Land use planning also encompasses the public—and often very contentious—process of decision making. Decision-makers attempt to weigh and balance various competing interests such as the following:

- private and public interests,
- different private interests, and
- present and future needs.

For example, a land use decision typically involves a contest between the long-term protection of environmental resources and proposals by private interests to maximize the income-generating value of property. Often no clearly right or wrong answers exist. Land use planning therefore requires not only the application of planning principles in a scientific way, but also a fair and open decision-making process that considers the different stakeholders' needs and values.

Land use planning regimes typically carry out four functions:

1. establish broad land use planning policies, including designation of geographic areas for certain uses and settlement patterns through the establishment of official plans;

2. impose specific rules to control the use of land, including the form and location of buildings and structures on the land through zoning bylaws or ordinances;

3. control the division or partitioning of lands into smaller parcels by making decisions on land severances and plans of subdivision;

4. create procedures, including public consultative and adjudicative processes, to ensure that stakeholders and other affected individuals and agencies have a role in land use decision making.

Each of these four functions is performed by a separate land use planning instrument. Respectively, these instruments are (1) land use plans, including official plans; (2) zoning bylaws; (3) subdivision and land severances; and (4) decision-making processes. Each instrument is discussed in detail below.

Land Use Plans

Both the provincial and municipal governments may produce plans, as described below.

PROVINCIAL PLANS

While the role of establishing planning policies has historically been given to local municipalities, provincial governments sometimes create planning documents of broader application. Consider the following plans of the Ontario government, which provide broad planning policy direction across southern Ontario:

1. The Niagara Escarpment plan imposes land use planning controls across the Niagara Escarpment, a geologically and ecologically significant landform with a lateral extent of over 750 kilometres that has been designated by the United Nations as an international biosphere reserve.

2. The Oak Ridges Moraine conservation plan provides a similar level of provincial land use control over a large moraine feature that runs 165 kilometres from Peterborough to Brampton across the greater Toronto area, and requires protection as a recharge area for drinking water for many communities north of Toronto.

3. The Greenbelt plan builds on the land use planning protections provided by the Niagara Escarpment and Oak Ridges Moraine plans. It establishes strict land use policies in rural areas across the lands known as the "Golden Horseshoe," which ring Lake Ontario from Toronto to Fort Erie.

REGIONAL AND MUNICIPAL OFFICIAL PLANS

Regional and **municipal official plans** establish general land use policies across large geographical areas, which are usually based on municipal political boundaries. These differ from plans such as the Niagara Escarpment and Oak Ridges Moraine plans, which are based on ecological features and landforms. In most provinces, land use plans arose from the need to establish municipal jurisdiction over settlement patterns and land use control. The official plan therefore generally encompasses the whole of the municipality that has formulated the plan. Where there are two tiers of municipal government, there may be larger regional official plans that provide overall guidance for more specific municipal plans. The Capital Regional District in British Columbia, for example, has a regional growth strategy that must be followed by the official plans of Victoria, Saanich, Esquimalt, and the other municipalities in that regional district.

PURPOSE   Official plans establish a formal set of policies and principles governing the nature, pattern, extent, and timing of future growth and development within a municipality. The plans are developed with a time frame in mind, typically about 20 years. An official plan usually sets out a series of policies concerning key areas that affect growth and development within a municipality, including the following:

- range and types of housing;
- settlement patterns;
- industrial and commercial development;
- provision of necessary services, including transportation and highways, public utilities such as water and sewage treatment, and waste management;
- protection of environmental resources, including flood plains, wetlands, and aggregate extraction;
- conservation and protection of agricultural lands and activities;

- provision of health, policing, and school services;
- restrictions on land severance and subdivision;
- economic development; and
- rules governing public participation in land use planning decisions.

Most importantly, the document serves as a blueprint for guiding land use across the municipality and managing the estimated population growth. Thus, one of the most important aspects of any official plan is the land use map attached to the plan. This map indicates the lands on which urban growth and redevelopment are intended to occur and designates the ultimate land use or function that the municipality considers appropriate for each geographical area within its boundaries.

AMENDMENT   Official plans, like all planning tools, are not cast in stone. Mechanisms are in place to amend official plans to respond to changing information, ideas, and desires about how land development should occur. In Ontario, for example, there are four mechanisms available to amend official plans:

1. *Municipality-initiated amendments.* Municipalities may initiate amendments to their own plans. In Ontario, although most official plans are designed for at least a 20-year planning horizon, the *Planning Act* requires municipalities to review their official plan once every five years and consider whether changes are needed. Typically, this involves a comprehensive municipal review of relevant information about population growth projections, demand for municipal services, industrial and commercial growth, and the status of environmental resources within the municipality. On the basis of this information, the municipality determines what, if any, changes are required to the plan, and initiates a public process for developing and approving a new official plan.

2. *Secondary plans.* Municipalities, particularly in urban areas, sometimes identify the need for detailed planning policies within an official plan. **Secondary plans** cover specific areas within a municipality. For example, if an official plan designates an area for residential use, a secondary plan may provide additional detailed policies and mapping to show areas where high-, medium-, and low-density residential development is permitted.

3. *Private amendments.* Amendments to an official plan may be initiated any time to permit specific development projects that do not conform with the existing official plan. Typically, this type of amendment is initiated by private landowners or developers and is accompanied by applications to establish zoning and/or plans of subdivision to permit a particular develop-

ment to proceed. For example, a developer who wishes to build a shopping mall in a residential area must apply to the municipality to change the official plan designation from residential to commercial, and to establish specific policies to govern the commercial uses.

4. *Provincial amendments.* The provincial government has the power to amend an official plan to address a matter of provincial interest. In Ontario, provincial interventions in local planning decisions are rare but not unprecedented.

LEGAL FORCE AND EFFECT Regional and official plans set out policies that guide municipal councils and other government decision-makers in making planning decisions. Policies are not generally considered by the courts to be legally enforceable against individuals. For example, official plans do not directly impose legal requirements on property owners. A municipality may not lay charges against a property owner for carrying out a land use that does not conform to the official plan.

In many jurisdictions, however, official plans indirectly impose property use restrictions on individuals. In Ontario, for example, no municipality may pass a zoning bylaw that does not conform to its official plan. (Zoning bylaws are discussed in greater detail below.) Unlike official plan policies, zoning bylaws are legally enforceable instruments that restrict land use activities and impose planning rules on individual property owners. If an individual seeks a zoning amendment to change the existing rules, or to expand the permissible uses on her property, the municipality is legally bound to refuse the amendment if it does not conform to the official plan. This example demonstrates how official plans can exert significant planning control over the way individuals can use their property, albeit indirectly.

MULTIPLE LAND USE PLANS

Some areas are governed by two, or even three, land use plans. In the City of Burlington, for example, in order to determine the land use policies governing a particular property, a landowner might need to look first at the Niagara Escarpment plan and/or the Greenbelt plan, then the Region of Halton official plan, and finally the City of Burlington official plan.

In cases where more than one plan governs land use, a hierarchy is typically established. For example, the Niagara Escarpment plan creates land use designations to protect escarpment features, to which all regional and local official plans must conform. The Region of Halton official plan also provides a general policy direction, including direction on permitted land uses to which the local (City of Burlington) official plan must conform. Finally, the city's official plan provides still more specific direction on permissible land uses and the other aspects of land use planning described above. In the event of conflict between the city and regional plans, the policies of the regional plan govern.

Zoning Bylaws

Official plans establish general policies and direct the locations where growth and development will occur. **Zoning bylaws** provide the specific, legally enforceable rules and requirements for the use of land, and for the use and location of buildings and structures on land. Zoning bylaws influence how buildings are constructed by setting rules about the height, bulk, location, size, floor area, spacing, and general character and use of buildings or structures.

FUNCTIONS

Generally, local municipalities are responsible for passing zoning bylaws, which have the following functions:

- *Land use.* Zoning bylaws may restrict the specific land uses permitted on certain lands. For example, a zoning bylaw may prohibit the commercial or industrial use of a particular property.
- *Setback requirements.* Zoning bylaws may establish rules for locating buildings by means of setback requirements. For example, zoning bylaws typically establish the amount of frontage required for each building within a zone, the spacing between buildings through side yard zoning, the depth of lots, and the size of front and rear yards.
- *Density control.* Zoning bylaws usually control density by establishing minimum lot sizes and the number of dwelling units permitted on each lot within a zone. Within a particular zone, for example, a zoning bylaw could permit individual dwelling units in one area, medium-density townhouse development in a second area, and high-density apartment buildings in a third area.
- *Building height.* Zoning bylaws may establish the maximum height permitted for buildings within a zoning category. Through this mechanism, the municipality has the ability to establish a range of community types and densities.
- *Parking requirements.* Zoning bylaws may set parking requirements, which raise important considerations for residential, commercial, and industrial development.

Zoning bylaws provide a mechanism for detailed regulatory control over land use. They implement and give the force of law to the environmental and land use planning protections that municipalities seek to establish through official plan policies.

FACTORS CONSIDERED

Factors considered in the drafting of bylaws primarily include the following:

- whether the zoning conforms to the policies and land use designations set out in the official plan, and
- whether land use conflicts might be created by the bylaw.

For example, a decision to rezone in order to permit a high-density development within a residential area typically involves consideration of the development's impact on the neighbourhood, including the adjacent properties. Studies might be required to determine the probable effects, and whether or not they are acceptable, before a zoning change is approved.

LEGAL NON-CONFORMING USES

It is common, particularly in older areas, to find lands or buildings that are being used for purposes other than those permitted by the current zoning bylaw. This situation arises when a zoning bylaw is imposed after an existing use is already established. Hardship would result for users of land if they were suddenly required to cease using their property in the legal manner in which they had been using it. Rather than disrupting businesses or residents in this way, governments give property owners relief from latterly imposed planning rules through a concept called **legal non-conforming uses**.

According to this principle, a pre-existing use on a property is allowed to continue, even though it does not conform to the existing zoning requirements, provided that the use is maintained uninterrupted. If the use is discontinued temporarily, the current zoning requirements come into effect. In most jurisdictions, a legal non-conforming use cannot be expanded without permission.

A legal non-conforming use differs from a non-conforming use bylaw because it relates to a historical use. A non-conforming use bylaw, on the other hand, is a bylaw passed to permit a new use, usually by a developer, that is not otherwise allowed by an official plan.

Subdivision and Land Severances

A critically important tool available to government to protect environmental resources and manage growth is the regulation of the subdivision of land. The potential environmental impacts of permitting unchecked division of properties into increasingly smaller individually owned parcels are obvious. Municipalities therefore are empowered to decide whether or not new lots may be created and built on. In Ontario the *Planning Act* establishes the following two mechanisms for lot creation:

- grant of consent to sever, and
- approval of plans of subdivision.

Generally, owners apply for **consent to sever** if a proposal involves the creation of only one or two lots. In cases involving more complex lot creation patterns, such as a new housing development, a **plan of subdivision** is required.

During the 1980s, a number of rural Ontario municipalities permitted residential growth through the granting of severances. In Grey County the number of severances rose from several hundred per year in the early 1980s to almost 2,000 in 1989. Consider the problems that were created:

- The government agencies responsible for reviewing severance decisions and key issues, such as the adequacy of septic systems and the impacts on water supply and wetlands, were not able to respond in a timely way.
- Lots were established on major concession roads, and not through the use of internal secondary road systems, leading to traffic and safety issues.
- The creation of lots adjacent to agricultural operations created the potential for land use conflicts arising from the impacts associated with standard farming activities, such as odour, dust, and noise.
- Continuing severances caused gradual fragmentation of farmland, mounting pressure on environmental resources as a result of incremental decision making, and ultimately the loss of high-quality farmland.

In most municipalities, the granting of severances is closely regulated, particularly in rural areas. In Ontario the current provincial policy discourages lot creation of any kind on agricultural lands. New residential lots in prime agricultural areas are permitted only in very limited specified circumstances. In addition, most municipalities in Ontario place significant restrictions on the number of severances that may be granted in rural areas.

By contrast, plans of subdivision provide the opportunity for a more comprehensive community-planning approach. For example, the creation of a series of residential lots through a plan of subdivision requires consideration of the overall impacts: the adequacy of utilities, such as drinking water and sanitary sewage treatment; the need for infrastructure, such as roads; and the provision of municipal services, such as policing, education, and health services.

Consents to sever remain useful in the context of existing areas, where severances sometimes provide an opportunity for further development of a particular lot within an established neighbourhood. This procedure is consistent with the policy of increasing residential density in urban areas, an undertaking known as **residential intensification**.

Decision-Making Processes

On the one hand, land use decision making lends itself to rational policy and rule-making. On the other hand, decisions about land use can involve high drama and high stakes. Behind many planning or zoning decisions are judgments about how best to reconcile or balance private property rights, economic objectives, larger community interests, and long-term environmental land stewardship.

There are many stakeholders with an intense interest in the outcome of this balancing act. Consider the following examples:

- Private developers want a return on their investment in lands that they have purchased or acquired rights to. Restrictive planning policies or zoning rules can mean a loss of revenue.
- Neighbouring property owners may object if a vacant lot is turned into an apartment building complex that fundamentally alters the nature and character of the community, and creates traffic, noise, and visual changes.
- Municipalities are concerned because planning decisions affect municipal resources, demands on municipal services, and the municipal vision for community-building.
- A planning decision may have broad implications for the mandate of provincial government agencies. For example, the decision to permit a golf course in an ecologically important wetland complex would run directly against the mandate of the Ontario Ministry of Natural Resources to protect these provincially significant natural features.

Given the potential tensions and conflicts associated with land use planning decisions, and the environmental and economic issues at stake, it is important that the decision-making process be seen as accessible, rational, and fair to all stakeholders. Because land use decisions are generally associated with local decision making, local political accountability is also an important component of the process.

ONTARIO PROCESS

Ontario is used here as an example of how the decision-making process works at the municipal level. Land use planning decisions are triggered in the following two ways:

1. by municipal action to establish new land use policies or zoning rules, or

2. by private action through an application to change land use rules to permit a land development project on a specific property.

The approval processes for municipally and privately initiated proposals are similar, although there are some differences. A land use change triggered by a municipal action—such as a proposed new official plan, secondary plan, or municipality-wide comprehensive zoning bylaw—begins with extensive studies to establish the need for the new planning rules.

MUNICIPAL PROPOSALS   In developing a new official plan, a municipality may be required to carry out municipality-wide studies concerning the following matters:

- population growth projections;
- current demands on municipal and other services, including policing, hospitals, schools, and municipal sewage treatment and water supply facilities;
- transportation needs and current traffic levels on municipal roads;
- inventories of current environmental resources within the municipality, including wetlands, aggregate resources, and agricultural lands;
- inventories of existing employment lands and employment opportunities in the municipality;
- market studies to determine the existing and future need for retail stores and services within the municipality; and
- existing and projected future settlement patterns.

All of this information is analyzed by municipal planners on behalf of the municipality, and translated into a series of policy objectives.

Municipalities usually consult various stakeholders before and during the development of a proposed new official plan or comprehensive zoning bylaw. Stakeholders include businesses, prominent environmental and neighbourhood interest groups, and a long list of government agencies responsible for various environmental and public resources that could be affected by land use planning changes.

The *Planning Act* presents formal opportunities for both written and oral submissions. For example, the Act gives members of the public an opportunity to make submissions directly to municipal councils at public meetings.

PRIVATE PROPOSALS   Private development proposals go through a similar process, most often on a smaller scale. Developers or landowners are required to apply to the municipality to seek the amendments to the official plan that are necessary to allow a particular development to proceed.

Municipalities generally require studies to support these applications. Under the *Planning Act*, a municipality may refuse to review a planning application if sufficient information is not provided. If a private development involves a significant land use change, such as a plan of subdivision or a major industrial or commercial proposal, applications must be accompanied by technical studies covering a range of disciplines.

For example, a residential subdivision usually requires a study to show that the new homes to be built in the subdivision will be adequately serviced with water, sanitary sewage treatment, and traffic access. If the project involves potential effects on environmental resources—such as wetlands, woodlots, or the natural habitat of significant wildlife or plant species—studies must be provided to show that unacceptable impacts will not occur.

The level of study and the amount of detail required by the municipality depend on the nature and scale of the development proposal. For example, a consent to sever one or two lots does not generally require as extensive a study as a plan of subdivision that will create a new residential community with 100 homes.

Once a municipality determines that the information provided in support of a study is acceptable, it begins the circulation process to relevant government agencies. The developer has an opportunity to respond to agency concerns and to make changes to the development or proposal to address these concerns. The municipality also makes the application material available to the public, and gives the public a chance to make submissions, either in writing or orally before council at a public meeting.

COUNCIL DECISION   The municipal council makes a decision on a proposed land use change after reviewing a report from its planning staff on the application and all of the public comments. Notice of the decision is provided to the public.

APPEAL TO THE ONTARIO MUNICIPAL BOARD   Ontario, unlike most jurisdictions in Canada, provides an opportunity for stakeholders who are unhappy with council's decision to appeal to an independent tribunal—namely, the Ontario Municipal Board (OMB). The OMB hears appeals of land use planning decisions by municipal councils with respect to the following:

- official plans and official plan amendments,
- zoning bylaws and amendments,
- approval of consents,

- approval of severances and plans of subdivision, and
- other municipal and planning-related issues.

Hearings at the OMB are less formal than in courts, but they are run in accordance with specified rules and procedures. Most parties are represented by lawyers, and witnesses are subject to cross-examination.

Tribunals other than the OMB may also have a mandate related to land use and environmental matters. For example, in Ontario the Niagara Escarpment Hearing Office hears appeals of development permit applications and conducts Niagara Escarpment plan amendment proceedings under the *Niagara Escarpment Planning and Development Act.* The Environmental Review Tribunal has specific review powers under the *Oak Ridges Moraine Conservation Act, 2001* and the *Greenbelt Act, 2005.*

Land Use Planning as a Growth Management Tool

In some parts of Canada, a critically important function for government-led land use planning is the proper management of growth and development.

Urban Sprawl

A particular concern is the impact of **urban sprawl**, some of whose detrimental effects are the following:

- encroachment on prime agricultural land;
- encroachment on natural habitats;
- need for greater expenditures on infrastructure, such as roads, electricity, water, and sewers, to support low density; and
- reliance on cars for transportation as a result of low density.

The current thinking is that good planning focuses population growth within existing urban areas and adjacent lands. This approach is a response to the economic inefficiencies and environmental impacts of low-density residential growth in rural areas.

Intensification

Focusing growth within existing urban areas, through redevelopment and intensification, allows more people to live within the current urban boundaries, helps to support improvements in public transit, and better uses other existing services and infrastructure. Redevelopment to add density also provides opportunities to avoid additional consumption of good agricultural lands and extension of human activities into natural areas.

Ontario has taken specific steps to manage population and growth at the macro level. Consider the following examples:

- creation of the Greenbelt plan, which imposes restrictive land use policies on rural areas across a portion of southern Ontario, in conjunction with the Niagara Escarpment and Oak Ridges Moraine plans;
- passage of the *Places to Grow Act, 2005,* which allows the province to establish growth management plans that identify where and how growth should occur in the province; and
- preparation of the first growth plan for the Greater Golden Horseshoe area.

These measures direct population and employment growth to existing urban areas. The **growth plan** for the Greater Golden Horseshoe area sets out specific intensification objectives for municipalities.

Placing controls on the expansion of existing settlement area boundaries is a priority in Ontario. For example, the growth plan states that a settlement boundary expansion can occur only as part of a "municipal comprehensive review" that clearly demonstrates the need for such an expansion. This review must show, among other things, that insufficient opportunities currently exist to accommodate forecasted growth through intensification within the existing settlement boundary.

Growth plans also identify urban growth areas, and municipalities must ensure that certain density targets for both residence and jobs are met. Municipalities are mandated to plan urban growth centres as the focal points for investment in public services as well as commercial, recreational, cultural, and entertainment uses. The growth plan directs municipalities to bring jobs closer to where people live by allocating an adequate supply of lands for employment uses.

These new policies are largely focused on a single objective: to reverse the trend of urban sprawl that has emerged in Ontario over the last 40 years and reduce or eliminate the pressure on environmental and agricultural land resources in rural areas.

Remaining Challenges

Planning direction at the provincial level ushered in through the *Places to Grow Act, 2005* and the *Greenbelt Act, 2005* is unprecedented. Ontario is clearly aiming to close loopholes that led to inefficient and environmentally expensive development in the rural parts of the province. It remains to be seen whether these measures will be effective.

For example, we do not yet know what will happen if municipalities fail to meet the provincially set growth targets or veer away from provincial policies. There is no clear provincial enforcement mechanism.

Further, there may yet be a backlash against the restrictive nature of these policies. Some development interests have argued that the policies are not fair to rural communities included in the Greenbelt plan area and artificially limit the availability of a full range of housing types and locations because of the focus on urban redevelopment and intensification.

Brownfields Redevelopment

One principle of land use policy that has won broad acceptance in recent years is the value of brownfield redevelopment. **Brownfields** are abandoned, underused, or derelict sites of previous human activity. They may include crumbling factories, old railway yards, or condemned apartments. These sites are often located within or near urban centres.

From the perspective of efficiency and resource management, it makes more sense to explore opportunities to redevelop lands that have already been subject to the long-term stresses of human activity than to expand the human footprint into greenfield locations. Within Canada's existing urban areas, there are estimated to be between 30,000 and 100,000 brownfield sites that could be redeveloped. While the concept seems sound—even obvious—implementation has proven to be a great challenge.

Environmental Liability

The key challenge facing the redevelopment of brownfields is environmental liability. Before obtaining land use planning approvals from a municipality, a developer must conduct investigations to assess the environmental quality of a site by testing soils and groundwater, for example. Few developers are willing to take on the unknown risks associated with ownership of sites that may be seriously contaminated. Consider the following:

- *Unforeseen contamination.* Investigation can be expensive, and the level of thoroughness required is usually difficult to assess at the outset. For example, a routine investigation of an abandoned apartment complex might, on closer inspection, reveal that the lot had also been used as a dumping ground for toxic chemicals.
- *Unforeseen cleanup costs.* The result of an investigation can impose new financial obligations on a developer and landowner. For example, if contam-

ination in groundwater is found to be affecting neighbouring properties, the current property owner may be ordered by the Ministry of the Environment to clean it up.

- *Unforeseen legal claims.* The potential for off-site contamination also raises the possibility of private legal claims from neighbours whose properties are affected.

In order to redevelop brownfield sites, developers must initiate a process that has much cost, risk, and uncertainty associated with it. All of these costs, risks, and liabilities come with no guarantee that the redevelopment will even be approved. It is not surprising that developers prefer fresh clean sites.

Ironically, when developers are deterred from brownfield redevelopment, not only is the opportunity for redevelopment lost, but buried environmental problems are also left unaddressed, and greater harm may result from the migration of contaminants. As time goes on, it becomes even less likely that the original polluter will be found and required to pay any of the cleanup costs.

Ontario Amendments

Most governments recognize both the value of brownfield redevelopment and the circumstances that discourage private investment. Consequently, governments wishing to advance brownfield redevelopment have been moving to reduce the costs and risks of environmental liability. Ontario has taken a number of steps to reduce these risks and costs:

- *Records of site conditions.* Records of site conditions must be filed with an environmental site registrar to certify that a development site meets appropriate standards for soil and groundwater quality. This involves a minimum amount of investigation and sometimes site cleanup. However, once a record of site conditions is registered, it provides current and future owners with limited protection from orders made by the Ministry of the Environment.
- *Grants and loans.* The Ontario *Planning Act* provides for grants and loans to developers to defray the costs of cleanup.
- *Tax cancellation.* The *Municipal Act* permits the passage of bylaws cancelling property taxes on contaminated properties under certain conditions.
- *Mortgage incentives.* The *Environmental Protection Act* provides incentives for mortgages to extend funding to developers of brownfield properties by protecting them from orders made by the Ministry of the Environment.

Innovative developers, in cooperation with forward-looking municipalities, have succeeded in a few cases in advancing major redevelopment projects. In most cases, however, the risks of incurring environmental liability, costs of investigation, and costs of cleaning up contamination have discouraged positive action. To encourage redevelopment, conditions have to be right: the site must have a high revenue-generating potential, and the risks of environmental liability must be known and manageable.

While governmental measures provide some relief from risks, they are not likely to lead to significant private sector investment in brownfield redevelopment.

Electric Power Supply and Demand Management

Not too long ago, governments and electricity generators thought that ensuring a reliable supply of electricity simply meant planning for and building more generating units—usually big new plants powered by hydroelectricity, nuclear technology, or fossil fuels—and transmission lines. Now, virtually everyone understands that all of the old solutions are problematic, and that there are two additional components to be included in electricity planning if we want systems that are more cost-effective, less threatening to human health and environmental integrity, less vulnerable to catastrophic breakdown, and more viable over the long run. These components are demand management and conversion to renewable energy sources.

Demand Management

Demand management is based on the recognition that every kilowatt reduction of demand for electricity is a kilowatt that does not have to be generated and transported through the transmission system. Governments and electricity providers in many jurisdictions have found that it is often cheaper to encourage investment in more efficient industrial processes, home appliances, and lightbulbs than to build more generating plants and transmission lines to service inefficient demand.

Moreover, while new supply initiatives add to increased resource demands, contaminant emissions, waste production, and land disturbance, demand reductions avoid these problems and often have beneficial side effects. These effects include lower costs, more dispersed employment, and reduced dependency.

Measures to promote energy efficiency and conservation have been facilitated, encouraged, or required through law-based actions by all levels of government. The federal *Energy Efficiency Act*, for example, allows the federal government to make regulations prescribing efficiency and labelling requirements and to initiate programs fostering efficiency research and education. Both federal and provincial governments have used building code standards to require efficiency improvements in new construction, have imposed minimum appliance efficiency regulations, and have adjusted tax policies to encourage the purchase of energy-efficient products.

Provincial governments have more direct authority than the federal government over electricity systems, often through provincial Crown corporations that are major players or monopolies in the provincial electricity market. The provinces therefore have greater ability to set pricing regimes and use other tools to encourage conservation and efficiency steps by industrial, commercial, and residential consumers. Provincial initiatives are estimated to have increased energy efficiency in Ontario by 16 percent during the 1990s.

Renewable Energy Sources

The second major new area of electricity policy interest emphasizes renewable and otherwise green energy sources for new supply. Renewable and green sources include the following:

- wind energy,
- solar arrays,
- small-scale hydroelectricity plants, and
- thermal generators burning biomass wastes or landfill gases.

While all of these sources have some undesirable aspects, they are generally much less damaging to the environment than nuclear plants, which leave highly toxic radioactive wastes; big hydro projects, which disrupt watershed ecosystems; and fossil fuel plants, which discharge smog-producing emissions that cause climate change. Especially when combined with demand management initiatives, the green and renewable options are also more diverse than other sources, less vulnerable to system failure, and more likely to provide employment opportunities in or near existing population centres.

Federal, provincial, and even municipal governments have a wide variety of law-based tools available to facilitate and encourage greater electricity production from renewable sources. They can, for example, require utilities to include at least a minimum percentage of renewable-sourced electricity in their portfolios, ensure secure base prices for renewable energy suppliers, contract directly for construction of renewable energy facilities, or purchase electrical power from these facilities.

Governments can also make price competition among energy sources fairer by reducing subsidies to conventional generators and by requiring substantial abatement of health- and climate-threatening emissions from fossil fuel plants. Consider the fact that the Canadian nuclear power industry has long been heavily subsidized by the federal government through research and development funding, trade support, and insurance cost avoidance. In 2000 researchers with the Campaign for Nuclear Phaseout estimated that the Canadian government had given $16.6 billion to Atomic Energy of Canada Limited (this figure does not include costs such as the $1.5 billion in financing for the sale of two CANDU reactors to China in 1996). As mentioned in chapter 9, the federal *Nuclear Liability Act* limits the liability of nuclear power generators in the event of any accident to $75 million.

Transition

It is not easy to move from the relatively simple practice of building big new supply plants to meet rising demand, to a more complex system that combines conventional sources with a wide range of demand management efforts and renewable and green generating facilities. Several levels of government and a variety of legal, financial, and other tools are involved. Moreover, the electricity-focused purposes overlap with other considerations, including broader programs addressing climate change, energy efficiency, national security, and international trade and competitiveness.

Ontario's experience illustrates some of the challenges. Consider the following primary sources of energy in Ontario today:

- several old and inexpensive hydroelectricity sources, including a station at Niagara Falls;
- a set of nuclear power plants, several of which have been closed because of breakdowns or are nearing the end of their useful lives; and
- several large coal-fired thermal power plants that are major sources of smog-producing emissions and greenhouse gases.

Challenges facing Ontario include the following:

- a growing population that is not tuned into energy efficiency,
- the cost of retiring the debt of the former Crown corporation Ontario Hydro,
- the need to keep electricity prices low enough to avoid offending industrial users and voters, and
- the need to minimize the risks of system failure.

Ontario's major options include some combination of the following:

- costly repairs to major nuclear generating units,
- building of new nuclear plants,
- conversion from coal to natural gas for the thermal plants,

- encouragement of new generation from renewable sources, and
- initiation of more ambitious demand management measures.

New legislation, the *Electricity Restructuring Act, 2004*, established an annual regulated price-setting system managed by the Ontario Energy Board through a multi-stakeholder process. A major element of the new approach is the use of **smart meters** to support time-of-day electricity pricing. The Act also established the Ontario Power Authority, which has now developed and submitted to the Ontario Energy Board an "integrated power system plan" that includes addressing government goals relating to demand management. Specifically mentioned as matters for ministerial directives to the Ontario Power Authority are conservation measures and the phase-out of coal-fired generation.

As with decision making in many of the other areas discussed in this book, planning and managing a transition to more sophisticated and sustainable electrical energy demand and supply systems involve choices among multiple options and trade-offs. These are choices that can be informed by experts and facilitated by well-structured decision-making processes. However, they are ultimately matters of public preference. The laws that ensure public access to information and effective opportunities to participate in the deliberations can be just as important as the laws that support regulatory requirements and pricing rules.

CHAPTER 12

Corporations and Harnessing Market Forces

Introduction

This chapter examines corporate law as it relates to environmental protection, and considers some approaches that attempt to work with, rather than against, market forces. Economic instruments that have been adapted for environmental purposes, such as subsidies to assist companies in developing

or purchasing new environmentally friendly equipment, are also considered. The chapter concludes by discussing the role of environmental law in so-called voluntary initiatives that are undertaken by the corporate sector and encouraged by governments.

Corporate Law

It is often the activities of corporations that cause harm to the environment. Corporate law is generally viewed as unfriendly to environmental concerns for two primary reasons:

1. it protects shareholders from liability, and

2. it mandates that corporations operate in their own best interests.

However, there are exceptions to these general precepts, which are discussed in the following section. In addition, the corporate mandate of self-interest may even be used to advance environmental protection.

Liability and the Corporate Veil

Lawyer M.F. Crust has described corporate law as "a shell that does not address environmental protection." Corporate law protects shareholders from liability for torts committed by a corporation. In essence, this means that owners of corporations may avoid personal liability for corporate activities because lawsuits must be directed at the corporation itself. If a corporation has no assets, those who bring lawsuits against it may find themselves unable to recoup losses caused by the corporation.

Despite these challenges, environmental law has chipped away at the protective shell of corporate law. The corporate veil does not protect against environmental liability in certain circumstances:

- *Personal liability for officers and directors.* Environmental statutes hold corporate officers and directors personally liable for environmental offences committed by corporations in some circumstances, whether or not the corporation is convicted or even charged with an offence.
- *Vicarious liability for acts of employees.* Corporations are **vicariously liable** for the environmentally damaging acts of their employees if the action occurs on the site of employment. They are also liable when one of their agents (such as a lawyer or consultant) commits an environmentally damaging action that lies within the authority given by them to the agent.
- *Parent's liability for acts of subsidiary.* A parent corporation may be liable for contamination caused by the actions of a **subsidiary**, a second corporation whose shares are owned by the parent company.
- *Owner's liability for contaminated site.* Environmental legislation may impose liability on an owner of a contaminated site.

Corporate Mandate

The **corporate mandate** requires corporations to operate in their own best interests; this requirement is legislated in statutes such as the *Canada Business Corporations Act*. Corporations must operate in a self-serving manner, and maximize returns for shareholders.

There is a very important purpose to this rule—namely, to protect minority shareholders from officers, directors, or controlling shareholders who might otherwise use the corporation to further their own financial or other personal interests. However, the duty to serve the corporation's best interests may also curtail activities that benefit the environment. Any such secondary activities must always serve the ultimate corporate objective of profit maximization.

This mandate does not necessarily prevent corporations from behaving in an environmentally responsible manner. In fact, responsible environmental behaviour may best advance the corporation's interests in many circumstances. For example, it is generally in the corporate interest to achieve the following objectives, all of which are consistent with environmental protection:

- comply with environmental laws and regulations in order to avoid fines and lawsuits,
- conserve energy in order to reduce costs,
- participate in emission reduction programs in order to qualify for tax reductions and subsidies, and
- preserve and promote an environmentally friendly image in order to satisfy customers and clients.

Some corporations, such as the Body Shop and Ben & Jerry's, have made support of environmental causes part of their successful marketing campaigns. As environmental issues become more urgent, consumers may become more inclined to support environmentally friendly businesses, and even demand minimum standards of environmental responsibility from the businesses that they patronize. In some small measure, consumers' concerns could begin to align market forces with environmental goals.

Although not yet implemented, corporate codes of environmental principles have been proposed as part of self-regulatory corporate governance codes. In the United States, citizens and some politicians have even called for the revocation of the corporate charters of companies that have failed to comply with environmental laws. Revocation of a corporate charter essentially dismantles a corporation and prevents it from continuing to operate if it fails to comply with the law.

Economic Instruments

Externalities are the public costs of environmental degradation. For example, the environmental and health costs of smokestack emissions are borne by the public, not by the factory that pollutes or the customers who purchase the factory's products. This means that businesses are subsidized by the public and by future generations, who are forced to shoulder the burden of present day environmental harm.

When the cost of doing business, such as the cost of manufacturing a product, is measured without considering environmental costs, the rational behaviour assumed by free market economics does not occur. For example, imagine that it costs Smokestack Inc. $4 to produce a widget. Every year 200,000 customers are willing to pay $10 per widget, providing Smokestack with a generous $6 profit per widget and a total annual profit of $1,200,000. What no one has thought about is the externalized costs of widget production. A closer look reveals that the cost to the environment of widget production approximates $3 per widget.

If these externalized costs are absorbed by Smokestack, what is likely to happen?

- Smokestack may pass on the additional cost to the consumer, charging $13 per widget. In this case, fewer customers will be willing to pay the higher price. If only 100,000 customers remain, Smokestack's profits will be reduced by half to $600,000.
- Smokestack may continue to charge $10 per widget and retain its customer base; however, its profit will drop to $3 per widget, and its overall profit will again be reduced by half to $600,000.

Given these numbers, which are based on an accurate and full picture of all costs, Smokestack may alter its business choices. It may spend more money on research and development to improve its processes. It, or one of its competitors, may develop a substitute for the widget that satisfies customers and does less harm to the environment.

Public costs can be reduced or eliminated by regulating or prohibiting an activity that is causing damage, and by imposing penalties for non-compliance. This is the standard command and control model, which was discussed in chapter 8. However, many economists argue that the same goal can be reached most effectively by using **economic instruments** that provide companies with flexibility and permit them to minimize costs, and allow these costs to be reflected in the market.

Types

Economic instruments require that companies absorb at least some of the environmental costs of doing business. There are two primary types of economic instruments: **fixed-price measures**, which use tax and subsidy incentives to reduce pollution, and tradable emission rights, which are also called "cap and trade." Tradable emission rights create "rights" to pollute up to a prescribed limit or cap, and permit the trading of these rights at a price established by supply and demand.

Fixed-Price Measures

There are two types of fixed-price measures: emission taxes and subsidies. The amount of tax or subsidy is fixed by the government per unit of pollution.

Emission taxes are taxes charged on units of contaminants released into the environment. These taxes encourage polluters to discharge less by increasing the total costs of production. The taxes collected can be used by the government for other environmental protection initiatives.

Subsidies are grants, loans, or tax breaks provided to polluters for reducing discharge by basing the size of the subsidy on the amount of the reduction. Like the pollution tax, subsidies provide a direct financial incentive to reduce pollution. It is a "carrot" approach, in contrast to the "stick" approach of emission taxes.

Both emission taxes and subsidies work by raising the relative cost of producing the polluting product. When this cost is passed on to the consumer, there may be less demand for the product. Customers will either use less of the product or find cheaper alternatives to it. Emission taxes and subsidies also cause polluters to research and invest in new methods of reducing pollution—for example, by acquiring new technology.

A criticism of fixed-price measures is that they do not provide for a limit or cap on the total amount of pollution discharged. It is possible to impose a cap on allowable discharge for individual businesses by using regulation in addition to fixed-price measures; however, it is not possible to impose a cap on the aggregate levels within a jurisdiction or industry. Polluters may choose to pay the tax or forgo the subsidy in preference to curbing emissions.

Tradable Emission Rights

Tradable emission rights are rights representing specified quantities of emissions that are issued to polluters. An aggregate cap on allowable emissions, called a **baseline**, is set, and it is divided into units. The units are allocated to polluters on the basis of their previous polluting history, by auction, or by a combination of these two methods.

Once an emission right is owned by a polluter, it may be used to discharge pollutants, traded at a price determined by the marketplace, or saved for use later. Businesses with the lowest abatement costs actually reduce emissions. Those with higher abatement costs purchase pollution rights. The objective is to meet emission reduction targets by setting a sufficiently low baseline, and to ease the burden on industry by facilitating pollution abatement where it is least expensive. In theory, provided that a market is competitive, overall abatement costs are minimized, and the baseline objective can be achieved.

A criticism of this model is that the baseline is often set too high, thereby redistributing pollution but not reducing it. How rights are allocated can also be problematic. If rights are given to established businesses on the basis of their pollution history, an unintended consequence is that new businesses are at a disadvantage when entering the market because they are forced to purchase rights.

When used wisely, economic instruments may be important tools; unfortunately, they are not a panacea for environmental challenges.

Non-regulatory Instruments

For decades now, regulatory requirements of various kinds have been the main political means of getting industry to improve its environmental performance. This is still the case. However, over the last 15 years or so, a variety of non-regulatory "voluntary" instruments have been introduced through government–industry cooperation.

Types

Non-regulatory instruments are sometimes used as supplements to regulation, and sometimes as alternatives to regulation. The most important of these tools include the following:

- *Organizational structure.* Companies may change their organizational structure—that is, their reporting hierarchy and job descriptions—as part of an environmental management system. These changes are intended to place more attention on environmental issues for the purpose of preventing serious problems and identifying opportunities for environmentally desirable initiatives.
- *Pollution reduction agreements.* Agreements to reduce pollution may be negotiated between governments and either industries or industrial sectors. These agreements commit industry to environmental protection actions that exceed prevailing regulatory requirements.
- *Industry association performance obligations.* Industry associations may push their members to meet higher environmental standards. Marketing by the association on behalf of its members may include reference to these goals or achievements.
- *Sectoral abatement challenges.* Governments may set informal targets or "challenges," often in cooperation with polluting industries in a particular

sector, and encourage businesses within the sector to meet these targets without regulatory obligation.

- *"Profit from pollution prevention" educational programs.* Educational programs, usually initiated by government, are intended to inform businesses of opportunities to reduce pollution while saving money; an example of such a program is one that advocates the reduction of wasted materials and energy.
- *Eco-labelling programs.* Eco-labelling programs involve labelling the products and services of businesses that comply with specified environmental standards. This provides a competitive advantage to participants when marketing to environmentally concerned customers and clients.
- *Green consumer education programs.* Green consumer education programs focus on educating the consumer, and can work in conjunction with eco-labelling programs. Consumers are given information about various products and are encouraged to choose those whose manufacture involves fewer negative environmental effects, and whose use or disposal is less environmentally dangerous. By raising consumer awareness and changing purchasing decisions, governments hope that informed consumers will affect corporate behaviour.

Many of these non-regulatory instruments are likely to increase in importance as environmental issues become more urgent, and as growing numbers of consumers appreciate this urgency. New programs and approaches are likely to arise as well.

Voluntariness

Non-regulatory measures are often called "voluntary," which is technically correct. None of them involves direct regulatory obligation. However, measures such as pollution reduction agreements are effective only in conjunction with an implicit threat of more stringent and less flexible regulation in the event that the voluntary initiative fails.

Likewise, industry associations that push their members to improve environmental performance beyond regulatory requirements are acting voluntarily in the sense that they are not required to do so by regulation. However, these initiatives are usually driven by fear of tough regulations or other financial consequences if the sector does not take action to improve its environmental behaviour. For example, the Canadian Chemical Producers' Association introduced its responsible care program after a series of nasty chemical industry accidents had darkened the industry's reputation, made investors and insurers nervous, and inspired calls for tougher regulation.

Indirect regulatory pressures may also encourage compliance with voluntary measures. Indirect pressures include concerns about liability if a serious environmentally damaging event occurs. In order to prove due diligence and avoid penalties under environmental protection statutes, businesses must demonstrate that they have taken every reasonable precaution to avoid these damaging incidents. Proving due diligence is much easier when an offending business can show that it had an environmental management system in place.

Perhaps the only initiatives that are truly voluntary are the ones that focus on profitable pollution-reducing actions. These rely on the core financial motives that private sector firms are expected to apply. We might expect profit-driven companies to be naturally good at finding ways to cut expenses in environmentally desirable ways. However, unless a company is organized to look for these opportunities, it may well miss them.

Consider the example of Nortel Networks. Some years ago, Nortel invested $1 million in an initiative to eliminate use of an environmentally damaging solvent. As a result of the process changes involved, the company saved $4 million in three years. This initiative was undertaken in anticipation of a regulatory requirement, and the fact that it was a cost-saving opportunity was recognized only later.

Advantages and Disadvantages

Non-regulatory measures have been attractive for several reasons. They are flexible, may raise overall performance at a lower cost than regulatory action, can be easier to implement than regulations, and may help persuade businesses that environmental improvements can serve their economic self-interest. Non-regulatory measures also make use of a wide range of motivations and pressures—from bankers, insurers, employees, and customers, as well as governments.

At the same time, non-regulatory measures tend to be less well defined, more difficult to test for adequacy and effectiveness, less open to public scrutiny, and less evenly applied than regulations. They are most problematic when adopted as alternatives to regulatory action, since the threat of effective regulation and the indirect influence of legal obligations are probably the most powerful motivators of voluntary action.

We are likely to see continued, and perhaps increasing, use of non-regulatory tools in combination with government's continuing core reliance on regulation. The two primary reasons for this trend are described below.

1. *Regulatory initiatives are not enough.* Governments increasingly recognize that regulatory initiatives have never been, and are unlikely ever to be,

sufficient by themselves. Regulatory authorities are facing increasing challenges as technologies become more ambitious and as economic activities develop more complex linkages from local producers to global trade systems. Most governments are under pressure to do more in many areas while not increasing tax burdens, and this situation creates a powerful impetus for experimentation with combinations of regulatory and non-regulatory instruments.

2. *Pressure from public interest groups.* Public interest or "civil society" organizations have gained prominence in recent years. Governments are no longer the only significant source of pressure for better corporate performance on environmental matters. Public interest organizations have become much more numerous and influential. They are using the Internet and other modern technologies to organize in effective coalitions that exert direct pressure on the private sector to improve environmental performance. Campaigns by these groups have included boycotts of targeted environmentally undesirable products or environmentally irresponsible companies and have increased public awareness of the unsustainability of current practices. Public interest groups have greatly contributed to the rising public expectations that are pushing industry to adopt at least the green mantle of corporate social and environmental responsibility if they wish to maintain consumer respect, investor confidence, and employee loyalty.

As a result of these trends, the direct influence of environmental regulation has combined with non-regulatory measures and civil society actions to establish a number of drivers of change. In addition to simple command and control obligations and penalties, these drivers now include the following:

- incentives to reduce costs, especially by cutting resource use and waste generation;
- desire to avoid, or at least delay, additional regulatory action that would impose undesirable administrative and compliance costs;
- concern about negative reaction from environmentally informed consumers;
- fear of damage to public image and associated customer and investor confidence (or desire to enhance public reputation and associated customer and investor confidence);
- desire to minimize risk of costly surprises;
- expectation of competitive advantage through exclusion of new competitors and access to new markets;

- requirements imposed by banks and/or insurers that do not wish to inherit environmental liabilities;
- demands of suppliers and customers who wish to avoid environmental costs and liabilities;
- pressure from staff or fellow industry members; and
- personal commitment of corporate leaders.

So far there have been few steps to approach regulatory and non-regulatory initiatives in a coordinated way that mobilizes all of these drivers effectively and ensures that each strengthens the other. Indeed, we have still only an incomplete understanding of how regulatory efforts must be designed and focused to provide a firm foundation for a larger and more powerful environmental regime. But increasingly the building blocks are in place.

PART V

Using Courts and Tribunals to Protect the Environment

CHAPTER 13

Using the Courts to Protect the Environment

Introduction

The very first environmental protection court cases were civil lawsuits based on private property rights. Neighbours sued neighbours for damage caused to their land.

After providing a historical context, this chapter examines the current role that civil actions play in protecting the environment. It also addresses some of the obstacles encountered in civil litigation, such as obtaining standing (the right to sue), identifying a cause of action, proving causation, proving damages, and suffering the costs consequences of losing a case.

History of Private Actions

Canadians are blessed with a wide array of rights and freedoms. However, these rights and freedoms are not unlimited, and ultimately it is up to the courts to determine what the limits are. In the environmental context, the courts must reconcile the rights of owners and occupiers of property to use and enjoy the property with the rights of their neighbours to do the same. Consider the following issues:

- Can you build a tall fence to create privacy in your backyard if your fence deprives your neighbour's award-winning rosebush of sunlight?
- Can a factory near your home continue its manufacturing process if the noise it emits at night is so loud that you have problems sleeping?
- What can a farmer do when the groundwater she uses for irrigation is being contaminated by a neighbouring landfill?
- What can residents do when tunnels dug by a mining company under their land begin to cave in?
- Can a factory emit a pollutant that affects the health of residents downwind?
- What can residents do if their drinking water smells bad and is discoloured?
- Can residents stop the migration of contaminants from an abandoned site?

Similar issues were litigated as far back as the 1800s, although they were not called "environmental matters" at that time. There was scant, if any, legislation on these subjects. The courts were therefore required to apply general principles of the common law to the particulars of each case.

Today there are many environmental court actions. Most do not make the front pages of newspapers; however, each and every one of them adds to the growing body of law that governs the environment. While the courts remain the primary forum for the adjudication of environmental rights in lawsuits initiated by individuals, litigants face many challenges in pursuing environmental claims in the courts.

Standing

Not just anyone may go to court to bring a lawsuit. A person must have standing, or status to sue. Under traditional rules, it was always difficult for persons who wanted to protect the environment to attain status to sue, but, over the years, the courts broadened the rules and developed rules for public interest standing.

Traditional Standing Rule

Courts are generally willing to hear only from people who are directly involved in or affected by the matter in dispute. To open the courthouse doors to anyone who wants to be heard would be cumbersome and very costly. Therefore, standing, or permission to participate in a lawsuit, is reserved only for people with a recognized legal interest.

The traditional **"three p" rule** for determining whether a person has standing requires that would-be litigants demonstrate that they have one of the following three interests:

1. *Property interest.* The person's property has allegedly been harmed.

2. *Personal (health) interest.* The person's health has allegedly been harmed.

3. *Pocketbook or pecuniary (financial) interest.* The person's business or economic interests have allegedly been harmed.

The "three p" rule limits standing to those individuals with a direct and measurable interest in the dispute. However, sometimes it is appropriate to allow wider participation in a lawsuit, and this matter is explored in the following sections.

Public Interest Standing

Consider the following cases where groups and individuals want to bring a legal action to protect a common or public interest:

- A community member is concerned about city council's decision to build fire stations in local parks, thus removing valuable greenspace from neighbourhoods.
- A passerby notices that trees are being cut down on lands owned by the province, and wants to have it stopped.
- A conservation group wants to challenge a bureaucratic decision to allow the draining of a wetland.

In all these cases, the groups and individuals who want to bring an action do not satisfy the traditional "three p" standing rule because their property, health, and pocketbooks are not directly affected.

The standing rule has often stood in the way of environmentalists who seek redress in court. This issue was raised in the US Supreme Court in the early 1970s, when an environmental group tried to bring an action to prevent a development activity near a national park. One of the submissions, a law review article by Christopher Stone entitled "Should Trees Have Standing?," remains a persuasive treatise about why rules of standing should be relaxed for environmental litigation.

Since that time, the courts have carved out an exception to the traditional standing test by applying a **public interest standing** test in certain circumstances. This new broader test requires that three questions be answered in the affirmative:

1. Is a serious issue being raised?

2. Does the applicant have a "genuine interest" in the litigation, as demonstrated by

   a. his having worked on the issue for a long time, and

   b. his being knowledgeable about it?

3. Is the applicant in a better position to bring the action than anyone else—that is, is there no other way to bring the issue before the court?

Public interest standing is now well recognized in Canadian courts. However, the granting of public interest standing remains discretionary. Hence, in each case the proposed public interest plaintiff must make a very persuasive argument for standing.

Class Actions

A **class action** is a procedural mechanism that is used when large numbers of plaintiffs sue over the same event or set of facts. Class actions do not give plaintiffs any additional rights; rather, they are intended to facilitate the efficient progress of the case.

Assume, for example, that a company negligently allowed a contaminant to leak from its facility and affected over 40 landowners in the immediate vicinity such that their groundwater was contaminated.

Using the traditional lawsuit method, every landowner affected by the contaminated groundwater would bring a separate action. However, in a class action, one plaintiff (called the **representative plaintiff**) brings one action on behalf of all the affected landowners. Usually there is a notice posted in newspapers informing the public of the class action. In our example, the notice would ask the affected landowners to contact the plaintiff's lawyer.

The representative plaintiff must have the class certified, or approved, by the court. The lawsuit then carries on in much the same way as any other. The difference is that the result of the action by the representative plaintiff binds all members of the class. The win or loss by the representative plaintiff is a win or loss for all of the members of the class. Rules of court procedure usually permit plaintiffs to opt out of the class at the beginning of the process if for any reason they do not want to be bound by the class action. A plaintiff might opt out if he wanted to start a separate action, for example.

Interventions

Standing is the right to initiate a legal action against someone else. However, once a legal action is already under way, other interested parties may want to become involved. These parties may wish to intervene in the case to protect their interests, or to have their concerns and points of view heard by the court.

Intervention is a procedural device that allows persons or organizations that are not plaintiffs or defendants to participate in a legal proceeding. Intervention is particularly relevant in environmental law cases since businesses, environmental groups, community organizations, and others may want to participate in cases that could set binding precedents or raise important policy implications for the present and future of environmental law.

Most of the provinces have the same general procedural rules and tests for intervention. Two types of intervention are usually recognized: intervention as an added party and intervention as a friend of the court. Each type of intervention has its own common law heritage and its own test for status. An intervenor as an added party becomes a party to the legal action and is thus afforded greater rights than an intervenor as a friend of the court. An intervenor as a friend of the court remains a non-party to the proceeding, but enjoys limited participation rights. In practice, the distinction between these two types of intervention may become blurred. Because courts carefully define the rights of each intervenor, some intervenors may be given rights that are broader than a friend of the court but narrower than an added party. There are also specific rules for interventions at appeal courts, federal courts, and the Supreme Court of Canada.

Added Party

A person or organization may apply to a court to gain intervenor status as an added party. If the application is successful, the person or organization becomes a party to the proceeding with a fairly broad array of rights, including the right to file pleadings, introduce evidence, examine and cross-examine witnesses at trial, present arguments, and appeal an adverse ruling. These rights are attractive to prospective intervenors who want to present evidentiary material. However, with the rights of a party come the potential risks, such as an adverse costs order if the case is unsuccessful.

To attain the status of an intervenor as an added party, the rules usually require that applicants establish that one of the following situations applies to them:

- they have an interest in the subject matter of the proceeding, or
- they may be adversely affected by a judgment in the proceeding.

Traditionally, the interest test required that the applicant's direct legal interests would be affected—for example, when a case involves the interpretation of a forestry licence held by a company and a First Nations wants to intervene to protect its land claim or treaty rights or when the applicant would be directly affected commercially. Gradually, courts widened the test to include a less direct interest in the subject matter of the case by using such terms as "vital," "legitimate," or "substantial" interests. This broader interpretation of the rule is important since it creates the possibility of adding public interest litigants—such as community groups or environmental organizations—as parties to the litigation.

The second test deals with whether the prospective intervenor will be "adversely affected." Courts have not made much of an effort to distinguish between having a "direct interest" and being "adversely affected." However, it is usually safe to assume that if applicants meet the direct interest test, they will also be directly affected by the outcome of the proceeding.

Friend of the Court

If a person is granted the status of an intervenor as a **friend of the court**, which is sometimes known as an *amicus curiae*, the person does not become a party. Rather than having the full rights of a party, this type of intervenor has the right to present oral and/or written submissions to the court.

To gain intervenor status as a friend of the court, the applicant must demonstrate that she will assist the court in resolving the issues before it. Historically, a friend of the court would assist the court by informing it of a relevant fact or circumstance or by advising it on a point of law. It is fair to say that this narrow notion of "assistance" has widened. It now involves a consideration of whether the applicant can address an issue that the parties are not fully canvassing, bring a different or unique perspective to the issues at hand, or add expertise or specialized knowledge that will make the ultimate decision more informed.

Public Interest

The categories of added party and friend of the court at times become blurred because of a gradual trend to broaden the scope of both types of intervention in recognition of the need to consider the public interest. As a result, **public interest intervention**, for all practical purposes, has become a category in itself.

Public interest intervention is commonly recognized where a provision of the *Canadian Charter of Rights and Freedoms* is being interpreted and applied and the court would benefit from submissions about the implications of various interpretations. Apart from Charter cases, many environmental law cases have intervenors since so many of the cases have broad public interest implications.

Public interest intervention allows different stakeholders in society—such as environmental groups, business associations, and informed individuals—to participate in important litigation that may have implications far beyond the four corners of the dispute.

Causes of Action

Not all grievances can be litigated. For example, if the smell of your neighbour's barbecue disturbs you, it is unlikely that you have grounds to sue. Causes of action are categories of grievances that are recognized by the common law and can be litigated.

Causes of action are distinguished from criminal offences, which are prosecuted by the state. In a civil lawsuit, the onus is on the plaintiff to prove that

- the defendant did something that falls within an established cause of action, and
- the defendant's action caused harm to the plaintiff.

The most recognized and relevant causes of action in environmental matters are discussed in the following sections.

Nuisance

Nuisance occurs when one person unreasonably interferes with the use and enjoyment of someone else's property. What is reasonable in one circumstance may be unreasonable in another. Courts consider such circumstances as the gravity of the harm and the nature of the neighbourhood. The annoyance of occasional barbecue smells is not a serious enough harm to amount to nuisance. However, a neighbour who is raising pigs in his backyard might be liable for nuisance (as well as guilty of violating zoning bylaws).

One of the defences to a nuisance claim is that the government authorized the activity that led to the nuisance by issuing a permit or an approval. Hence, a person living beside a factory would have a major hurdle to overcome in bringing a successful civil action against the company if the emissions are squarely within the terms of the approval issued by the government.

Public Nuisance

A public nuisance occurs when a whole community, rather than merely one person, is annoyed. It may arise as a result of noxious or offensive smells, or because of exposure to a serious infectious disease.

Trespass

A **trespass** is traditionally defined as an "invasion" of property; however, simply walking over property without the owner's permission may amount to trespass. Examples of trespass include fences encroaching past a property line, snowmobilers crossing into private property to find a trail, and advertisers posting flyers on someone else's property. In most other causes of action, plaintiffs must establish that they suffered harm in order to collect damages (monetary compensation). However, the mere act of trespass is sufficient to give rise to damages, and plaintiffs are not required to establish that any real harm occurred. Plaintiffs may be awarded only nominal damages in trespass cases where the act of trespass is of a minor nature.

Whether pollution can be considered a trespass is a contentious issue. There are some cases suggesting that a trespass must involve an invasion by a "physical mass" rather than invisible pollutants.

Negligence

Negligence is the basis of many environmental lawsuits. There are several elements to negligence that must be proven by the plaintiff:

- *Duty of care.* The defendant had an obligation to the plaintiff to act reasonably.
- *Standard of care.* The defendant did not act reasonably in the circumstances.
- *Causation.* The plaintiff would not have suffered harm if not for the defendant's conduct.
- *Forseeability.* The harm suffered by the plaintiff was a foreseeable consequence of the defendant's breach of the standard of care.

Negligence occurs when someone acts less than reasonably, and as a result causes harm to someone to whom a duty of care is owed. The harm suffered by a plaintiff must be foreseeable—for example, a bleach manufacturer would not be held liable if a purchaser used the bleach to poison a neighbour's tree. This result is too remote from the actions of the manufacturer.

Generally, everyone has a **duty of care**—the legal obligation to act reasonably—toward others. For example, if you are driving your neighbour to an environmental convention, you owe a duty of care to your neighbour to drive in a reasonable manner. You also owe a duty of care to other drivers, bicyclists, and pedestrians.

What is a reasonable manner? The standard of care owed to others varies depending on the circumstances. For example, a taxi driver, who solicits a fee for the service, may be held to a higher **standard of care** than a neighbour, who is doing you a favour. Similarly, the standard of care required with respect to storing chemicals may be lower for a homeowner than for a major industrial facility.

Causation must also be demonstrated to prove negligence, and this is not always obvious. For example, could the fact that your neighbour was not wearing a seatbelt have been the cause of her injuries? The rule of causation is usually expressed as follows: causation is established when the harm suffered by the plaintiff would not have occurred "but for" the defendant's action. Causation must be established on a balance of probabilities—that is, the defendant's activities probably caused the harm complained of by the plaintiff.

Establishing that the injury or harm complained of was the direct result of the actions of the defendant is one of the most formidable challenges in environmental litigation. Consider the example of a population living near a lead smelter, where the residents suffer from a higher rate of cancer than the general population. It is exceedingly difficult to prove that a particular case of cancer would not have occurred "but for" the existence of the smelter.

In *Berendsen v. Ontario*, a farming family was successful in proving causation, as well as the other elements of negligence, in its lawsuit against a provincial government that refused to take responsibility for road waste dumped on the farm. In the mid-1960s, the Ontario Ministry of Transportation undertook roadwork near a small town in Ontario. The ministry's contractor buried truckloads of the road surface waste of concrete and asphalt beside a watercourse on a nearby farm. A family bought the farm and ran a dairy operation close to the place where the wastes were buried. Soon after they started the farming operation, the family noticed that their cattle and other farm animals were refusing to drink water from a creek near the barn. As a result, the cattle became dehydrated and ill, which resulted in poor milk production. Some of the cattle, as well as chickens and rabbits, died prematurely. Some family members also experienced health problems. Eventually the family moved to another farm. Since the family was unable to sell the property with its suspected environmental problems, the land remained vacant and abandoned.

The family brought a lawsuit against the Province of Ontario, claiming that the buried road waste contributed to the damages that occurred. They sued the province in negligence for burying potentially toxic wastes near a source of water and failing to remediate the situation once the problem became known.

The province denied all liability. It challenged several of the elements of negligence, and made the following claims:

- It owed no duty of care to the family and it was not liable for the acts of an independent contractor.
- It did not breach the standard of care because the burial of waste material on rural property was a common practice in the 1960s.
- There was no causal connection between the road waste and the water contamination. The health problems experienced by the cattle were the result of poor farm management.
- It was not foreseeable that burying the waste would cause harm to cattle and humans.

The court ruled in favour of the plaintiffs, and found that they had established all the elements of negligence on a balance of probabilities:

- The defendant did owe a duty of care to the plaintiff. There was a clear relationship of proximity between the defendant that deposited the waste materials, and the occupiers of the land on which the waste was deposited.
- Policy considerations favoured upholding a high standard of care. The public obviously derived a benefit from the defendant's road maintenance and repair activities, and these activities included the incidental disposal of waste materials. The defendant breached the standard of care both by depositing and burying the harmful waste close to a natural watercourse and dairy farm well and residence, and by conducting an inadequate investigation and remediation of the harmful environmental effects of the buried waste.
- The deposit of the roadside waste was the cause of the harm suffered by the plaintiffs. The expert evidence presented at trial was reviewed extensively in the court's decision. The court noted that not only was there evidence of a substantial connection between the buried materials and the contamination of the well water, but the evidence also persuasively eliminated other potential causes of contamination. For example, the dioxin detected in the water would not have emanated from other sources on the farm, such as debris from fires or residue from chemical storage.
- The harm was foreseeable. The defendant knew or ought to have known that asphalt was a petroleum-based product containing potentially harmful residue. The defendant would have known that care and common sense had to be exercised both in the placement of the waste on private lands and in its duty to investigate and eliminate the continuing harmful effects in the 1980s, when it was called on to remedy the situation.

In the end, the court held the defendant liable for business loss, loss of farm property value, economic loss, and other damages totalling over $1.7 million.

Statutory Causes of Action

The causes of action mentioned above, such as nuisance, trespass, and negligence, are grounded in common law—that is, legal principles that have evolved through case law. In some cases, legislatures create new causes of action to give people the specific right to commence a lawsuit if certain conditions are met. For example, the *Canadian Environmental Protection Act, 1999* and the Ontario *Environmental Bill of Rights, 1993* both create statutory causes of action. The causes of action enacted by these statutes are quite narrow and limited in scope. They are also essentially the same and can be summarized as follows:

- any person may bring an action if someone has violated an identified environmental law;
- before bringing an action, litigants must request an investigation in accordance with the procedures outlined in the statute;
- defendants will not be found liable if they can prove due diligence—that is, that they took reasonable care to prevent the incident;
- no damages are available; and
- remedies may be ordered to address any harm done.

Because of the limited scope of these causes of action, the federal and the provincial provisions have rarely been used to date.

Damages and Remedies

Generally speaking, court cases are divided into two parts: liability and remedy. Liability involves proof of the elements of the cause of action, and **remedy** relates to compensation. What form of remedy is appropriate? If a remedy involves monetary compensation, how much money is adequate?

Most often, plaintiffs want monetary compensation and therefore must attach a monetary value to the harm they have suffered. In other circumstances, plaintiffs may simply want a court to order a defendant to do or to refrain from doing something.

Monetary Damages

Establishing the appropriate amount of monetary damages to compensate a plaintiff is often very challenging. The plaintiff may need to bring evidence through expert witnesses and documentation to prove the amount of damages.

Imagine, for example, that a company is found liable for spilling a toxic chemical and contaminating the groundwater under your property. However, if your water source is the municipal system, and you do not use the groundwater, what are your damages? You may argue that the value of your property has suffered depreciation, although a new buyer may neither notice nor care about the state of the groundwater. In the case, you will have to establish that in fact the groundwater contamination did affect the value of your property.

Now imagine the situation of a farmer who is complaining about dust and odour from a nearby landfill. However, the nuisance affects neither the farmer's ability to farm nor the farmer's enjoyment of his land. The farmer's monetary damages may be very small even though a nuisance has been established.

Generally speaking, there are three categories of damages: special damages, general damages, and punitive damages.

- **Special damages** are damages directly caused by the defendant's behaviour, and are easily and objectively quantifiable. Examples include costs of repair, remedial measures, and cleanup; costs of monitoring and testing water; and medical bills. They are out-of-pocket expenses incurred by the plaintiff.
- **General damages** are subjective and not as easily quantified. They include loss of enjoyment; pain and suffering; future effects, such as future monitoring and testing of water; depreciation of land value; and loss of business. Expert witnesses are often required to make a convincing case regarding the appropriate amount of general damages. When determining the size of damages awards, courts consider the size of awards in similar cases.
- **Punitive damages** go beyond the usual purpose of damages—that is, putting the plaintiff back into the position she was in before the event. Instead, they focus on punishing the defendant and setting an example. Punitive damages are rarely awarded because they are warranted only when a defendant acts in a particularly malicious, grossly reckless, or violent manner, and when the defendant has not been punished by other means, such as by fines.

Equitable Relief

Equitable relief may be available at the discretion of a court when monetary compensation is inadequate or inappropriate. For example, a plaintiff who is suffering from a nuisance caused by his neighbour may be more interested in having the nuisance stop than in receiving monetary compensation.

An **injunction** is a court order that requires a defendant either to do something (a mandatory injunction) or to refrain from doing something (a prohibitory injunction). For example, a mandatory injunction may be employed to order a polluter to install a pollution control system, and a prohibitory injunction may be employed to order a polluter to stop its environmentally harmful activities.

Injunctions are ordered at the discretion of the court and are not granted routinely. One of the barriers encountered by plaintiffs who apply for injunctions is the possibility that courts may require them to provide security for costs. In the event that the defendant is successful at trial, the costs arising from the imposition of the injunction will be paid to the defendant out of the amount that the plaintiff has posted as security.

Another form of equitable relief is a declaration. A **declaration** is simply a finding of a court. For example, a court may make a declaration that a defendant has not complied with an environmental assessment process or has not provided proper monitoring data. Although in and of itself a declaration may not provide relief to a plaintiff, it may assist in further private or public action.

Costs

In Canada the costs of a lawsuit are awarded to the winning party. This means that the losing party must pay the costs of the winner. The purpose of this rule is to protect defendants against frivolous lawsuits, and to encourage parties to settle their differences before expending court resources. However, a costs award usually represents only a portion of the total costs incurred. Furthermore, a court has the discretion not to award costs—for instance, in a test case or a case that raises a matter of general public interest. Obviously many environmental groups attempt to bring their cases within these exemptions. However, the matter always remains within the discretion of the court.

Mandatory Mediation

Mediation and pretrial negotiations are almost always attempted for the purpose of resolving a matter before it is necessary to incur the expense and expend the energy involved in a lengthy trial. By far the majority of cases are settled before trial begins.

In some jurisdictions, mediation and pretrial negotiations are mandatory. Trained mediators attempt to find common ground among the parties and resolve the dispute. Only if this process is exhausted without a successful resolution may the matter proceed to trial.

Court Action as an Environmental Protection Tool

Much is written about the adequacy and effectiveness of courts in resolving matters in society. Many of the challenges that arise in any court action are compounded in environmental matters. Environmental harm and damage to public health may not be obvious immediately; years may elapse between the offending conduct and the resultant impacts. For example, low levels of pollutants in drinking water may not produce adverse results that are recognized by consumers until years after consumption of the water began.

Further, there is the age-old problem of attempting to establish the causal link between the environmentally damaging conduct and the resultant harm. Establishing such a link can be a daunting task since the impact on the environment can be compounded by other factors. There is also the issue of quantifying damages. The legal system has not yet evolved to recognize or measure the inherent value of nature: pristine water, natural heritage features, or old-growth forests. Instead, it has concentrated on nature's market value.

Therefore, the court system may simply not be equipped in many circumstances to respond to environmental protection challenges. Indeed, there are many individuals and groups from across Canada that can well describe their frustration with the process. Nevertheless, it would be unwise to give up. Over the years, many courts have slowly become sensitized to the environmental plight. The Supreme Court of Canada, for example, has described the environment as "one of the major challenges of our times" and a "fundamental value" of Canadians.

Despite the growing sensitivity of courts, however, legal rules concerning standing, causation, and costs may require further changes to better respond to the challenges of environmental protection litigation.

CHAPTER 14

Using Administrative Decision-Making Processes to Protect the Environment

Introduction

Many years ago, a story appeared in a Vancouver newspaper by a reporter who attended a public hearing of the British Columbia Pollution Control Board (the environmental regulatory tribunal of the day). The hearing concerned an application by a mining company for an approval to discharge mine waste into a northern Vancouver Island coastal inlet. The reporter described how company experts explained and were questioned about scientific and technical issues, while nobody else in the community hall "understood a thing." Environmental groups, whose members included knowledgeable specialists, had not been granted standing to participate in the hearing. These specialists were reduced to whispering questions to several citizens who had been permitted to participate, and who tried to put the specialists' questions to the company's experts. It was bad theatre and a very ineffective public hearing. Many participants in various kinds of public hearings in different parts of Canada can relate to this frustrating procedure.

On the other hand, citizen participants have played major roles in hearings and their contributions have influenced results. The evidence and arguments of environmental groups and First Nations participants in the Mackenzie Valley Pipeline Inquiry in the 1970s were reflected in Commissioner Thomas Berger's report. Berger ultimately recommended protection for the caribou on the Yukon north slope and delay of the proposed northern pipelines to permit Aboriginal land claim negotiations to continue toward resolution.

Through environmental assessment public review processes, citizen participants have contributed to more complete and better balanced environmental assessments. For example, environmental groups have promoted the idea of assessment of cumulative effects in a number of panel hearings under the *Canadian Environmental Assessment Act*. Though results are mixed, these interventions have assisted developments in the scope of cumulative-effects assessment under the Act. In Alberta citizens have been active participants in hearings on well licence applications that were denied by the Energy and Utilities Board. Noteworthy cases include applications by Amoco Canada Ltd. (decision September 6, 1994) and Polaris Resources Ltd. (decision December 16, 2003). The board noted the potential environmental impacts in the sensitive montane region of the Rocky Mountain eastern slopes and the corporation's failure to address community concerns, including cumulative environmental effects.

Much environmental law, including the Amoco and Polaris cases, involves administrative decision making. It is therefore worthwhile to acquire a basic understanding of the principles and practices of administrative law. This chapter explains different types of administrative decisions, with particular attention on decision making by tribunals. It also introduces the environmental public hearing processes and the common law concept of procedural fairness with its attendant safeguards. The importance of examining the particular statute that governs each administrative decision-maker is emphasized, and the role of the courts in overseeing administrative decision making is explored.

Types of Administrative Decision Making

Administrative decisions are decisions made pursuant to a statute, which sets out the requisite decision-making process. They differ from judicial decisions, which are made by courts. There are two basic types of administrative decisions:

1. decisions made by a government employee or Cabinet minister; and

2. decisions involving a public hearing, where both sides make submissions before an impartial decision-maker called a tribunal or a board.

Environmental statutes often provide for administrative decisions. For example, initial decisions about whether or not to approve projects are usually delegated to environment ministries or sometimes to ministers, who make decisions in a perfunctory manner on the basis of the advice of ministry personnel. Applicants for approvals are usually required to inform and engage interested members of the public and provide their feedback to the decision-maker; however, public hearings are not commonly held at this stage. There is no formal process beyond requirements that applicants provide specific information and that decision-makers exercise procedural fairness by receiving and considering the information submitted, and by providing reasons to affected persons. There is no general legal obligation to allow public participation through hearings.

The procedure at a public hearing is similar to the procedure in a court, and is often called quasi-judicial. Anyone who walks into a hearing by some environmental tribunals—and most energy and natural resource tribunals, which have the statutory power to grant approvals for natural resource and energy developments—will think she is in a courtroom. Tribunal members sit at the front on a raised dias, and participants rise when members of the tribunal enter and exit the hearing room. Lawyers formally examine and cross-examine witnesses, make objections, and present arguments. Nevertheless, the process is less formal than the process of a court, with relaxed rules of procedure and evidence. Non-governmental organizations and members of the public are generally permitted to participate. Typically, decisions are based on statutory powers to decide whether proposed developments are in the public interest.

Other tribunals are less formal. Hearings are conducted in the manner of a meeting or seminar with an agenda, interactive proceedings, and sometimes a round-table format. Often the degree of formality is determined by statutory requirements. Some tribunals, such as environmental appeal boards, are required to hold oral hearings in accordance with the legal dictates of procedural fairness (see below). Others, such as assessment panels under the *Canadian Environmental Assessment Act*, are required by their statutes to conduct their proceedings informally.

Tribunal Procedures

The law governing the procedures of administrative tribunals attempts to balance two competing interests: efficiency and fairness. An informal process is much quicker and less expensive than a formal court process, and it allows for the admission of a broader range of evidence from a wider scope of sources. However, too much informality may compromise fairness and the impartiality of the decision-maker by not, as a formal legal requirement, providing affected citizens with notice, information, and an opportunity to respond.

Natural Justice and Procedural Fairness

The fundamental procedural concept is **natural justice** or, as it has become more commonly known in the last two decades, **procedural fairness**. This common law concept was developed by the English courts in the early 18th century. Elements of procedural fairness have since been codified in many statutes; however, unless a statute is clear and explicit in changing or excluding one of the common law rights of procedural fairness, the common law rights continue to apply and fill any gaps. For example, a statute may state that "personal written notice is not required" for a particular decision; however, the common law may still require that some form of notice—through advertising, for example—be given to persons affected by the decision.

There are three main elements of procedural fairness that a tribunal must employ:

1. reasonable notice of a proposed decision;

2. a fair opportunity to be heard, orally or in writing; and

3. an impartial and independent decision-maker.

Whether specific formal procedural rights—such as cross-examination, questioning of witnesses, or representation by legal counsel—apply depends on the circumstances, including the mandate of the empowering statute and the procedure that is followed. For example, there may be a right to cross-examine when a formal quasi-judicial procedure is used, but no such right when a hearing assumes an informal meeting-type format.

Evidence

Evidence refers to facts, objects, and (in some circumstances) opinions that are presented to a decision-maker for the purposes of reaching a decision. To be admissible, evidence must be relevant to the subject of the decision, and it must be reasonably reliable.

Tribunals do not usually observe the stringent rules of evidence that apply in courts. This means that tribunals often receive **hearsay** evidence (statements about what a witness heard from another person) and opinions, even though a witness may not be formally qualified as an expert on the subject about which he expresses the opinion. Tribunals are generally less concerned than courts about assessing the relevance of evidence when deciding whether it is admissible. Often tribunals prefer to listen to the evidence and assess its relevance later when they decide how much weight, if any, to give to it.

Tribunals may also have the coercive powers to summon witnesses and compel production of evidence. These powers may be derived either from the statute governing a particular tribunal or from the general powers of commissions of inquiry under public inquiries statutes. To compel the appearance of witnesses and documents, tribunals may issue subpoenas, usually on the application of a party to the proceeding.

Record

The **record** of proceedings includes all evidence and arguments presented at a hearing. Decisions are usually required to be based on the record, and not on extraneous information. For example, members of the tribunal may not base decisions on their own independent research, unless they invite input and response from hearing participants by requesting written comments or reopening the oral hearing. However, tribunals may take **official notice** of obvious and well-accepted facts—such as the fact that the Don River flows into Lake Ontario—without requiring formal proof.

The importance of a record is less obvious in proceedings such as **public inquiries**—that is, investigative proceedings that result in recommendations to government. Recommendations may be based on the record of any hearings that such an inquiry decides to hold or on the results of its own investigations. This broad-ranging mandate makes sense because public inquiries result merely in recommendations to government, rather than in enforceable decisions.

Parties

In the context of administrative law, a party is a person or organization that is recognized by a tribunal as a participant in a decision-making process. Obtaining party status may depend on meeting a statutory test, such as being "directly affected" by a decision. If there is no statutory test for obtaining party status, tribunals may create their own tests or categories, provided that the principles of procedural fairness are respected. They may, for example, invite persons to decide whether they want to be full parties—that is, participants who are present throughout the hearing, submit evidence and arguments, and question witnesses—or whether they merely want to make a presentation or file a written submission.

Decision and Reasons

Tribunals must, as their statutes require, reach explicit final decisions. In making their decisions, they must give due consideration to written and oral evidence that the parties have provided. They must also issue written reasons for their decision, at least if directly requested to do so by persons significantly affected by it. This requirement is particularly important if affected persons need reasons to exercise their right to appeal the decision.

Costs

Funding for hearing participation by members of the public and non-governmental organizations is often essential to ensure full and effective involvement. Like courts, some tribunals have the authority to force unsuccessful parties to pay the **costs** of successful parties.

Other tribunals, such as the National Energy Board, have no power to award costs. Still other tribunals, such as Alberta's Energy Resources Conservation Board, have the power to award participation costs, win or lose, to affected landowners. The Ontario Energy Board can award participant costs, and can also assess costs against intervenors whose intervention is, in the board's opinion, "frivolous or vexatious." It is necessary to examine the empowering statutes to determine the extent of the cost-awarding powers of particular tribunals.

Environmental tribunals, such as environmental appeal boards, often have powers to award costs after a hearing depending on the nature of the proceeding. In assessing costs requests, the tribunal's primary criterion is whether the costs applicant has made a substantial contribution to the appeal and focused on the important issues that needed to be addressed.

Participant funding, on the other hand, is funding made in advance of a hearing to assist parties in the participation of the hearing process and is not usually tied to the outcome of an appeal. Participant funding is available in some types of proceedings. In assessing funding requests, tribunals have tended to consider criteria such as:

- whether a funding applicant is in a position to make a substantial contribution to the appeal;
- whether the funding sought is directly related to the specific issues in the appeal or to broader environmental issues; and
- whether the applicant is in financial need.

The application of these criteria has often resulted in the drastic reduction of costs claims, particularly the costs of legal and other professional assistance. Sometimes members of the public and non-governmental organizations have, with the encouragement of a tribunal, made agreements directly with industry applicants for participant funding. A limited-budget participant funding program, based on a federal government fund, has been developed for environmental assessment processes under the *Canadian Environmental Assessment Act.*

Appeals

There is no automatic right to appeal an administrative decision, whether it is made by a government official or results from a formal hearing. A right of appeal must be provided by statute, and if there is no statutory right to appeal, there may be no appeal.

Where a statute does provide a right of appeal, it sets out the particulars of that right: what body hears the appeal, what issues are to be considered by the appellate decision-maker, and what preconditions must be met before the appeal is heard. Sometimes, particularly in appeals to courts, it is necessary to obtain permission, or leave, to appeal before presenting a case. The court hears arguments and decides whether there is a serious arguable point with a reasonable prospect of success.

There are two possible forums for appeals:

1. appeals to another administrative tribunal, such as an environmental appeal board established by a provincial government; and

2. appeals to a court.

Statutes dictate whether it is necessary to appeal an administrative decision to a court or an appellate tribunal.

There are two types of appeal processes:

1. *Appeals de novo.* These appeals are new hearings in which a court or appeals tribunal rehears and reconsiders everything that was before the original decision-maker, as well as any fresh evidence or new arguments.

2. *Appeals on questions of law and jurisdiction.* These appeals are limited to legal arguments; no new evidence is submitted.

Again, the scope of the appeal depends on the wording of the applicable statutory appeal provision.

Environmental Appeal Boards

There are a number of specialized tribunals established under provincial environmental legislation to hear appeals from administrative decisions, including the following:

- Alberta's Environmental Appeals Board;
- British Columbia's Environmental Appeal Board; and
- Ontario's Environmental Review Tribunal.

These appeal boards are required to hold hearings *de novo*.

Appeals may sometimes consist of written submissions only. They may include reconsideration of decisions to grant or deny approvals or to make enforcement orders. Administrative decisions suspending or revoking approvals, requiring clean-up or remediation, or imposing monetary penalties are typical subjects of appeal.

Operators against whom orders have been made and individuals who meet statutory standing requirements have a right to appeal. The test for standing varies from jurisdiction to jurisdiction. For example, in Alberta a person has standing to appeal when he is "directly affected" (provided that he files a notice of objection to the original decision). In British Columbia a "person aggrieved" has standing to appeal. And in Ontario, standing to initiate an appeal is granted to a "person to whom an order was directed." As well, others who have an interest in an approval can seek leave to appeal, and, if successful, can file an appeal.

Environmental appeal boards have significant advantages over courts. Their members have a range of environmental expertise. Their procedures are less formal than those of courts, and usually include well-developed mediation processes that make it possible for appellants to negotiate satisfactory results without resorting to hearings and receiving board decisions. Boards review negotiated settlements, and approve them as board decisions. Even if appeals do go to hearings, the process is likely to be faster and less costly than court proceedings.

However, there is a disadvantage to environmental appeal board appeals. Board decisions may, as in Alberta, be subject to approval by environment ministers, which gives these decisions a political dimension. Although ministers do not often reverse or modify board decisions, they nevertheless have the power to do so. Parties do not have the right to make submissions to the minister, but reasons for any ministerial decision must be given.

In *Fenske v. Alberta (Minister of the Environment)*, the Alberta Environmental Appeals Board allowed an appeal by local residents challenging an Alberta Environment decision to approve the massive expansion of a rural landfill. The board sent the matter back to the department for a proper environmental assessment, with additional information to be submitted by the developer. However, the minister stepped in and granted the approval, with conditions requiring additional studies and information. A lower court overturned the minister's decision on the ground of procedural fairness, but the Alberta Court of Appeal upheld it. The Court of Appeal held that the decision was neither outside the minister's jurisdiction nor procedurally unfair, even though the minister failed to hear from the residents.

While it is possible to challenge board decisions in courts, it is not easy. As the section below demonstrates, grounds for judicial review are narrow. Courts give great weight to the expertise of environmental appeal boards and to ministerial expertise, which derives from departmental staff experts. Generally, courts defer considerably to environmental decision-makers. In addition, courts usually require that all internal appeals be exhausted before they accept an application for judicial review.

Judicial Review

Even if there is no statutory right to appeal, anyone with standing may challenge an environmental decision in a judicial review application. Judicial review is neither an appeal based on a decision-maker's error of law nor a rehearing of the facts of the case. There are two possible grounds for judicial review; both are based on errors allegedly made by an administrative decision-maker. On an application for judicial review, courts assess the merits of a decision and the process used to reach a decision:

1. *Reviewing the merits of a decision.* Courts look at whether the decision-maker acted outside its statutory jurisdiction or made any other error of law. In some cases, where a great deal of deference is not owed to the decision-maker, courts also look into whether any factual errors were made.

2. *Reviewing the fairness of the decision-making process.* Courts look at whether the decision-maker used improper procedures, lacked impartiality, or committed any other error that rendered the proceeding unfair.

Reviewing the merits of a decision is the most complicated category of judicial review. It involves application of one of two standards of review: correctness or reasonableness; both are described below. Generally, it is not the role of a court to second-guess administrative decision-makers.

Procedural fairness is a commonly used ground for judicial review. In an application for judicial review that is based on an allegation that a decision-maker failed to exercise procedural fairness, the process by which the tribunal reached its decision is assessed by a court.

Reviewing the Merits of a Decision and Standard of Review

Courts have developed sometimes complex and confusing theory and methodology for deciding to what extent they will review the decisions of regulatory tribunals and officials. Where the application for judicial review is based on an allegation that there was an error in the merits of a decision, the court must first determine the **standard of review**—that is, the scope of the review. The court asks itself how much deference it must give to the administrative decision-maker. Fortunately, this process was recently simplified by the Supreme Court of Canada in *Dunsmuir v. New Brunswick*. In this case, the court reduced the standards of review from three to two:

1. *Correctness.* Correctness is a broad scope of review where the reviewing court does not show deference to the decision-maker's reasoning process. Rather, it substitutes its own analysis of the issues and legal principles, and makes its own decision.

2. *Reasonableness.* Reasonableness is a narrower scope of review that focuses on the reasonableness of the decision-making process. A court does not engage in its own assessment and reasoning; rather, it reviews the decision-maker's reasoning to evaluate the analytic method, logic, and consistency. It then determines whether the decision falls within a range of reasonable outcomes, having regard to the facts and the law. In other words, the court defers to a decision it does not agree with, provided that the decision is not unreasonable.

To determine which standard of review applies in a particular case, courts look to the governing statute and any relevant cases. The factors that the court considers when determining the standard of review are the following:

- *Privative clause.* A **privative clause** is a provision that is sometimes included in a governing statute that specifically limits judicial review of administrative decisions made under that statute.
- *Expertise of decision-maker.* Expertise does not refer to the academic achievements or other formal qualifications of tribunal members; rather, it refers to the statutory responsibilities of tribunal members and the experience and "field sensitivity" that they develop.
- *Policy versus technical issue.* Looking at the statutory scheme and the particular provision under which the decision-maker acted, a court asks itself whether the decision is technical or based on policy. Administrative decision-makers, rather than courts, should make policy decisions.
- *Law versus fact.* Is the issue a matter of law—for example, how a common law principle should be applied or how an ambiguous statutory provision should be interpreted? Alternatively, does the matter involve finding and assessing facts—for example, who put what contaminant in the water, when, and how? The courts are the experts on questions of law, while environmental regulators, who are closer to what happened and have heard directly from the parties, are better placed to decide factual questions.

The court then weighs these factors and decides whether the standard of review should be correctness or reasonableness, as illustrated in table 14.1.

Table 14.1   Two Standards of Review

Least deference ⟵ ⟶ Greatest deference	
Correctness	Reasonableness
The court uses legal analysis to determine whether the administrative decision is legally correct. If the court concludes that the decision was not correct, it sets the decision aside.	The court determines whether the decision was irrational or clearly wrong. Only if the court concludes that the decision was not reasonable will it set the decision aside.

Environmental decisions made by tribunals usually require more deference than the correctness test allows. This is the case because the decision-makers are likely to have experience; the issues are often technical and scientific; there are privative clauses in many environmental statutes, such as the Alberta *Environmental Protection and Enhancement Act*; and statutory powers are often discretionary—broad and open-ended so there is no single legally correct interpretation.

On judicial review, a court may find that an environmental decision-maker made a reviewable error on grounds such as:

- It acted outside its statutory powers.
- It failed to consider relevant matters or considered irrelevant matters.
- It acted for an improper purpose by, for example, using a statutory power to establish restricted development areas for "conservation purposes" to approve a corridor for transportation and utility purposes.
- It unlawfully delegated statutory powers to another person or authority.

Generally courts are unlikely to set aside environmental decisions unless the environmental decision-maker misinterpreted a statute or legal principle, or unless a discretionary decision strikes a reasonable person who knows the facts and circumstances as seriously flawed.

Procedural Fairness

Judicial review of an administrative decision may also be sought by a party who asserts that the hearing procedure was unfair. In this case, the court's role involves an examination of the hearing procedure, and an assessment of its fairness. Courts may also review and set aside environmental decisions as procedurally unfair because affected persons were not given

- reasonable notice of a proposed decision,
- a fair opportunity to be heard, and
- a reasonably impartial and independent decision-maker.

In hearing such an application for judicial review, courts place emphasis on the adverse effects suffered by an affected person as a result of the denial of fairness.

Here there is no analysis of the appropriate standard of review. Decisions must be procedurally correct, and courts show little deference to the administrative decision-maker. However, the relative statutory formality of the procedure and the decision-maker's choice of specific procedures are taken into account. The courts are the experts on procedural fairness.

Many environmental decisions have been set aside on procedural grounds. When this happens, the case is usually reheard by a tribunal composed of different members.

Public Inquiries

Public pressure may cause a government to establish a public inquiry into an environmentally sensitive matter. However, public inquiries are rare. They occur only in the case of significant proposed developments that catch the attention both of governments and of the public. A famous example was the Berger inquiry of the early 1970s, which held hearings on proposals to build major natural gas pipelines from the Arctic.

Public inquiries are more commonly used to investigate and provide recommendations to government when environmental problems emerge or disasters, such as the Walkerton water system tragedy, occur. Public inquiries operate independently of governments and usually hold public hearings that provide a public forum for discussion about the environmental problems under investigation. The creation of public inquiries is entirely a matter of government discretion.

CHAPTER 15

Environmental Bill of Rights and Access to Information

Introduction

This chapter examines notable legislation that provides rights to members of the public, empowering them and improving the accountability of governments. In particular, Ontario's *Environmental Bill of Rights, 1993* and access to information legislation in various jurisdictions are considered.

Ontario's Environmental Bill of Rights, 1993

By the early 1970s, a number of new non-governmental groups had formed across Canada to respond to the lack of public involvement in environmental decision making. Groups that spearheaded the movement toward more transparency and accountability in environmental decision making included the following:

- the Canadian Environmental Law Association,
- Pollution Probe,
- the West Coast Environmental Law Association, and
- the Environmental Law Centre (Alberta) Society.

Various proposals were published for new and bold initiatives to increase public participation. Perhaps one of the best-known proposals was for an environmental bill of rights. The environmental bill of rights movement called for legislation reform that included the following:

- access to information legislation;
- whistleblower legislation;
- the right to notice and to comment on new environmental approvals, policies, laws, and environmental impact assessments; and
- the right to sue when there are violations of environmental requirements.

At the time, these were wide-ranging and progressive reforms—a wish list for environmentalists, community leaders, and others who felt excluded from environmental decision making.

Even after two decades of effort, neither the provinces nor the federal government enacted an environmental bill of rights. In 1984 the federal minister of the environment, Charles Caccia, supported the enactment of an environmental bill of rights for Canada. However, he was unable to gain adequate political support before the 1984 election and his aspiration was not translated into concrete action. In Ontario there were at least six private members' bills put forth by opposition parties between the late 1970s and the late 1980s. Although private members' bills are rarely enacted, they do serve to create an atmosphere for discussion and debate.

By the early 1990s, no environmental bill of rights had yet been passed by a provincial or federal government, but two territorial governments (the Yukon and the Northwest Territories) had enacted environmental-bill-of-rights laws. As well, numerous provinces had made progress in responding incrementally to some of the proposals. Many provinces enacted laws or adopted policies throughout the mid-1970s, 1980s, and early 1990s to incrementally provide either limited and specific environmental rights or broader public rights. Consider the following examples in Ontario:

- in 1983, environmental laws were enacted to create whistleblower legislation to protect workers who exposed the environmental violations of their employers;
- access to information legislation was enacted in 1987; and
- a class action statute was passed in 1992.

Many other provinces also made incremental reforms on a variety of issues. By the early 1990s, most jurisdictions had some sort of environmental assessment regime in place.

In 1990 the New Democratic Party formed the government in Ontario after campaigning for environmental rights. Shortly following the election, Ruth Grier was appointed environment minister in 1990. In the spring of 1991, she appointed an Environmental Bill of Rights Task Force that was composed of environmentalists, industry, and government to draft a new rights bill. The bill was introduced into law in February 1994.

Purposes

The *Environmental Bill of Rights, 1993* (EBR) was enacted to fulfill the following purposes:

- protect, conserve, and (where reasonable) restore the integrity of the environment;
- provide sustainability of the environment;
- protect the right to a healthful environment;
- prevent, reduce, and eliminate the use, generation, and release of pollutants that pose an unreasonable threat to the integrity of the environment;
- protect and conserve biological, ecological, and genetic diversity;
- protect and conserve natural resources, including plant life, animal life, and ecological systems;
- encourage the wise management of our natural resources; and
- identify, protect, and conserve ecologically sensitive areas and processes.

To further these purposes, the Ontario EBR can best be viewed as a menu of rights given to the public. Some of these rights are focused on enhancing the ability of the individual to protect the environment and to make the government more accountable for its actions.

Public Participation Rights

The EBR provides a number of rights for the public to participate in environmental decision making. They include the right to notice and comment, to request a review of an existing law or instrument, to request leave to appeal an approval, to request an investigation, and to sue for harm to a natural resource. The EBR also removes a traditional barrier to nuisance lawsuits and provides protection for employees who report environmental violations of their employer.

Right to Notice and Comment

One of the key rights given in the EBR is the right of the public to receive notice of environmentally significant proposals for legislation, regulations, instruments, and policies. The term **instruments**, in this context, refers to certificates of approval (for a facility's air emissions, waste management sites, and sewage works, for example); permits (for taking water from the ground for bottled water, for example); and licences (for mineral extraction, for example).

The public is notified through the posting of information on an online registry maintained by the Ministry of the Environment. The registry has been substantially revised a number of times to keep pace with new technology, and its use continues to grow. The emergence of the registry as a vehicle for public notification about new proposals has contributed to greater participation in the government's environmental decision making, thereby contributing to what is called **e-democracy**. According to a 2006 case study by Allan Gunn and Jim Lewis, there are approximately 10,000 site visitors per month with over 3,400 postings per year, over 3,100 of which are postings for proposals and decisions.

There is a minimum 30-day notice and comment period, and the ministry must take into account comments submitted. As required by the EBR, the ministry posts the final decision on the registry and summarizes the comments made. It also includes responses that explain how the comments were or were not addressed in the final decision.

Right to Request Review of Existing Law

The right to request a review gives the public an opportunity to voice concerns about existing laws and instruments. Any two residents of Ontario may file an application for review, requesting that a law, policy, or instrument be reviewed by the appropriate ministry. This right is discretionary—that is to say, the ministry may decide that a review is not appropriate. Nevertheless, there are a number of instances where an application for review has been influential. For example, residents of Hamilton, Ontario sent a request to review ministry approvals for a local incinerator; the provincial government granted the review, at least in part, and then amended the approvals for the incinerator. As a result of the amendments, the city decided that the new requirements were too onerous and decommissioned the incinerator.

According to a 2004 report from the Environmental Commissioner's Office, there were 109 applications for review submitted between 1995 and 2003 and 13 percent of them were accepted for review. By 2008 the acceptance rate had risen to approximately 30 percent.

Right to Request Leave to Appeal an Approval

Before the EBR was enacted, only a person who sought an environmental or natural resource approval was allowed to appeal a decision by the Ministry of the Environment to a tribunal such as the Environmental Review Tribunal (ERT). Now any person who meets all of the following criteria may seek leave to appeal before the ERT:

- the person is a resident of Ontario;
- the person has an interest in the decision—that is, a relationship, history, or involvement with the subject matter of the decision;
- it appears that there is good reason to believe that the decision is unreasonable, having regard to the relevant law and government policies; and
- it appears that the decision could result in significant harm to the environment.

According to a 2004 study by the Environmental Commissioner's Office, there were 96 applications for leave to appeal between 1995 and 2003; 21 percent of the applications resulted in leave to appeal being granted. It is suspected that this percentage is marginally higher now.

Right to Request Investigation

Another right given to the public under the EBR is the right of any two Ontario residents to ask the relevant ministry to investigate the violation of 18 specified environmental or natural resource statutes or certain provisions of those statutes. The process requires the government to consider the request. If it chooses not to investigate, it must provide an explanation. If the request is successful, the ministry then investigates and decides whether or not to prosecute. It is interesting to note that the right to request an investigation was closely mirrored in the 1999 amendments to the federal *Canadian Environmental Protection Act, 1999*.

The Environmental Commissioner's Office reported in 2004 that there were 140 requests for investigation between 1995 and 2003; approximately 36 percent of them resulted in investigations.

Right to Sue for Harm to Natural Resources

In the United States most environmental laws have provisions that allow the public to bring a civil lawsuit to enforce the provisions of the statute. Similarly, the EBR allows any person to sue where a public resource in Ontario is at risk of harm as a result of the contravention of a statute, regulation, or instrument. A precondition of exercising this right of action is that the plaintiff must first request an investigation, as described in the preceding section.

Another challenge for plaintiffs is the availability of the defence of due diligence. If the defendant is able to demonstrate that all reasonable care and precautions were taken to avoid the transgression, it has a valid defence to the claim. No damages award may be granted, although the EBR provides for a broad range of other remedies, including restoration plans. Like the right to request an investigation, the right to sue for harm to natural resources is closely mirrored in the federal *Canadian Environmental Protection Act, 1999*. Probably because of the complexity of the governing provisions, it has rarely been used.

Removing the Public Nuisance Barrier

Historically, the common law prevented private nuisance claims by individuals who suffered the same harm as the harm suffered by the rest of the community. In these cases of public nuisance, only the government could bring a claim, and this restriction raised a significant barrier against environmental nuisance claims. The EBR removed this barrier; now any person who suffers a direct loss is entitled to bring a claim.

Whistleblower Protection

Whistle blowers are people who report information about violations of the law to enforcement agencies or the media. Often they are people with inside information, such as employees of a polluting company, or employees of a government agency that is not properly doing its job.

Whistle blowers are often concerned about reprisals by employers, colleagues, or others who stand to lose when incriminating information is disclosed. Threats by employers of discipline or dismissal may prevent many potential whistle blowers from coming forward. To address these concerns and encourage whistle blowers to disclose important information, some—although not all—environmental protection statutes include provisions to protect whistle blowers. For example, employees who act in compliance with the Ontario *Environmental Protection Act* or the *Canadian Environmental Protection Act, 1999* are protected against unjust dismissal or coercive action by their employers.

Ontario's EBR is more specific. It prohibits employer reprisals—through dismissal, harassment, or intimidation, for example—against employees who have used the rights provided to them under the bill. It protects employees who seek enforcement of environmental statutes, give information to enforcement agencies, or give evidence in environmental proceedings.

Government Accountability

The EBR also seeks to make the government more accountable for its environmental decision making by appointing an environmental commissioner and requiring government ministries to draft a statement of environmental values (SEV).

The Environmental Commissioner

The EBR establishes a watchdog to monitor and report on how the legislation is working. This official, known as the environmental commissioner, is an independent officer who reports directly to the Legislative Assembly of Ontario and is appointed for a five-year term. The commissioner's role is to review the implementation of the EBR to ensure that ministries comply with its requirements and report annually to the legislature, and thus the public. Examples of the issues reported on by the commissioner include the following:

- the exercise of discretion by ministers under the EBR;
- appeal rights under the EBR; and
- the receipt, handling, and disposition of applications for review and applications for investigation under the EBR.

The commissioner's office produces and publishes an annual report online through which its evaluations of the EBR's implementation, and the ministries' compliance, are shared with the general public. The commissioner's office also handles more than 1,300 inquiries per year from the public.

Statements of Environmental Values

An innovation of the EBR is its requirement that designated ministries develop a statement of environmental values. These documents are legally required ministry policies stating how the purposes of the EBR will be applied. They are intended to facilitate the application of the EBR and to integrate its purposes with social, economic, and scientific considerations, when a ministry is making environmentally significant decisions.

The status of the SEV was recently canvassed in *Lafarge Canada Inc. v. Ontario (Environmental Review Tribunal)*. In that case, the tribunal granted leave to appeal to a number of groups and individuals on a number of grounds, including the failure of the Ministry of the Environment to consider the SEV in granting an approval. The court held that the tribunal was reasonable in finding that the SEV was part of government policies developed to guide decisions of that kind.

Access to Information

Access to any information held by others is not automatic. Businesses generally have the right to protect information such as trade secrets, manufacturing processes, customer lists, and financial data. Individuals have privacy rights that protect their personal and health information. Governments are required to protect confidential information in many circumstances.

However, the right to protect information must be weighed against the rights of interested parties to obtain it. Some kinds of information are very difficult to acquire independently, and there are often good reasons why they should be shared.

There are three kinds of access to information rights that are applicable to environmental information:

1. *Notice and disclosure.* In civil and criminal proceedings, the parties have the right to notice and disclosure of the case against them. In civil cases, these procedural rights are available only to persons who meet the relevant legal standing test.

2. *Environmental statutes.* Federal and provincial environmental statutes include general rights of any resident to have access to specified kinds of environmental information. There is usually a procedure for determining whether particular information must be disclosed.

3. *Access to information statutes.* Federal and provincial access to information statutes give general rights of access to all residents, regardless of whether they have a direct personal stake in the issue. Canadian citizens may even have information access rights under the US *Freedom of Information Act.*

Access to information granted to the general public by statutes often involves exceptions under which information need not be disclosed. It is important to keep in mind that these exceptions do not apply to the common law procedural rights of litigants, which are necessary for reasonable notice and a fair opportunity to be heard.

Access to Information Statutes

Under the federal *Access to Information Act*, members of the public may request disclosure of environmental information held by the government and its agencies. Provincial statutes, such as the freedom of information acts of Alberta, British Columbia, and Ontario, are broadly similar to the federal statute.

Difficulties sometimes arise in exercising rights to information. The need to clearly identify the information requested, the difficulties of delay, and the high cost of photocopying may all be problematic for those who seek to exercise their access rights. Most significant, however, are the broad categories of exemptions in the Act.

Exemptions and Exceptions to Exemptions

General exemptions from the government's obligation to disclose under the federal *Access to Information Act* can be sweeping. Section 18 of the Act exempts

- "advice or recommendations" by and for government,
- confidential private business information, and
- information relevant to the economic interests of Canada.

Typical exemptions from disclosure in the provincial statutes include

- advice and recommendations to government (but not facts or statistical information), Cabinet records, and information that may harm law enforcement, intergovernmental relations, or government economic interests;
- unreasonable interference with personal privacy; and
- potential harm to private economic interests.

The exemptions become even more complicated as a result of the exceptions. For example, the public health and safety exclusions do not apply to heritage conservation and endangered or threatened species in the legislation of provinces such as Alberta (under section 28), British Columbia (under section 18), and Ontario (under section 21.1).

The **public interest override** is another important exception to the exemptions. The exemptions may be overridden where it is in the public interest to do so. Examples of cases in which the override may be used include situations where public health, safety, or protection of the environment outweighs potential financial, competitive, or other consequences of disclosure.

The public interest override may permit disclosure of private information, such as that collected by environmental regulators, even if confidentiality is claimed. Under the federal statute, the public interest override does not apply to government information; therefore the government may refuse access. The Ontario *Freedom of Information and Protection of Privacy Act*, on the other hand, provides that access can be refused only in the case of Cabinet documents and law enforcement information where it is in the public interest not to disclose.

Finally, section 17(3) of the British Columbia statute and section 18 of the Ontario statute create an exception to the economic interest exemption for the results of product or environmental testing. Unless the testing is done as a service for someone outside government for a fee or for the purpose of developing methods of testing, the exception applies.

With these categories of exemptions and exceptions to exemptions, it is not hard to imagine the kinds of disclosure disputes that can arise. For example, imagine that a statute contains exemptions from disclosure for "advice or recommendations to government" as well as "economic interests of the province"; it also contains no exception from the exemption for environmental test results. Are the toxicity test data produced by private consultants for a government committee developing environmental standards exempt from disclosure? Would it make any difference if there is a provision indicating that "public interest outweighs likely public harm"?

Information Commissioner

Information seekers who are not successful in obtaining the information they want may make a complaint to the information commissioner. The commissioner may investigate, and under the federal legislation may make non-binding recommendations to departments. This situation differs from the role of commissioners under the Alberta and Ontario statutes, which permit commissioners to make binding rulings.

Information commissioners are called on to interpret exemptions and exceptions to exemptions. Examples of rulings by Alberta's information commissioner include the following:

- A report about the effects of oil and gas activities on the cattle industry, prepared by a consultant for the Alberta Environmental Center (a government agency), was not exempt from disclosure, even though the consulting contract contained a confidentiality clause.
- Information about the operation of a natural gas processing plant was not exempt from disclosure, although it contained only facts and no advice to a public body.

PART VI

Into the Future of Environmental Law

CHAPTER 16

The Evolution of Environmental Law and the Challenges Ahead

The Last 40 Years

We have come a long way since the late 1960s, when the current wave of attention to environmental law began to rise. Back then, the most prominent environmental concerns were, or at least seemed, obvious. Newspaper cartoonists drew pictures of factories belching black smoke, effluent pipes dumping evidently toxic liquids into rivers, fish floating upside down with little Xs where their eyes should have been, piles of litter, and heaps of barrels with skull and crossbones markings. Pollution was something you could see and smell.

Not everyone was prepared to worry about this. A British Columbia Cabinet minister, responding to complaints about the stinking air downwind from pulp and paper mills, famously said, "Pollution is the smell of money, and I love it." However, increasing numbers of people were refusing to tolerate the smell, the ugliness, and the associated threats to health and well-being.

The imposition of new laws was initially considered to be the best means of forcing the perpetrators to clean up their mess. Polluting companies (and municipalities and public utilities) resisted, claiming that the costs of cleanup would be too great, jobs would be lost, and the economy would be ruined. But the emerging environmental organizations countered with claims that the costs of inaction would be even greater: nature would be lost, and environmental contamination would kill us too. Governments wavered, but were slowly pushed to take action.

Especially at first, government action was hesitant, piecemeal, and incomplete. Sometimes and in some places, there were retreats. But overall, the past 40 years have seen a gradual extension and strengthening of environmental law and practice. Few of the old problems have been entirely solved. There are still worrisome air and water discharges, waste management failures, and contaminated lands yet to be cleaned up. Nevertheless, on many of these fronts, there have been important and hard-won achievements.

It is not just that we now rarely see factories belching black smoke or rivers turned bright orange with industrial effluent. Scientific understanding and public awareness are much improved. Most of the old polluting industries now have employees dedicated to environmental responsibility, or at least to avoiding costly environmental liabilities. Pollution control technologies are much more sophisticated. There have been similar gains in the broader field of environmental concern and response: in the management of water, forests, and wastes; the regulation of pesticides and other hazardous chemicals; the planning of land use; and the evaluation of new undertakings.

At the same time, new difficulties have emerged. Two have been particularly important:

1. As we began to pay serious attention to environmental issues, we learned that both problems and solutions were a good deal more complicated than we expected.

2. While dealing (often quite successfully) with particular abuses, the overall situation still became more worrisome. The combined effects of growing populations, increasing consumption, and more invasive technologies put pressures on ecological systems and imperilled human well-being.

On the environmental front, we have been winning battles but losing the war. While there are fewer of the obvious nasty local abuses that the cartoonists found easy to depict, we now recognize many bigger problems that are harder to comprehend, resolve, or even describe in ordinary language:

- ozone layer depletion;
- global climate change;
- biodiversity loss;
- hydrological system disruption;
- zoonoses (transfers of disease from animals to humans);
- an asthma epidemic and increases in other immune system disturbances;

- trace chemical contamination and long lists of known and possible carcinogens, mutagens, and teratogens.

Environmental law today therefore faces challenges that are different from those that inspired the first wave of legislative and enforcement action in the 1960s and 1970s. We have also learned a good deal and changed in important ways since then. We have different understandings, different capabilities, different institutional arrangements and cooperative possibilities, a different global context, and (in some ways at least) different relations between environmental issues and the larger set of factors that affect our prospects for the future.

Effectively, what has happened is a co-evolution of environmental law and the world of challenges and possibilities that surrounds it. This co-evolution can been seen in the main themes of change in environmental law over the past four decades.

Ten Themes of Change

In chapter 6, we identified four phases and five trends associated with the evolution of environmental law in Canada. Looking back over the last 40 years and considering the main areas of law covered in this book, we now can expand the discussion a little. The following 10 interrelated themes do not capture all of the significant changes we have seen over the past four decades. They are meant only to describe the main elements of change, incorporating the most important issues, pressures, expectations, and trajectories of change that we have seen and are still seeing in the development of Canadian environment law. Taken together, they provide a useful foundation for considering where we now stand and how we are moving into the future.

Scale

Environmental law first focused on mainly local pollution from individual smokestacks and discharge pipes. This focus led to the regulatory regimes discussed in chapter 8. It soon became evident, however, that environmental problems were not just local. We would also need to deal with the environmental damages and risks of whole industrial sectors, as described in chapter 9, and areas of planning and management, as described in chapter 11.

Today, while we are still concerned about local threats to human health and ecosystems integrity, more attention is being paid to larger scale issues, as illustrated by the following examples:

- *Regional.* Legislation is now in place to combat urban sprawl and associated problems in the Greater Golden Horseshoe area of southern Ontario, and the major growth areas of southern British Columbia.
- *National.* Federal species at risk legislation has now been enacted in compliance with Canada's commitments under the international Convention on Biological Diversity.
- *Global.* Obligations to cut greenhouse gas emissions have been much debated at the federal level and have spurred important provincial and municipal initiatives.

These larger scale issues are important but challenging. As the scale of issues increases and more governments and other stakeholders are involved, achieving consensus and cooperation becomes more difficult.

Timing

In the early days of environmental law, most initiatives were reactive rather than preventive. The first environmental laws responded to the most obvious and destructive abuses and were designed to force after-the-fact cleanups.

Newer initiatives have increasingly focused on more anticipatory, preventive measures, such as

- requirements for pre-construction certificates of approval,
- environmental assessments, and
- better planning and management regimes.

This trend toward prevention has evolved in part because we have learned from bitter experience that environmental damage is costly and that cleanup and repair, when they are possible at all, tend to be prohibitively expensive.

We are also finding that anticipatory planning gives us more numerous options. For example, instead of building somewhat less noxious landfills, we can plan better integrated waste management systems with waste reduction initiatives, composting and recycling programs, and smaller landfills for the residuals. Earlier interventions have brought opportunities to avoid problems, save money, make more substantial changes, and obtain greater benefits.

Complexity

Many of the old regulatory regimes assumed that the world was a very simple place. They addressed particular contaminants one by one as if they did not interact and as if controlled laboratory studies would tell us all we needed to know about the effects of the various soups of substances we are now breathing and ingesting. They considered impacts in the traditional silos of air, land, and water without accounting for the subtle and interrelated natural pathways for pollution. Often, they also seemed to assume that contaminants and other environmental abuses do not cross political and administrative boundaries and do not require integrated interjurisdictional responses.

Much the same is true of the old approaches to planning and management. Forest management regimes, for example, were typically based on the assumptions that forests existed chiefly to supply us with lumber and pulp fibre, and that other roles and purposes—such as traditional harvesting, ecological services, recreational opportunities, wildlife habitat, and carbon sink provision—could be safely ignored.

While the old thinking still underpins a significant portion of environmental law and practice today, we now know better. The best of the new environmental laws recognize that the most important effects on nature and our health and well-being come from combinations of contaminants, development projects, and planning decisions. They act across the lines of municipal, provincial, and national jurisdiction, through a host of mechanisms from watershed-based planning and landform protection to global environmental agreements. And they recognize that even with the best scientists, and unlimited resources, we will never know all we need to know to make fully competent decisions. The world is too complex for that.

Precaution

A consequence of a greater awareness of complexity and uncertainty is the growing acceptance of precautionary approaches to environmentally significant decisions. As described below, precaution in the face of complexity is most appropriate in cases where the harm that could result from a certain action is severe, or where the risk of the harm occurring is particularly difficult to measure.

1. *Severity of possible harm.* Sometimes we must act to restrict possibly dangerous substances and activities even though we have no certain proof of damage, because of the importance of what is at risk—for example, children's health—and the practical impossibility of getting the necessary proof in a highly complex world.

2. *Unmeasurable risk.* Because we often cannot predict the future effects of some initiatives very accurately, and cannot safely assume that we will be able to clean up or repair unexpected damage, we have good reason to avoid undertakings and options that may threaten things we value greatly. We have good reason also to design our activities in ways that allow us to make adaptive changes, or resort to fallback alternatives, if nasty surprises emerge.

Transparency and Participation

Most of the major advances in Canadian environmental law have been driven by public concern and the efforts of public interest environmental organizations. Governments have merely responded, often with evident reluctance. In this, advances in environmental law share characteristics with initiatives in other areas, such as health programming, urban planning, energy policy, and international development projects. Citizens have become skeptical of government assurances and insistent in demanding access to information, opportunity for involvement, and responsiveness from those in authority.

Some steps forward in these areas have been made through laws of general application—for example, laws that provide public access to government information. Citizen pressure has also ensured that many specifically environmental laws have been designed to make environmental decision making more transparent and participative—for example, environmental bills of rights.

The trend toward more open and accessible decision making is also related to the growing awareness of complexity and uncertainty. In a world of difficult choices about what risks should be accepted or avoided, it is no longer accepted that environmental decisions can or should be left to "the experts."

Specialists can provide scientific and technical information and analysis that is important for environmental decision making. They can present the existing range of policy options and project design alternatives. However, the key issues are about preferences and underlying values. In the more open deliberations that we now have on environmental policy matters, we often see competing teams of highly credentialed scientific and technical experts disagreeing on key issues. This has helped to reveal that while environmental decisions need to be based on good science, they are also exercises in public choice in which members of the public as well as governments, corporate interests, and the relevant experts play an important role.

Globalization

Just as legal provisions for transparency and participation were forcing governments to give up a little power to their own citizens, other pressures were pushing effective authority from the national to the international level. Especially over the past two decades, a mixture of phenomena—trade liberalization and economic globalization, security concerns, global health threats, the transboundary nature of many pollution problems, and the growing awareness of environmental perils at the planetary scale—has led to an increasing emphasis on problems and responses that are beyond the competence of national governments acting alone.

The results include more numerous and more powerful international institutions at work influencing environmental decision-making options or acting on important environmental mandates. Some of these bodies can limit national government actions for environmental protection. For example, the World Trade Organization may block environmental regulations that it sees as barriers to international trade. Others—for example, the bodies assigned to assist implementation of the growing number of international environmental agreements—are crucial facilitators of global environmental action.

Globalization also includes, and has been accelerated by, the rise of new communications media and their powerful effects on the global sharing of information, opinions, and ideas. For example, the increasing influence and effectiveness of environmental organizations and other public interest groups can be linked to their rapidly expanding and remarkably effective use of the Internet to organize international campaigns.

Efficiency

One side of the story of environmental law in Canada is the increasing scale and complexity of problems that it attempts to address, and the more anticipatory and participative processes that it applies. The other side, not surprisingly, is deepening concern about how to manage and pay for all this.

While in most areas environmental law is now much more sophisticated and ambitious than it once was, it is still inadequate to address the mounting problems. Greenhouse gas emissions are growing. Fisheries are in trouble. Agricultural land is being paved. The endangered species list is getting longer. Clearly there is a great deal more to be done. At the same time, governments are also under pressure to allocate more resources to hospitals, farm support, education, international aid, the arts, and a host of other worthy causes, and taxpayers are unenthusiastic about paying more.

Facing these competing demands, governments have looked to cut costs and introduce efficiencies. One target has been the law-based command and control model of environmental protection. This model involves creating scientifically based standards, and monitoring and enforcing environmental rules. These tasks require expensive contributions, including scientific expertise, data collection, environmental policing, and legal services.

To reduce command and control costs, governments have taken a variety of steps, including the following:

- harmonization of federal–provincial and international regulatory regimes,
- consolidation of approval processes,
- privatization of service delivery,
- streamlining of decision procedures,
- elimination of allegedly unnecessary requirements,
- downloading of responsibilities to lower-tier governments, and
- reliance on non-regulatory mechanisms.

At least a few of these have been adopted by governments that have been demonstrably more interested in pleasing corporate interests than in enhancing efficiencies of environmental law implementation. Certainly some governments have found it difficult to distinguish between making environmental agencies "lean and mean" and starving them into inaction. Still, the efficiency issue is a real one that is certain to play a role in the future of environmental law.

Governance

Governments have been and will remain central players in environmental law development and implementation. However, as we have seen, citizens organizations, often with media support, have won a central and important position as advocates, initiators, and monitors of environmental law. Private sector bodies, including trade organizations and industry associations, have also been influential. These bodies have often been opponents of environmental obligations that they expect to be costly, but they have also been proponents of laws that discourage fly-by-night competitors. In addition, they have acted as participants in alternative approaches, such as the "voluntary" measures discussed in chapter 12.

Some of the most innovative recent environmental initiatives, such as the Forest Stewardship Council's certification and labelling program, have centred on agreements negotiated by corporate, consumer, and environmental interests without direct government involvement.

At the same time, government roles have become more complex. Authorities have struggled to address the following matters:

- overlapping responsibilities under the Canadian constitution, and an expanding list of overlapping local, regional, national, international, and global issues;
- increasing demands for efficiency; and
- commitments to consult with industry, to ensure greater transparency, and to facilitate public participation.

Governments have responded by establishing a wide range of agency-specific mandates, processes for deliberation and decision, and mechanisms for implementing or complementing legal requirements. Ever-increasing pressures for greater efficiency as well as better results have encouraged additional innovation and the redistribution of traditional government responsibilities, not only to different levels of government but also to industry, citizens groups, and international agencies.

As a result, it is now necessary to understand environmental law not simply as a government activity but also, and more broadly, as a phenomenon of governance—the overlapping and sometimes cooperative engagement of many players, including different agencies and levels of government, corporate interests, civil society organizations, citizens, and others in making socially and environmentally important decisions.

Tools

The expansion of roles and players in environmental law development and implementation has been accompanied by an ever-lengthening list of law-based tools and related mechanisms. From the beginning, the formal statutory and regulatory requirements were often softened by ministerial or official discretion. Many of the rules were implemented with case-by-case variations after quiet negotiations with the polluters or resource extractors involved.

While greater transparency has led to more procedural consistency, case-specific approaches are still common—for example, in environmental assessments—and often appropriate. Meanwhile the old regulatory and resource management tools have been supplemented by additional law-based options, including economic penalties, environmental offence tickets, public-reporting requirements, and performance bonds.

In turn, these legal tools have been complemented by other regulatory or non-legislated but indirectly law-based mechanisms, such as civil law, tax incentives and subsidies, product labelling and other consumer-focused measures, insurance requirements, investor expectations, and environmental health and safety provisions in collective agreements. So far, legislators and other environmental law participants have rarely attempted to see all of these tools and mechanisms as a package, or to design the individual components so that they complement and support each other. However, given the pressures for greater effectiveness and efficiency in environmental initiatives, better overall design is likely to be a higher priority in coming years.

Sustainability

One of the early debates in environmental law centred on the proper scope of the agenda. Should we focus exclusively on the natural environment and the need for much better stewardship of ecosystems and the biophysical world? Alternatively, should we stress our role in and dependence on biophysical systems and focus on ensuring effective integration of environmental responsibility in all decision making?

Environmental lawmakers have sometimes taken apparently opposing positions, some focusing on "environment" in a narrowly biophysical way, others including social, economic, cultural, and other aspects. But it is probably best to act on both emphases. We need to ensure that ecological implications are taken seriously as special considerations *and* that they are integrated effectively in significant decisions.

The importance of this requirement has been deepened by lessons from practical initiatives and scientific studies on sustainability's challenges and needs. Two key insights have emerged:

- *The major prevailing global trends are not sustainable.* Human demands on the planet are probably already exceeding the earth's renewable carrying capacity—by about 25 percent according to the World Wildlife Fund—and these demands are still rising. But most of the extracted resources and other benefits are going to those who least need them. Billions of people are living in conditions of serious material privation and the gap between rich and poor is widening.
- *Responses must link environmental stewardship and social justice.* This is evidently a practical as well as moral truth. Experience in environmental law and in other areas has demonstrated that needed changes can rarely be made and maintained without engaging all parties actively and fairly. If we want durable environmental gains, we must also ensure progress in meeting human needs for physical well-being, security, opportunity, and equity—across races, religions, and genders today and between present and future generations.

Canada, an exceptionally though unevenly rich country in the global picture, has plenty of unsustainability problems to address. We are, collectively, using more than our proportional share of global material and energy resources, even taking our cold climate into account. We are eating away at our natural legacy: over-fishing, degrading soils, depleting non-renewable resources, compromising ecological systems, and losing biodiversity. And while we have improved social justice on some fronts, we are allowing deepening inequity between rich and poor.

In environmental law, we are still focusing just on reducing the specific damages of particular activities. We have not yet taken serious steps to cut our overall demands, even in the case of greenhouse gases, about which we have signed a global treaty. Furthermore, we are just beginning to experiment with requiring new undertakings to make a positive contribution to sustainability. Here too is a growing task for the years to come.

The Path Ahead

Predicting the future is a good way to look stupid in 10 years. The world is a complicated place and, especially because humans are involved, there will be surprises. The prognosticators today are warning of avian flu, a new round of nuclear proliferation, more extreme weather events, a shift of the Gulf Stream, terrorists with chemical weapons, more HIV/AIDs, uncontrolled nanotechnology, water wars, ocean fishery collapse, and a host of other perils. Perhaps most of them will be avoided. Perhaps there will be a healthy number of more cheerful developments. But certainly a few big things that we do not now expect are waiting for us around the corner.

That said, we can make some reasonably safe bets on the future of environmental law. In particular, it is likely that all 10 of the themes discussed above will remain significant considerations in the coming years. The themes themselves are suggestive of solutions. Well into the roughly foreseeable future, we will have to act on the following 10 requirements:

1. Address problems at all scales from the local to the global.

2. Emphasize anticipatory planning and design.

3. Respect the interactive and dynamic complexity of environmental problems, and respond with suitably well-integrated initiatives.

4. Take precautionary action.

5. Maintain and expand opportunities for citizens to participate effectively in environmental decision making and in monitoring the results.

6. Respond to the challenges and opportunities of globalized problems, political and economic power, communications, and joint action needs.

7. Enhance the efficiency of environmental law implementation in ways that also strengthen its effectiveness.

8. Make better use of the different motivations and capabilities of public interest organizations, private sector bodies, and informal citizens groups as drivers, complements, and monitors of government actions.

9. Coordinate application of the diverse tools available for pushing and facilitating environmental improvements.

10. Shift from a focus on damage reduction to consistent delivery of positive contributions to sustainability, combining environmental stewardship with social justice, and seeking mutually reinforcing ecological and socio-economic gains.

From one perspective, this is a daunting list of requirements. From another, it represents a situation exceedingly rich in creative possibilities. No one will be able to accomplish all of these goals. But virtually everyone will be able to contribute. Innovative design and use of environmental law will involve a wide range of players, institutions, areas of expertise, and openings for application. Certainly it is not a realm merely for lawyers and legislators. Moreover, environmental law is just one of many instruments in the tool box for environmental stewardship and sustainable futures.

As we noted in the introduction to this book, the long-standing guides and drivers of human behaviour include economic motives, informed moral choice, and the establishment of new habits and customs as well as authoritative legal requirements. These guides and drivers are most powerful when linked as complementary forces. We therefore need to design law reforms and innovative legal applications to mobilize supporting changes in economics, understanding, and culture. It also means that initiatives in economics, understanding, and culture will be necessary to strengthen legal measures.

Consider the case of tobacco smoking. Until quite recently, smoking was broadly accepted, even celebrated in film and other media. Now, in much of Canada and in many other parts of the world, smoking is usually treated as unhealthy, irresponsible, and anti-social. The shift was accomplished in part through the application of law and in part through changes in product pricing, public information, and social norms. Law played big roles both directly—for example, in anti-smoking bylaws and environmental health lawsuits against the tobacco industry—and indirectly—for example, in liability and access to information law. But scientific research, higher tobacco taxes, and public health promotion efforts were also major influences. And the various initiatives included an interweaving of individual and collective actions at all levels from the family to the World Health Organization.

We can see many of the same factors in campaigns for more sustainable forest management, greenhouse gas emission abatement, reduction of cosmetic pesticide use, responsible international corporate behaviour, promotion of renewable energy options, trade in endangered species, and a host of other areas of concern and possibility. In each case, gains have depended on combining the strengths of environmental law with a rich and diverse set of efforts by individuals and institutions using packages of legal and other tools.

Over the past 40 years, we have accomplished a great deal through the application of environmental law and related initiatives. But we have only just begun. The next necessary step is to initiate a fundamental shift to behaviour that is viable in the long run. For this we must design law reforms, innovative legal applications, and links to supporting efforts in other areas so that they

- clarify and strengthen obligations for more sustainable practices,
- realign our economic system and pricing messages so that the economically attractive choices are also the ones that are good for the planet,
- foster much greater public understanding of our challenges and options, and
- build a culture of ecological stewardship and social responsibility.

Doing this will require government initiatives pushed and facilitated by individuals who can consolidate objectives, collaborate with others, and find ways of using the law to strengthen a larger circle of capacities and motivations for stewardship and sustainability. But no less important will be individuals within the private sector who see legal obligations and potential liabilities as just two of many good reasons to profit from social and ecological sustainability. Equally significant will be public interest organizations and citizens who identify emerging needs, build awareness of opportunities, and initiate collective action.

How much progress we make in the coming years and decades will depend in part on the nature of emerging pressures and opportunities. It will also depend on the strength, speed, and agility of our growing resolve, and on the commitment and creativity of organizations and individuals who recognize the importance of environmental action and who understand the potential, and limitations, of the law. That is what built the foundations of environmental law in Canada over the last 40 years. It seems reasonable to place our hopes for the future there too.

References

Statutes and Regulations

Access to Information Act, RSC 1985, c. A-1.

Aggregate Resources Act, RSO 1990, c. A.8.

Bill C-30, *An Act to Amend the Canadian Environmental Protection Act, 1999, the Energy Efficiency Act and the Motor Vehicle Fuel Consumption Standards Act* (*Canada's Clean Air Act*), 39th Parl., 1st Sess., first reading October 19, 2006.

Bill C-52, *An Act Respecting the Safety of Consumer Products* (*Canada Consumer Product Safety Act*), 39th Parl., 2nd Sess., second reading May 1, 2008.

Canada Business Corporations Act, RSC 1985, c. C-44.

Canada National Parks Act, SC 2000, c. 32.

Canadian Charter of Rights and Freedoms, part I of the *Constitution Act, 1982*, RSC 1985, app. II, no. 44.

Canadian Environmental Assessment Act, SC 1992, c. 37.

Canadian Environmental Protection Act, 1999, SC 1999, c. 33.

Charter of Human Rights and Freedoms, RSQ, c. C-12.

Civil Code of Québec, RSQ c. C-1991.

Clean Water Act, 2006, SO 2006, c. 22.

Climate Change and Emissions Management Act, SA 2003, c. C-16.7.

Constitution Act, 1867 (UK), 30 & 31 Vict., c. 3.

Constitution Act, 1982, being Schedule B to the *Canada Act 1982* (UK), 1982, c. 11.

Criminal Code, RSC 1985, c. C-46.

Crown Forest Sustainability Act, 1994, SO 1994, c. 25.

Crown Lands and Forests Act, SNB 1980, c. C-38.1.

Electricity Act, 1998, SO 1998, c. 15, Sch. A.

Electricity Restructuring Act, 2004, SO 2004, c. 23.

Endangered Species Act, RSO 1990, c. E.15 [repealed].

Endangered Species Act, 2007, SO 2007, c. 6.

Energy Efficiency Act, SC 1992, c. 36.

Energy Resources Conservation Act, RSA 2000, c. E-10.

Environmental Assessment Act, RSO 1990, c. E.18.

Environmental Bill of Rights, 1993, SO 1993, c. 28.

Environmental Protection Act, RSO, c. E.19.

Environmental Protection and Enhancement Act, RSA 2000, c. E-12.

Farming and Food Production Protection Act, 1998, SO 1998, c. 1.

Feeds Act, RSC 1985, c. F-9.

Fisheries Act, RSBC 1996, c. 149.

Fisheries Act, RSC 1985, c. F-14.

Fisheries and Coastal Resources Act, SNS 1996, c. 25.

Food and Drugs Act, RSC 1985, c. F-27.

Freedom of Information and Protection of Privacy Act, RSBC 1996, c. 165.

Freedom of Information and Protection of Privacy Act, RSA 2000, c. F-25.

Freedom of Information and Protection of Privacy Act, RSO 1990, c. F.31.

Freedom of Information and Protection of Privacy Amendment Act, 2003, SA 2003, c. 21.

Greenbelt Act, 2005, SO 2005, c. 1.

Hazardous Products Act, RSC 1985, c. H-3.

Mining Act, RSO 1990, c. M.14.

Municipal Act, SO 2001, c. 25.

National Energy Board Act, RSC 1985, c. N-7.

National Environmental Policy Act of 1969, Pub. L. 91-190, 42 USC 4321-4347, January 1, 1970, as amended.

Niagara Escarpment Planning and Development Act, RSO 1990, c. N.2.

Nuclear Liability Act, RSC 1985, c. N-28.

Nuclear Safety and Control Act, SC 1997, c. 9.

Nutrient Management Act, 2002, SO 2002, c. 4.

Oak Ridges Moraine Conservation Act, 2001, SO 2001, c. 31.

Oil and Gas Conservation Act, RSA 2000, c. O-6.

Pest Control Products Act, SC 2002, c. 28.

Pesticides Act, RSO 1990, c. P.11.

Places to Grow Act, 2005, SO 2005, c. 13.

Planning Act, RSO 1990, c. P.13.

Quebec Act, 1774, 14 Geo. III, c. 83 (UK).

Rules of Civil Procedure, RRO 1990, Reg. 194.

Seeds Act, RSC 1985, c. S-8.

Species at Risk Act, SC 2002, c. 29.

Statutory Instruments Act, RSC 1985, c. S-22.

Transportation of Dangerous Goods Act, 1992, SC 1992, c. 34.

Transportation of Dangerous Goods Regulations, SOR/2001-286.

Wild Animal and Plant Protection and Regulation of International and Interprovincial Trade Act, SC 1992, c. 52.

International Agreements and Conventions

Agreement for the Implementation of the Provisions of the United Nations Convention on the Law of the Sea 10 December 1982 Relating to the Conservation and Management of Straddling Fish Stocks and Highly Migratory Fish Stocks (United Nations Fishing Agreement). (1995) 34 ILM 1542.

Bergen Ministerial Declaration on Sustainable Development in the ECE Region. UN Doc. A/CONF.151/PC/10.

Convention on International Trade in Endangered Species of Wild Fauna and Flora.

Great Lakes Water Quality Agreement.

Kyoto Protocol to the United Nations Framework Convention on Climate Change.

United Nations Convention on the Law of the Sea. UN Doc. A/CONF. 62/122 (1982).

North American Agreement on Environmental Cooperation.

Stockholm Convention on Persistent Organic Pollutants.

United Nations Convention on Biological Diversity.

United Nations World Heritage Convention.

Cases

114957 Canada Ltée (Spraytech, Société d'arrosage) v. Hudson (Town), [2001] 2 SCR 241, 2001 CanLII 40.

Attorney-General of British Columbia v. Attorney General of Canada, [1914] AC 153 (PC).

Berendsen v. Ontario, 2008 CanLII 1416 (Ont. SC).

Canadian Wildlife Federation Inc. v. Canada Minister of the Environment (1989), 99 NR 72, 27 FTR 159; [1990] 2 WWR 69 (FCA).

C.N. Railways Co. et al. v. Ontario (EPA Director) (1992), 8 CELR (NS) 1 (Ont. CA).

Dunsmuir v. New Brunswick, 2008 SCC 9.

Fenske v. Alberta (Minister of the Environment), 2002 ABCA 135.

Fletcher v. Kingston (City) (2004), 70 OR (3d) 577 (CA).

Friends of the Oldman River Society v. Canada (Minister of Transport), [1992] 1 SCR 3, 132 NR 321, [1992] 2 WWR 193.

Heppner v. Alberta (Minister of the Environment), [1979] WWR.

Lafarge Canada Inc. v. Environmental Review Tribunal et al., 2008 CanLII 30290 (Ont. SC).

Quebec (Attorney General) v. Canada (National Energy Board), [1994] 1 SCR 159.

R v. Hydro-Québec, [1997] 3 SCR 213.

Rylands v. Fletcher (1868), LR 3 HL 330.

Books, Articles, Reports, and Government Documents

Agreement Review Committee. "Report to the Great Lakes Binational Executive Committee," vol. 2 (December 2006). *Binational.net*. http://binational.net/glwqa/v2_glwqareview_en.pdf.

Campaign for Nuclear Phaseout. "Media Release: Nuclear Subsidies to AECL Total $16.6 Billion." *Campaign for Nuclear Phaseout*. http://www.cnp.ca/media/nuclear-subsidies-11-00.html.

Canadian Council of Ministers of the Environment. "A Strategy to Fulfil the CCME Commitment to Pollution Prevention." *CCME*. http://www.ccme.ca.

Clinton, Bill. "Federal Actions to Address Environmental Justice in Minority Populations and Low-Income Populations." Executive Order 12898, February 11, 1994, s. 1-101. In *Federal Register*, vol. 59, no. 32.

Commissioner of the Environment and Sustainable Development. "2004 Report of the Commissioner of the Environment and Sustainable Development to the House of Commons." *Office of the Auditor General of Canada*. http://www.oag-bvg.gc.ca.

Commissioner of the Environment and Sustainable Development. "2005 Report of the Commissioner of the Environment and Sustainable Development to the House of Commons." *Office of the Auditor General of Canada*. http://www.oag-bvg.gc.ca.

Conservation Ontario. http://www.conservation-ontario.on.ca.

Crust, M. F. "Green Business: Should We Revoke Corporate Charters for Environmental Violations?" (2003) 63 *Louisiana L Rev.* 175.

David Suzuki Foundation and Canadian Institute for Environmental Law and Policy. "Green Power Opportunities for Ontario." *David Suzuki Foundation.* http://www.davidsuzuki.org.

Environmental Commissioner of Ontario. "2006/07 Annual Report: Reconciling Our Priorities." *Environmental Commissioner of Ontario.* http://www.eco.on.ca.

Environmental Commissioner of Ontario. "Making a Difference: The First Ten Years of the EBR." *Environmental Commissioner of Ontario.* http://www.eco.on.ca/eng_pdfs/10years.pdf.

Franson, M.A.H., R.T. Franson, and A.R. Lucas. *Environmental Standards.* Edmonton: Environment Council of Alberta, 1982.

Gardner, M. *Linking Activism: Ecology, Social Justice, and Education for Social Change.* New York: Routledge, 2005.

Garner, Bryan A., ed. *Black's Law Dictionary*, 8th ed. Thomson West, 2004.

Georges Bank Review Panel. *Georges Bank Review Panel Report.* Ottawa/Halifax: Natural Resources Canada and Nova Scotia Petroleum Directorate, 1999.

Giroux, Lorne, and Paule Halley. "Environmental Law in Quebec." In E. Hughes et al., eds., *Environmental Law and Policy*, 3rd ed., chapter 4. Toronto: Emond Montgomery, 2003.

Government of Alberta. "News Release: Alberta to Cut Projected Emissions by 50 Per Cent Under New Climate Change Plan." *Alberta.* http://www.alberta.ca.

Government of Canada. "Guide to Making Federal Acts and Regulations," 2nd ed. *Privy Council Office.* http://www. pco-bcp.gc.ca.

Government of Canada. "Regulatory Process Guide: Developing a Regulatory Proposal and Seeking Its Approval." *Privy Council Office.* http://www.pco-bcp.gc.ca.

Government of Canada. "Turning the Corner." *Ecoaction.* http://www.ecoaction.gc.ca/turning-virage/index-eng.cfm.

Government of Ontario. "Environmental Registry." *Ontario.* http://www.ebr.gov.on.ca.

Gunn, Allan, and Jim Lewis. "Ontario's Environmental Registry: A Case Study in Public Participation." November 12, 2006, PowerPoint presentation.

Muldoon, Paul. *The Law of Intervention: Status and Practice.* Aurora, ON: Canada Law Book, 1989.

Muldoon, Paul, and Burkhard Mausberg. "The Regulation of Biotechnology." In David Estrin and John Swaigen, eds., *Environment on Trial: A Guide to Ontario Environmental Law and Policy*, 3rd ed., chapter 11. Toronto: Emond Montgomery, 1993.

National Energy Board. *Canada's Oil Sands: Opportunities and Challenges to 2015.* Calgary: National Energy Board, 2004.

National Energy Board. *Canada's Oil Sands: Opportunities and Challenges to 2015—An Update.* Calgary: National Energy Board, 2006.

O'Connor, D.R. *Report of the Walkerton Inquiry: A Strategy for Safe Drinking Water.* Toronto: Queen's Printer for Ontario, 2002.

Royal Society of Canada. *Elements of Precaution: Recommendations for the Regulation of Food Biotechnology in Canada: An Expert Panel Report on the Future of Food Biotechnology prepared by The Royal Society of Canada at the request of Health Canada, Canadian Food Inspection Agency and Environment Canada.* Ottawa: Royal Society of Canada, 2001.

Sands, Philippe. "Liability for Environmental Damage." In Sun Lin and Lal Kurukuiasuryia, eds., *UNEP's Way Forward: Environmental Law and Sustainable Development.* Nairobi: United Nations Environment Programme, 1995.

Weidemann, I., and S. Femers. "Public Participation in Waste Management Decision-Making: Analysis and Management of Conflicts" (1993), 33 *Journal of Hazardous Materials* 355.

World Wildlife Fund (WWF). "Living Planet Report 2006." *WWF International.* http://www.panda.org/livingplanet.

Glossary

Absolute liability offences   minor offences where the intention of the offender is not a required element

Actus reus   an element of an offence, namely, the doing of the prohibited act

Administrative decisions   decisions made pursuant to a statute, which sets out the requisite decision-making process

Administrative law   the legal rules and processes that govern administrative decision-makers

Administrative orders   orders made by ministry officials or employees, rather than by a court

ALARA   acronym for "as low as reasonably achievable" with respect to risk, which is the approach to safety used in the nuclear industry

Alternative dispute resolution (ADR)   settlement of a conflict through a process other than the court system

Aquaculture   fish farming

Balance of probabilities   the standard of proof in a civil proceeding, whereby the plaintiff must convince the court that the allegations are more likely true than untrue

Baseline   an aggregate cap on allowable emissions, which is divided into units that may be traded

Beyond a reasonable doubt   the standard of proof in a criminal proceeding

Bill   draft statute, subject to change and not yet passed into law

Biotechnology   the use of living organisms for the production of goods and services

Brownfields   abandoned, underused, or derelict sites of previous human activity, such as crumbling factories, old railway yards, and condemned apartments

Bylaws   legally enforceable rules created by municipalities according to the powers given to them by municipal statutes

CANDU technology   a nuclear power generation technology that uses heavy water to moderate the uranium fuel fusion reaction and requires fast, redundant shutdown systems to be available in various circumstances

Carbon offsets   the use of carbon sinks to offset emissions of carbon dioxide; used in emissions-trading systems

Carbon sinks   areas created by removing or "sequestering" carbon dioxide by growing trees, reducing soil tillage, and injecting carbon dioxide into depleted hydrocarbon formations; used in emissions-trading systems

Causes of action   legal grounds for a civil lawsuit

Certificates of approval   site-specific legal instruments required under the Ontario *Environmental Protection Act* in certain circumstances, containing site-specific requirements

Civil law   in Quebec, a system based on the Custom of Paris and later codified using French civil law and the Code Napoléon, which applies to private disputes between citizens

Civil law jurisdictions   most of Europe, but only Quebec and Louisiana in North America, where courts make decisions based on a civil code, not precedent, and there is no doctrine of *stare decisis*

Civil law system   deals with disputes between private parties, whereby the party pursuing the claim, usually called the plaintiff, must establish that the defendant committed a wrong (applies to both common law and civil law jurisdictions)

Class action   procedural mechanism used when a large number of plaintiffs sue over the same event or set of facts

Class environmental assessment process   an environmental assessment procedure that applies to undertakings that are part of a group of similar undertakings (for example, highway construction projects or forest management planning processes)

Cleanup laws   laws designed to minimize discharge of human and industrial waste into the environment

Command and control   state intervention involving the creation of rules and the enforcement of those rules

Common law   rules contained in judge-made decisions about similar cases stretching back in time

Common law jurisdictions   most of North America, with the exception of Quebec and Louisiana, where prior court decisions on similar facts may be binding law

Consent to sever   permission to divide a lot into a few lots that may be separately sold and bought

Conservation authorities   local watershed management agencies that deliver services and programs that protect and manage water and other natural resources in partnership with government, landowners, and other organizations

Conservation easement   legal tool used to protect natural habitats on privately owned land

Constitution   document that establishes the basic framework under which all other laws are created and the basic principles to which all laws must conform

Construction standard   an approved pollution control system mandated by the government for use by certain industries

Corporate mandate   the statutory requirement that corporations operate in their own best interests

Costs   part of legal expenses that a court or tribunal may order the losing party to pay to the winning party at the conclusion of the case

Criminal law system   deals with violations of the laws designed to protect the interests of society in general

Criminal liability offences   serious offences under the *Criminal Code*, such as murder

Crown land   land owned by the provincial or federal government, which controls its use and sale (also called public land)

Customary international law   a set of international rules that have evolved over time and been accepted by states as effective law

Damages   the monetary award that a defendant may be ordered by the court to pay to a successful plaintiff

Declaration   a finding of the court, given without other relief

Defendant   an individual or corporation that is sued in a civil action by another, called the plaintiff

Demand management   approach to energy that recognizes that it is often cheaper to encourage investments in more efficient industrial processes and products, such as home appliances and lightbulbs, than to build more generating plants and transmission lines

Dilution solution   the idea that air or water pollutants do not pose a problem if they are spread out widely enough, such as by the wind or ocean currents

Director   an appointee under the Ontario *Environmental Protection Act* who may issue an administrative order in certain circumstances

Discretionary decisions   decisions whereby the decision-maker has considerable latitude concerning the basis for a particular decision and the factors that can be taken into account in reaching the decision

Domestic law   the law within a particular country

Due diligence   defence to a strict liability offence requiring the accused to demonstrate that he took all reasonable steps to avoid committing a prohibited act

Duty of care   the legal obligation to act reasonably such that harm does not occur to others

Ecological integrity   approach adopted for national parks, which considers the needs of nature as the first priority

Economic instruments   instruments designed to require business to absorb at least some of the environmental costs of doing business

E-democracy   the use of the Internet to facilitate broad public participation in government decisions

Emission taxes   taxes charged on units of contaminant released into the environment

Emissions intensity reduction   emission limits based on emissions per unit of production, rather than a set limit

Enforcement ladder system   approach to responding to environmental law violations that increases in intensity, and involves inspections and progressively more serious warnings, monetary penalties, shutdowns, and prosecutions

Environmental assessment   requirement to predict and evaluate the potential effects of environmentally significant projects, such as hydro power stations, airports, mines, roads, and landfills, and to seek government approval

Environmental assessment law   law requiring careful attention to environmental considerations in the planning and approval of new undertakings

Environmental law   the body of legislated statute and judge-made common law that can be used to protect and improve environmental conditions

Environmental regulatory law   law governing the discharge of harmful substances into the air and water and onto land

Evidence   facts, objects, and opinions that are presented to a decision-maker for the purpose of making a decision

Exclusive economic zone   area of ocean adjacent to coastline belonging to the coastal state

Externalities   the public costs of environmental degradation

Fixed-price measures   tax and subsidy incentives designed to reduce pollution

Friend of the court   intervenor with the right to present oral and/or written submissions to the court, but not the full rights of a party (also called an *amicus curiae*)

General damages   damages that are subjective and not easily quantified, such as pain and suffering

Genetic engineering   genetic modification of a microbe, plant, or animal to serve a new or enhanced purpose

Governor in council   federal member of Cabinet vested with power to create regulations and rules pursuant to a statute

Growth plan   plans that identify where and how growth should occur

Health risk assessment standard   a quality-based standard that involves linking the standard under consideration to the health risks posed

Hearsay   statements about what a witness heard from another person

Hydrocarbons   the organic compound of hydrogen and carbon atoms that produces energy when burned; found in fossil fuels such as oil, natural gas, and coal

Industrial farming   large farms operated by corporations, distinct from traditional family-run farms

Injunction   a court order that requires a defendant either to do something (a mandatory injunction) or to refrain from doing something (a prohibitory injunction)

Instruments   certificates of approval for a facility's air emissions, waste management sites, etc., as referenced in the *Environmental Bill of Rights, 1993*

International law   a collection of rules governing countries

Intervention   procedural device that allows persons or organizations that are not plaintiffs or defendants to participate in a legal proceeding as added parties or friends of the court

Judicial review   a court's review of an administrative tribunal's decision to ensure that it acted within the powers granted under the legislation and to ensure that it respected the common law rules of fairness and natural justice

Jurisdiction   power to legislate or make a decision

Land use planning   determining how a parcel of land will be used by defining objectives, collecting information, identifying problems, and analyzing alternatives

Laws of general application   laws that apply to everyone and to all activities

Legal non-conforming uses   pre-existing uses of a property that are allowed to continue, even though they do not conform to existing zoning requirements

Liability   legal obligations and responsibilities

Liability rating system   a system for ensuring that a company can pay for the costs of possible contamination before a licence is granted for a new facility, by comparing the assets of the company with the estimated risk of contamination liability

Licences and approvals   permission to pollute, provided that certain conditions are met

Lieutenant-governor in council   provincial member of Cabinet vested with power to create regulations and rules pursuant to a statute

Media-based regimes   statutes based on a particular environmental medium, such as air, water, or land

Mens rea   an element of a criminal offence, namely, a guilty mind or intention to commit the act

Microbes   single-celled organisms such as bacteria, algae, and fungi

Monoculture   production of a single species or genetic variant crop in a particular area

Natural justice and procedural fairness   common law concept requiring the following procedural safeguards for all administrative decisions: reasonable notice of a proposed decision, a fair opportunity to be heard, and an impartial and independent decision-maker

Negligence   failure to act reasonably, with the result being harm to someone else

Novel product   product that has an intentionally selected characteristic that is "not substantially equivalent" to an existing organism in terms of its specific use and safety with respect to human health and the environment

Nuisance tort in which the defendant interferes with the use and enjoyment of the plaintiff's property

Official notice the allowance of obvious and well-accepted facts by an administrative decision-maker, without the need for proof

Oil sands crude bitumen deposits found in an area of northern Alberta and a small area of Saskatchewan

Orphaned sites oil wells and other facilities abandoned by oil and gas operators

Participation rights rights of private individuals to be informed and consulted as part of the environmental approval process

Performance standard a pollution limit imposed on a polluter, where the rule-maker is unconcerned with how the result is achieved

Persistent organic pollutants (POPs) about a dozen chemicals identified as having long-lasting toxicity

Pesticides a range of products that have in common the control of living organisms

Plaintiff an individual or corporation that brings a civil action against another, called the defendant

Plan of subdivision plan for dividing a parcel of land into many lots to be sold and bought separately

Planning and management regimes legislative schemes that govern a sector, such as forests, fisheries, farmlands, and watersheds, with the purpose of maximizing the long-term benefits obtainable from the resource while minimizing the detrimental effects of its exploitation

Point of impingement the impact of a pollutant, such as air pollution, at a property boundary

Pollution prevention an approach emphasizing prevention rather than control of pollution, using methods such as product reformulation, chemical substitution, and changes to processes

Precautionary principle the proposition that caution should be paramount when an activity raises threats of harm to health or the environment, and that the proponent of the activity should bear the burden of proving that it is safe; further, where the threat of serious or irreversible damage exists, a lack of full scientific certainty should not be used as a reason for postponing measures to prevent environmental degradation

Private law law pertaining to personal rights, such as the right to protect one's own property and interests

Privative clause a provision that is sometimes included in a governing statute that specifically limits judicial review of administrative decisions made under that statute

Provincial officer (PO) government official who gathers evidence about an environmental incident and prepares a report

Provincial officers' orders (POOs) orders that may be issued by provincial officers along with a report following an investigation, compelling an individual or company to carry out certain actions to prevent or respond to an environmental problem

Public inquiries investigative proceedings that result in recommendations to government

Public interest intervention category of intervention that blurs the added party and friend of the court categories, and which is commonly recognized where the Charter is an issue in the case

Public interest override provision in the *Access to Information Act* that allows for disclosure of confidential information where public health, safety, or protection of the environment outweighs the consequences of disclosure

Public interest standing new and broader test for determining whether a person has standing, requiring that the person either has a genuine interest in the litigation or is in a better position to bring the action than anyone else

Public law law enforced by the state against those who fail to abide by it

Punitive damages damages intended to punish the defendant and set an example

Quasi-criminal offences provincial offences punishable by heavy fines and up to six months in jail

Ratification agreement to the terms of a convention by the domestic legislatures of the countries signing the convention

Reasonable person a hypothetical person recognized as having a level of maturity and responsibility common to most people in the community, and used as an objective standard for determining liability

Record all evidence and arguments presented at a hearing

Regional and municipal official plans plans that establish general land use policies across large geographical areas delineated by political boundaries

Regulations legally enforceable rules created by the governor in council (federal) or lieutenant-governor in council (provincial) providing practical details of how a statute is to be implemented

Remedy court-ordered redress to a plaintiff in a civil case, such as monetary compensation

Representative plaintiff in a class action, the plaintiff who brings the action on behalf of the class of plaintiffs

Residential intensification redevelopment to add density in residential areas

Right to know the most basic of the participation rights, namely, the right to be informed

Secondary plans plans that cover specific areas within a municipality, and provide more detailed planning policies for those areas

Sectoral laws laws dealing with a resource sector such as water or forests, or an industrial sector such as fisheries or waste management

Sector-based regimes laws and policies that apply to a particular sector or specific area, such as energy, endangered species, or agriculture

Smart meter device that enables energy providers to charge more for consumption during peak usage hours

Special damages damages directly caused by the defendant's behaviour that are easily and objectively quantifiable, such as the costs of repair

Species at risk collective term that includes five categories: extinct, extirpated, endangered, threatened, and special concern

Standard of care the degree or level of care that is required—what is reasonable in the circumstances

Standard of proof degree to which a party must convince a judge or jury that the allegations are true

Standard of review the scope of a judicial review—the broader correctness standard (was the tribunal's decision correct?), or the stricter reasonableness standard (was the tribunal's decision reasonable?)

Standing the right to sue

Stare decisis principle that requires judges to follow decisions of higher courts in similar cases

Statutes codified laws passed by legislatures

Stay the temporary suspension of a court order, usually pending an appeal

Strategic level assessment an approach to big policy issues that applies environmental assessment requirements to government policies, plans, programs, and other broad-scale initiatives

Strict liability offences offence in which proof that an accused performed the prohibited act is sufficient to sustain a conviction, regardless of intention, unless the accused demonstrates that he took all reasonable care to avoid committing the prohibited act

Subsidiary   a second corporation whose shares are owned by the parent company

Subsidies   grants, loans, or tax breaks provided to polluters for reducing discharges; the size of the subsidy is based on the amount of the reduction

Sustainable development   an approach intended to ensure that resources continue to be available and that the environment is protected for future generations

Territorial waters   belt of water adjacent to a coast, over which the coastal state holds jurisdiction

"Three p" rule   traditional rule for determining whether a person has standing, requiring the person to demonstrate a property interest, a personal (health) interest, or a pecuniary interest

Tort   civil wrong other than a breach of contract, for which damages may be sought to compensate for any harm or injury sustained

Toxics control laws   laws designed to control the manufacture, use, sale, transport, storage, and disposal of toxic substances

Tradable emission rights   rights representing specified quantities of emissions that are issued to polluters

Transgenes   genetically modified genes

Transgenic crops   genetically engineered crops given specific characteristics to improve taste, appearance, nutritional value, and rate of growth

Treaty or convention   an agreement between two or more sovereign states, binding only those states that sign it

Trespass   a physical presence on someone else's property, without permission

Tribunal   specialized quasi-judicial board, commission, panel, or some other decision-making body that makes decisions pursuant to particular statutes

Urban sprawl   low-density residential growth in rural areas

Vicariously liable   legally responsible for the actions of someone else, such as an employee

Voluntary compliance   an approach that relies on industry and individuals to do the right thing, motivated by conscience, public relations, or a desire to avoid regulation

Waste control laws   laws designed to control discharge of waste using permits and approvals

Watershed   an area of land from which all water drains into a common body of water, such as a lake or river

Watershed planning   a scale of planning that is based on natural watershed boundaries and hence extends beyond political boundaries

Whistle blowers   insiders, such as employees, who report information about violations of the law to enforcement agencies or the media

Whole facility permitting   an approach to granting permits that involves a review of all the environmental exposures from a particular facility

Zoning bylaws   legally enforceable rules and requirements for the use of land, and for the use and location of buildings and structures on land

Index

law
  historical foundation, 3–4
  society, and, 5-7
Law of the Sea Treaty, 42
laws of general application, 16–17
leave to appeal, 205, 206
legal non-conforming uses, 159
legal systems, 19
legislative process, 26–27
Leopold, Aldo, 15
liability, 31–32
liability rating system, 96
licences and approvals, 84
lieutenant-governor in council, 24
Linking Activism, 69
London Dumping Convention, 53

mandatory mediation, 198
marine areas, 149
media-based regimes, 64
mens rea, 92
microbes, 116
mining, 104–106
Mining Act (Ont.), 105
monetary damages, 196
monoculture, 117
Montreal Protocol on Substances That Deplete the
  Ozone Layer, 53
Municipal Act (Ont.), 167
municipal–industry strategy for abatement, 80
municipal jurisdiction, 23
municipal law, 68
municipal official plans, 155

Napoleonic Code, 19
National Energy Board Act, 97
National Environmental Policy Act of 1969 (US), 125, 126
National Pollutant Release Inventory, 61
natural justice, 202
negligence, 46, 192–195
Niagara Escarpment Planning and Development Act
  (Ont.), 164
non-regulatory instruments, 178–182
North American Agreement on Environmental Coopera-
  tion, 112
novel product, 119
nuclear energy, 100–104
Nuclear Liability Act, 103
nuisance, 191
Nutrient Management Act (Ont.), 110

Oak Ridges Moraine Conservation Act, 2001 (Ont.), 164
O'Connor, Dennis, 151
official notice, 203
oil and gas, 95–96
Oil and Gas Conservation Act (Alta.), 95, 96
oil sands, 96–97
Oil Sands Conservation Act (Alta.), 95
Ontario Municipal Board, 163
Ontario Water Resources Act, 65, 77
opinio juris, 41
Organisation for Economic Co-operation and Development, 113
orphaned sites, 96

parks and protected areas, 147–149
participation rights, 60–62
performance standard, 77
persistent organic pollutants (POPs), 112
Pest Control Products Act, 48, 113, 114
Pest Management Regulatory Agency, 113
pesticides, 110, 111–115
Pesticides Act (Ont. and Que.), 114
Pipeline Act (Alta.), 95
Places to Grow Act, 2005 (Ont.), 165
plaintiff, 67
plan of subdivision, 160
Planning Act (Ont.), 106, 153, 156, 160, 162, 167
planning and management regimes, 50
point of impingement, 81
pollution prevention, 81–82
Pollution Probe, 211
precautionary principle, 80
preventive measures orders, 87
Priority Substances List, 48
private actions
  as environmental protection tool, 198
  causes of action, 191–195
  class action proceedings, 188
  costs, 197
  damages and remedies, 195–197
  history of, 185–186
  interventions, 189–191
  mandatory mediation, 198
  standing, 186–188
private landowners, 149
private law, 59–62
privative clause, 208
procedural fairness, 202, 209–210
prosecutions, 88–92
provincial officer (PO), 86